Ready-to-Run Visual Basic®
Code Library
Tips, Tricks, and Workarounds
for Better Programming

Ready-to-Run Visual Basic® Code Library
Tips, Tricks, and Workarounds for Better Programming

Rod Stephens

Wiley Computer Publishing

John Wiley & Sons, Inc.

NEW YORK · CHICHESTER · WEINHEIM · BRISBANE · SINGAPORE · TORONTO

Publisher: Robert Ipsen
Editor: Carol A. Long
Managing Editor: Marnie Wielage
Electronic Products, Associate Editor: Mike Sosa
Composition: Benchmark Productions Inc., Boston

Library of Congress Cataloging-in-Publication Data:

ISBN 0-471-33345-X

Printed in the United States of America.
10 9 8 7 6 5 4 3 2 1

CONTENTS

An example is worth a thousand words.

People naturally learn by example. Verbal or written instruction is valuable, but a good example conveys something more. Instruction must focus on one key concept, but an example can include extra information that shows the concept applied in a meaningful context. You learn not only how the concept works, but also how to apply it to a practical situation.

By providing background for itself, an example can be self-sufficient. A typical introductory book might be unable to explain certain topics, such as giving a form an irregular outline, because that topic does not fit properly within any of the book's chapters. Because an example provides its own context, it can stand alone, demonstrating concepts without fitting within a chapter's larger theme.

Examples are also more active than simple instruction. Instead of making you a spectator, listening passively to a description of a technique, an example makes you a participant. Instruction may convey important facts, but an example lets you experience the facts firsthand. If you take the time to modify an example and study the results, you can make the experience even more immediate and meaningful.

This book presents 173 examples that demonstrate useful programming concepts set within meaningful contexts. Each example shows how to accomplish some task that you might reasonably want to perform using Visual Basic. Each is also provided on the CD-ROM in a ready-to-run program. You can experiment with these programs to learn even more about the concepts they illustrate. You can use them as starting points for programs of your own, and you can cut and paste their code into your applications.

Intended Audience

This book is designed for programmers who already know the fundamentals of Visual Basic programming. Before you read it, you should understand basic concepts such as declaring variables, using controls, and writing simple subroutines. You do not need to be an expert, though. This book does not require any advanced programming knowledge. If you have read any introduction to Visual Basic programming, you will have no trouble reading this book.

Even if you know almost nothing about programming, you will find the examples in this book useful. Some are relatively straightforward, and you will be able to understand them with little difficulty. As you become more comfortable with the simpler programs, you can look at the more complicated examples to increase your knowledge of specific techniques and Visual Basic programming in general.

This book is intended for programmers who want to learn more than is taught in introductory books. It is meant for those who want to learn about the topics that slip through the cracks of other books, topics that often arise in real-world programming situations.

Visual Basic Version Compatibility

Many of the examples presented in this book use nothing more than standard Visual Basic features. These programs run in Visual Basic 4, 5, and 6. When future versions of Visual Basic are released, they will undoubtedly run in those as well. You can even translate some of them into Visual Basic 3 if you really must.

Some examples use features introduced by a particular version of Visual Basic. For instance, subclassing programs use features introduced to the language in Visual Basic 5. Those programs will not run in earlier versions of Visual Basic, though they should continue to work with future versions. Symbols next to each example's description indicate the versions of Visual Basic in which the example should work.

Programming languages often grow, but they rarely shrink. It is unlikely that Microsoft will remove important features from the language in future versions of Visual Basic. More techniques will become available, but few existing techniques will become useless. That means the examples presented here should be useful for many years to come. If any changes are necessary, they will be posted at this book's Web site: www.vb-helper.com/examples.htm.

What's on the CD-ROM

The CD-ROM contains the Visual Basic source code for all of the examples in this book. The code is stored in the earliest Visual Basic format that works. If a program works in Visual Basic 4, 5, and 6, it is stored in Visual Basic 4 format. If a program only works in Visual Basic 5 and 6, it is stored in Visual Basic 5 format. This lets you load the programs using as many versions of Visual Basic as possible.

When you load a program, the development environment may tell you it will convert the program into a newer version of Visual Basic. For instance, if you load a Visual Basic 4 program in Visual Basic 6, the environment tells you that it will save the files in Visual Basic 6 format. This message is for information only and is not an error, so you can safely ignore it.

If you try to open a project using an earlier version of Visual Basic, the development environment will claim the project is corrupted and cannot be loaded. For instance, if you try to load a Visual Basic 5 program in Visual Basic 4, you will see this message. The program is not really corrupted, but you still cannot load it in your version of Visual Basic.

You can either load the projects directly from the CD-ROM or copy them to your hard disk first. You do not need to worry about making changes that break the examples because you can always reload them later from the CD-ROM.

Some of the programs create files in the example's directory. Because you cannot write on the CD-ROM, those programs may not work if you load them directly from the CD-ROM. You should copy them into a directory on your hard disk and run the programs from there.

Files on a CD-ROM are always marked as read-only by the operating system. When you copy files onto your hard disk, they are also marked read-only. That means you cannot save changes you make to the files. It also means programs that modify the files may fail. To save changes and prevent this kind of error, you must remove the read-only flag from the files.

The easiest way to do that is to copy all of the subdirectories you want to use into one directory on your hard disk. Navigate to that directory with Windows Explorer. From the Tools menu, open the Find submenu and select the Files or Folders command. In the resulting Find dialog, enter *.* for the file name and click the Find Now button. The dialog will display a list of every file contained beneath the directory, as shown in Figure I.1.

Next, press Ctrl-A to select every file in the list. Right-click on the files, and select the Properties command from the popup menu. This presents the properties dialog shown in Figure I.2. Uncheck the Read-only check box and click OK. The files are no longer marked read-only, so you can save changes to them.

How This Book Is Organized

The chapters in this book describe groups of related programming examples. They are generally arranged in order of increasing scope. The early chapters work with items with smaller scope, such as variables and controls. Later chapters cover objects with a larger scale, such as forms, the file system, and the operating system. Within each chapter, the examples are mostly arranged in order of increasing difficulty. There are some exceptions, however, where chapters have been arranged to keep related examples together.

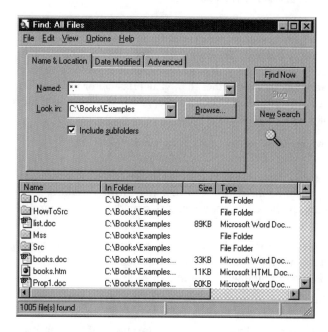

Figure I.1 Listing all the files in a directory.

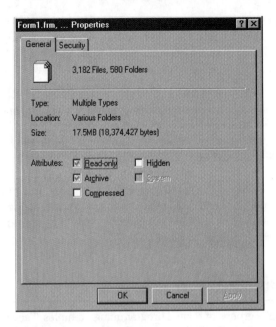

Figure I.2 Removing the read-only flag for selected files.

Each example begins with its example number, title, and the name of the directory that contains its files on the CD-ROM. It also includes the symbols ④, ⑤, or ⑥ to indicate the versions of Visual Basic that can run the example.

Each example is marked with one, two, or three stars to indicate its relative difficulty. Most of the examples with one star use only plain Visual Basic code. Examples with two stars use API functions and more complex program logic. The most complex examples have three stars. These include programs that demonstrate complicated logic, as well as those that use extra information about topics other than Visual Basic. For instance, subclassing requires knowledge of how Windows processes messages. It is confusing and dangerous, so subclassing examples have three stars.

The following list provides an overview of the chapters in this book.

Chapter 1, "Working with Variables" Variables are one of the most basic concepts in programming. This chapter describes tips that deal with variables. These topics include ways to load arrays easily, copy memory quickly, and compare the performance of arrays and collections.

Chapter 2, "Manipulating Numbers" Many programs use numbers extensively. This chapter explains some useful numeric techniques such as using random numbers, sorting lists, and performing simple encryption.

Chapter 3, "Handling Text" A lot of programs also use string manipulations extensively. This chapter demonstrates techniques that make text manipulation easier, such as methods for parsing delimited strings, determining if a string is blank, and allowing the user to find and replace text.

Chapter 4, "Formatting Output" Before it can present information to the user or to another application, a program must format the information properly. This chapter describes different ways to format output. It explains how to justify text output and convert between various data types before presenting information to the user. It also tells how to use the clipboard to make data available to other programs.

Chapter 5, "Tackling Timers" Visual Basic's Timer control lets a program perform actions periodically. The Timer is a useful control, but it is somewhat limited. This chapter explains ways to get the most out of the Timer control. It tells how to build such things as clocks, countdown timers, and alarms that can wait for very long times before triggering.

Chapter 6, "Starting and Stopping" Many programmers take a program's starting and stopping for granted. Actually there are several important starting and stopping issues that you should understand. This chapter explains these issues.

Chapter 7, "Network Programming" In recent years, network programming, the Internet, and the World Wide Web have become pervasive. All sorts of programs now include networking capabilities. This chapter covers a few of the simpler techniques for adding network features to a Visual Basic program. These include the ability to map a network drive, display a Web document, and search a Web document for specific strings.

Chapter 8, "Taming TextBoxes" The TextBox is probably the most commonly used control for gathering input from a user. This chapter explains ways a program can get more out of Visual Basic's TextBox control. It covers such topics as setting tabs and margins in a TextBox and automatically selecting text when focus enters a TextBox.

Chapter 9, "Using ListBoxes and ComboBoxes" In many ways the ListBox and ComboBox controls are better than a TextBox for obtaining user input. By allowing the user to select from a list of existing options, these controls reduce the chances of the user's entering invalid data. This chapter describes ways to enhance these useful controls. It tells how to change the size of a ComboBox's dropdown area, set tab stops in a ListBox, and select items in a ListBox based on text entered by the user.

Chapter 10, "Using ListView and TreeView" The TreeView and ListView controls provide complex views of data, but they are difficult to use. This chapter provides several examples showing how to use these powerful but confusing controls.

Chapter 11, "Using Other Controls" The first 10 chapters in this book describe some of the ways a program can use Timer, TextBox, ListBox, ComboBox, ListView, and TreeView controls. This chapter explains an assortment of topics covering other controls including the ProgressBar, StatusBar, Common Dialog, TabStrip, and Multimedia MCI controls.

Chapter 12, "Managing Controls" While previous chapters explained ways of using specific kinds of controls, this chapter describes ways to manage controls in general. It covers such topics as using control arrays, creating controls at run time, and using accelerators.

Chapter 13, "Generating Graphics" Forms and PictureBoxes allow a program to display complex graphics. This chapter explains several useful graphics programming techniques such as creating a color gradient, tiling a form with repeating copies of a picture, and allowing the user to select a region using a rubberband box.

Chapter 14, "Implementing Animation" Some concepts are best demonstrated to a user with animation. This chapter explains some simple methods for producing animation in Visual Basic. It also explains how a program can let the user drag complicated images around a form. Using a similar technique, a program can move complex objects programmatically.

Chapter 15, "Using Fonts" The majority of controls display text of some kind. The control's font determines the appearance of the text. This chapter presents some powerful techniques for creating and manipulating fonts. It shows how to build customized fonts that are tall and thin, short and wide, or rotated at an angle.

Chapter 16, "Making Menus" Visual Basic's menu editor makes creating simple menus easy. This chapter explains some of the more advanced ways a program can use menus. It tells how to create popup menus, how to add and remove menu items at run time, and how to modify a form's system menu.

Chapter 17, "Managing Forms" Forms are the basic unit of Windows programming in Visual Basic. Almost all of a program's user interface is displayed on forms. This chapter describes special ways a program can manipulate forms. It tells how to keep one form on top of another, manage wait cursors, and create irregularly shaped forms.

Chapter 18, "Using Files and Directories" Many programs manipulate files and directories. This chapter demonstrates powerful file management techniques including ways to determine if a file exists, read text files and arrays, search a directory hierarchy for files, and copy selected files in a directory hierarchy.

Chapter 19, "Using the Registry" With the introduction of Windows 95, Microsoft declared that programs should store configuration information in the system registry. This chapter explains ways a program can take advantage of the registry's features.

How to Use This Book

The chapters in this book are not closely related, so you can read them in any order. Some of the examples within a chapter build on each other, so in many cases it will be easiest if you read the examples in a chapter in order.

There are at least three approaches you can take to reading this book. First, you can read it from start to finish, covering each example in order. Second, you can study the examples that deal with a particular topic. For instance, if you are interested in TextBoxes, read all of the examples that deal with TextBoxes.

You can also read through the book at different levels. Make one pass through the book, studying the simpler examples that have one star. Then read it again, examining programs with two stars. Finish by reading the remaining examples. This approach may be particularly useful if you are relatively inexperienced and you would like to wait before tackling the more advanced examples.

Using API Functions

Visual Basic makes Windows programming easy by hiding many of the operating system details. It automatically processes the messages Windows uses to control the program. It also implements the main Windows event loop so that the program need not worry about it. It translates complex messages into relatively simple calls to event handlers.

This convenience comes at the price of reduced flexibility and sometimes performance. To make certain routine tasks easier, Visual Basic hides some of Windows' features. Some of those features provide services that are unavailable in Visual Basic itself.

Fortunately, a program can regain some of these features by using the Windows Application Programming Interface (API). These functions provide access to system utilities at a lower level than is available in Visual Basic itself.

Many of the more difficult examples in this book demonstrate techniques that take advantage of the API. This book does not explain everything there is to know about using the API, but you can learn a lot by studying the examples. A few points that apply generally to API functions are also worth mentioning here.

Before a program can use an API function, it must use a Declare statement to declare the function. It must also use Type statements to define any data structures the function needs. For instance, the following code defines the POINTAPI data structure and declares the Polygon API function. The POINTAPI structure contains two long integer fields, x and y. The Polygon function is contained in the gdi32 library. If you are running a 32-bit operating system, this library is in the file Gdi32.dll in your system directory.

Polygon's first parameter, hDC, is the handle of a device context (DC). This tells the function where it should draw. Visual Basic's Form and PictureBox objects both have hDC properties that a program can use for this argument.

The lpPoint parameter actually represents an array of POINTAPI structures. Because the declaration does not include the ByVal keyword, the function receives the address of a POINTAPI structure. The API function can use that address to find all the POINTAPI structures in the array.

The final parameter, nCount, indicates the number of POINTAPI structures in the array. Because the function uses addresses to search through memory for the POINTAPI structures, it must know when to stop so that it does not examine meaningless memory.

```
Private Type POINTAPI
    x As Long
    y As Long
End Type

Private Declare Function Polygon Lib "gdi32" (ByVal hDC As Long, _
    lpPoint As POINTAPI, ByVal nCount As Long) As Long
```

The following code shows how a program can invoke the Polygon function after it has been declared. To pass the address of the array to the function, the Visual Basic program uses the first item in the array. The address of the first item is the same as the address of the start of the array.

```
Private Sub DrawPolygon()
Const NUM_POINTS = 20
Dim pts(1 To NUM_POINTS) As POINTAPI

    ' Initialize the pts array.
        :

    ' Draw the polygon on the form.
    Polygon hDC, pts(1), NUM_POINTS
End Sub
```

For more information about API functions, consult the online documentation or a book about the API. Visual Basic also comes with text files that list Visual Basic declarations for API functions. Search the Visual Basic CD-ROM for files that contain the string api. In Visual Basic 4, the 32-bit version of this file is called Win32api.txt and is in the Winapi subdirectory.

Visual Basic also includes an API text viewer. This program can help you search for API data structure definitions, function declarations, and constant definitions needed by API functions.

One final word of caution: The API can be dangerous. API functions can access memory outside of the memory the program has allocated. For instance, if a program creates an array of 10 POINTAPI structures but tells the Polygon function to draw 100 points, the function will access memory outside of the array. In some cases, this will merely cause incorrect results. In other cases, it will crash the program, sometimes the Visual Basic development environment, and occasionally the entire operating system.

Be sure you pass API functions parameters of the correct data types. Pay particular attention to arrays. Be sure you pass in the first item and that the item count is correct. Finally, save your work often. If the development environment or operating system crashes, you will lose any changes you have made since the last time you saved.

Updates and Feedback

Updates to this book will be posted on the book's Web site at www.vb-helper.com/examples.htm. These will include modifications to make the examples work with future versions of Visual Basic, if necessary. This Web site also contains many other code examples at www.vb-helper.com/HowTo.htm, though they are not as completely explained as the ones described in this book.

If you have questions, comments, or suggestions, or if you want to share your programming tips and tricks with others, send e-mail to the author at RodStephens@vb-helper.com.

Working with Variables

Variables are one of the most basic concepts in programming. This chapter covers tips and tricks that deal with variables. It explores such topics as loading arrays quickly, creating and using nested user-defined data types, and copying memory from one array to another much more quickly than is possible using a For loop.

---

1. Initialize Arrays

Directory: InitArr

Ancient versions of Basic and FORTRAN included a DATA statement that let a program specify the initial values an array should hold. Visual Basic does not include this statement, but you can still initialize an array quickly.

Example program InitArr demonstrates methods for initializing variant and integer arrays. Enter the number of times you want the program to initialize the arrays and the number of times you want it to access every item in the arrays. You may need to pick large numbers to get timing results big enough to be meaningful. When you click the Run button, the program initializes the arrays and then accesses each item the indicated number of times. Initializing the integer array is usually slightly faster than initializing the variant array. Accessing the items in the variant array usually takes much longer.

Program InitArr.

How It Works

Variant variables can contain many different kinds of data such as integers, singles, Booleans, and so forth. They can also contain arrays of other variants. A variant can even contain an array of variants that each contains other things.

Visual Basic's Array statement takes a list of values and creates a variant array holding those values. This makes initializing a variant array simple. The Array statement can even take values of different data types and place them in the variant array's entries.

The following code shows how a program can initialize a variant array. In this example, the array contains two strings, an integer, and a double-precision floating-point number.

```
Dim my_array As Variant

    my_array = Array("Item 1", "Item 2", 3, 4#)
```

Unfortunately, variants are not very efficient. Working with them is slower than working with variables of other data types. They also take more memory than variables of other types.

To get both easy initialization and good performance, you can write a routine that initializes an array with a more specific data type. The following code shows a subroutine that initializes an integer array. It uses a ParamArray argument so it can take any number of integer parameters. It allocates the array and then uses a For loop to copy the values into the array.

```
' Initialize the values in an integer array.
Public Sub InitIntegerArray(int_array() As Integer, _
    ParamArray values() As Variant)
Dim i As Long

    ' Allocate the array.
    ReDim int_array(LBound(values) To UBound(values))
```

```
    ' Copy the values into the array.
    For i = LBound(values) To UBound(values)
        int_array(i) = values(i)
    Next i
End Sub
```

The following code shows how a program might use subroutine InitIntegerArray to initialize an array.

```
Private Sub Form_Load()
Dim my_array() As Integer

    InitIntegerArray my_array, 2, 3, 5, 7, 11
        :
End Sub
```

Program InitArr uses the Array statement to initialize a variant array and subroutine InitIntegerArray to initialize an integer array.

2.   Copy Memory Quickly Using the API   ☆ ☆

Directory: CopyMem

Copying an array using Visual Basic alone is fairly slow. The following code shows how a program might copy data from one array into another.

```
Dim i As Integer

    For i = LBound(from_array) To UBound(from_array)
        to_array(i) = from_array(i)
    Next i
```

This is simple but slow. The hmemcpy (for 16-bit systems) and RtlMoveMemory (for 32-bit systems) API functions are much faster. Example program CopyMem compares the speed of copying memory using a For loop with the speeds given by these two API functions.

Enter the size of the array and the number of times you want the program to run the test. Then click the Run button. The program allocates the arrays and then copies them using the two different methods. In a typical test, the For loop may take more than 100 times as long as the API functions.

Program CopyMem.

How It Works

The following code shows how to declare the hmemcpy and RtlMoveMemory functions. Notice that both are defined using the name MemCopy. Although they have different names in their API libraries, Kernel and kernel32, this program calls them both Mem-Copy. The program refers to the appropriate function using the name MemCopy no matter which API function it really uses.

```
' Declare the memory copying function.
#If Win16 Then
    Public Declare Sub MemCopy Lib "Kernel" Alias _
        "hmemcpy" (dest As Any, src As Any, _
        ByVal numbytes As Long)
#Else
    Public Declare Sub MemCopy Lib "kernel32" Alias _
        "RtlMoveMemory" (dest As Any, src As Any, _
        ByVal numbytes As Long)
#End If
```

These functions take the memory address to which the memory should be copied, the address from which the memory should be copied, and the number of bytes to copy. Visual Basic uses a variable in place of its address. For instance, the following code shows how to copy the data in one integer array into another.

```
Dim from_array() As Integer
Dim to_array() As Integer
Dim bytes_to_copy As Long

    ' Initialize the arrays.
        :

    ' The number of bytes to copy is the size of an entry
    ' in the array times the number of items in the array.
    bytes_to_copy = _
        Len(from_array(UBound(from_array))) * _
        (UBound(from_array) - LBound(from_array) + 1)
```

```
' Copy from_array into to_array.
MemCopy to_array(LBound(to_array)), _
    from_array(LBound(from_array)), bytes_to_copy
```

Note that the arrays do not need to have the same bounds. In fact, they do not even need to have the same sizes as long as to_array has room for all of the bytes copied. If there is not enough room, however, the function will happily try to copy values beyond the end of to_array. That will copy data into other parts of memory, probably corrupting other variables and possibly crashing your program or even the Visual Basic development environment.

You can also use this technique to copy items from one position to another within the same array. For instance, you could use the following code to insert an item at the beginning of an array full of values.

```
Dim my_array(0 To 99) As Integer
Dim bytes_to_copy As Long
Dim new_value As Integer

    ' Initialize the array and new_value.
        :

    ' The size of an entry times one less
    ' than the number of items in the array.
    bytes_to_copy = Len(my_array(0)) * 99

    ' Move the items over one position.
    MemCopy my_array(1), my_array(0), bytes_to_copy

    ' Insert the new value.
    my_array(0) = new_value
```

Program CopyMem compares the speed of copying an array using a For loop with the speed of using the hmemcpy and RtlMoveMemory functions.

3. Copy Memory Quickly in Visual Basic 6

Directory: CopyArr

The previous example shows how to copy data in an array quickly using API functions. In Visual Basic 6, you can assign one resizable array to another in a single step.

The CopyMem2 example program compares three methods for copying memory: using a For loop, using the API functions described in the previous section, and using array assignment. Enter the size of the array and the number of times you want the program to run the test. Then click the Run button to make the program perform the tests. The API functions are the fastest. Array assignment is a reasonably close second. Using a For loop is a distant third.

Program CopyMem2.

How It Works

The following code shows how array assignment works in Visual Basic 6. This code copies the data in from_array into to_array. The destination variable to_array is automatically allocated and redimensioned if necessary so its dimensions match those of from_array. That means the program does not need dimension to_array explicitly.

```
Dim from_array() As Long
Dim to_array() As Long

    ' Initialize from_array.
        :

    to_array = from_array
```

This code copies the data from one array to another; it does not make the arrays equivalent. For instance, if you change the value of to_array(1), the value of from_array(1) is not changed.

This technique has several advantages over the method used by the previous example. It uses only Visual Basic commands so you do not need to work with confusing and possibly dangerous API functions. It also will not write over random chunks of memory if to_array does not have room to hold all the data.

On the other hand, it does not allow you to copy one array into part of another. For instance, you cannot copy entries 1 through 10 in one array into positions 21 through 30 in another array. It also will not let you copy data from one part of an array to another. If you need these capabilities, use the API functions described in the previous example. Otherwise, use this technique.

4. Empty Collections Quickly

④ ⑤ ⑥

Directory: EmptyCol

There are many ways to empty a collection, and some are much faster than others. Example program EmptyCol compares three different methods. It removes the items in last-in-first-out (LIFO) order, first-in-first-out (FIFO) order, and by setting the collection to Nothing.

Enter the number of items you want added to the collection and the number of times you want the program to repeat the test. When you click the Run button, the program creates, fills, and destroys three collections using the three methods. The reported times do not include the time to create the collections, so the program actually takes much longer than the times displayed.

Program EmptyCol.

How It Works

The following code removes the items in a collection in last-in-first-out (LIFO) order.

```
Dim col As New Collection

    ' Add entries to the collection.
        :

    ' Empty the collection.
    Do While col.Count > 0
        col.Remove col.Count
    Loop
```

It may seem that the order in which items are removed should make no difference, but it does. The following code removes the items in first-in-first-out order and is much faster.

```
Do While col.Count > 0
    col.Remove 1
Loop
```

Finally, setting the collection variable to Nothing is faster still. This approach also frees the memory allocated for the collection itself.

```
Set col = Nothing
```

Because it is simple and fast, setting a collection to Nothing is the best way to empty a collection.

5. Use Arrays Not Collections

Directory: UseArray

Collections are convenient for storing information, but arrays are faster, particularly if you must store many items.

Example program UseArray compares the speeds of collections and arrays. Enter the number of items you want to store and the number of times the program should run its test. Click the Run button to make the program compare the times needed to fill a collection and two arrays. The fixed size array is initially allocated to have enough room for all the data items. The variable size array is incrementally enlarged as each item is added.

Program UseArray.

How It Works

If you know in advance how many items you will need to store, use an array. The program can make the array large enough to hold all the items. Use a variable to keep track of the number of items used in the array. This variable tells you where to add the next item.

If you do not know in advance how many items the array must hold, resize the array when necessary, as shown in the following code.

```
Private num_items As Long
Private item_array() As Double

' Add an item to the array.
Private Sub AddItem(ByVal new_value As Double)
    ' Make room for the item.
    num_items = num_items + 1
    ReDim Preserve item_array(1 To num_items)

    ' Add the item.
    item_array(num_items) = new_value
End Sub
```

Resizing the array frequently slows the program down, but not as much as using a collection. Using arrays is much faster. You should use a collection only if you need its special capabilities, such as searching for an item using a key.

6. Create Objects Quickly

Directory: MakeObj

In Visual Basic, you can declare an object reference and then allocate the object later using the New keyword. You can also declare and allocate the object at the same time. The following code shows these two methods.

```
Dim col1 As Collection          ' Declare col1.
Dim col2 As New Collection      ' Declare and allocate col2.

    Set col1 = New Collection    ' Allocate col1.
```

It may seem that these methods should have similar performance, but there is actually a significant difference. Example program MakeObj compares the performance of these methods. Enter the number of times you want to run the program's tests. Then click the Run button to make the program compare the two item allocation methods. The program allocates the items and then invokes two simple property procedures defined by the objects. In one set of tests, declaring and allocating the object separately was roughly 25 percent faster.

Program MakeObj.

How It Works

When you declare and allocate a reference in a single statement, Visual Basic does not actually allocate the object. Instead it waits until the first time the program accesses the object. As it works with the object, Visual Basic must constantly check whether the object has been allocated so it knows if it must create the object. This continual checking slows the program down.

The program runs more quickly if you declare and initialize the object separately. Then Visual Basic allocates the object when you tell it to do so. It does not need to check constantly whether the object is allocated. It relies on you to allocate the object before it is needed.

7. Use Nested UDTs

Directory: NestUDT

User-defined types (UDTs) let a program keep related information together in a single variable. Using UDTs to manipulate related data simplifies the program.

A program can also make a UDT that contains fields that are instances of other UDTs. That lets it treat different parts of the larger UDT uniformly.

Example program NestUDT uses nested UDTs to manage a simple customer list. Click the Name, Home Phone, Home Address, Work Phone, or Work Address option button to see a list of the appropriate customer data. The program uses the UDTs to pass as little information as possible into the routines that generate the lists.

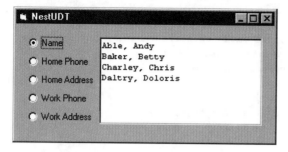

Program NestUDT.

How It Works

The following code shows how a program might create a Customer UDT to represent information about customers.

```
' Define the Customer UDT.
Type Customer
    CustomerID As Long
    LastName As String
    FirstName As String
    HomePhone As String * 12
    HomeStreet As String
    HomeCity As String
    HomeState As String * 2
    HomeZip As String * 10
    WorkPhone As String * 12
    WorkStreet As String
    WorkCity As String
    WorkState As String * 2
    WorkZip As String * 10
    ' More information about purchases, etc.
        :
End Type


' Create an array of customers.
Public Customers() As Customer
Public NumCustomers As Long
```

Using this UDT, a program can work with a particular customer as a single unit. For instance, suppose the program has initialized the Customers array. Then it might use the following code to make the PrintName subroutine print each customer's name on the printer. PrintName can work with a customer wrapped in a nice little package and ignore the address, phone number, and other fields it does not need.

```
Dim cust_num As Long

    ' Make PrintName print each customer's name.
    For cust_num = 1 To NumCustomers
        PrintName Customers(cust_num)
    Next cust_num
        :
Private Sub PrintName(cust As Customer)
    Printer.Print cust.LastName & "," cust.FirstName
End Sub
```

The Customer UDT contains several pieces of data that are very similar. It contains a street address, city, state, Zip code, and phone number for both the customer's home and office. You can make the Customer type a bit more compact and consistent with a new UDT that represents this contact information.

```
    ' Define the ContactInfo UDT.
Type ContactInfo
    Phone As String * 12
    Street As String
    City As String
    State As String * 2
    Zip As String * 10
End Type

    ' Define the Customer UDT.
Type Customer
    CustomerID As Long
    LastName As String
    FirstName As String
    HomeInfo As ContactInfo
    WorkInfo As ContactInfo
    ' More information about purchases, etc.
        :
End Type
```

Placing the contact information in a new UDT allows the program to treat the home and work information more uniformly. The following code shows how the program might print mailing labels for the customers' home addresses.

```
Dim cust_num As Long

    ' Make PrintLabel print each customer's home address label.
    For cust_num = 1 To NumCustomers
        PrintLabel Customers(cust_num).HomeInfo
    Next cust_num
        :
Private Sub PrintLabel(contact_info As ContactInfo)
    ' Do whatever is needed to properly position:
```

```
'        contact_info.Street
'        contact_info.City
'        contact_info.State
'        contact_info.Zip
       :
End Sub
```

Because the PrintLabel subroutine takes a ContextInfo UDT as a parameter, it is easy to write a new routine to print work address labels. The program would simply pass Print-Label each customer's WorkInfo value instead of the HomeInfo value.

8. Create Global Properties

Directory: GlobProp

Programmers who have used Visual Basic's classes know they can create properties for classes and controls. Many do not realize, however, that they can also create global properties that apply to the application as a whole. These properties play the role of global variables, but they give all the advantages of properties in a class or control. They let you control access to the property, validate its values when the program wants to change it, and make a property that is essentially read-only.

Example program GlobProp demonstrates global properties. Enter a value in the text box and click the Set Fahrenheit or Set Celsius button. The program uses property procedures to set the temperature and then display the new values in degrees Fahrenheit and Celsius. Try entering a value less than absolute zero (–273.18 C or –459.72 F) to see how the program catches and handles the error.

Program GlobProp.

How It Works

Use a private variable in a .bas module to store the property's actual value. Provide property let, set, and get procedures in the module to allow other parts of the program access to the property.

The following code shows how module Degrees.bas manages a temperature value. This module provides two sets of property procedures. One lets and gets temperature in degrees Fahrenheit, and the other allows access to the value using degrees Celsius. Note that the code validates the new value to verify that it is greater than absolute zero, the lowest possible temperature that makes sense.

```
' The real temperature in degrees Celsius.
Private temp_celsius As Single


' Set the temperature in degrees Fahrenheit.
Public Property Let DegreesF(ByVal new_value As Single)
    ' Use DegreesC to set the value.
    DegreesC = (new_value - 32) * 5# / 9#
End Property


' Return the temperature in degrees Fahrenheit.
Public Property Get DegreesF() As Single
    ' Use DegreesC to get the value.
    DegreesF = (DegreesC * 9# / 5#) + 32
End Property


' Set the temperature in degrees Celsius.
Public Property Let DegreesC(ByVal new value As Single)
    ' If the value is not greater than absolute zero,
    ' raise an invalid parameter error.
    If new_value <= -273.18 Then _
        Err.Raise 380, "Degrees", _
            "Temperature must be at greater than absolute zero."

    ' Save the new value.
    temp_celsius = new_value
End Property


' Return the temperature in degrees Celsius.
Public Property Get DegreesC() As Single
    DegreesC = temp_celsius
End Property
```

Using property procedures, an application can control access to a value.

9. Hide Data Inside Modules ④ ⑤ ⑥

Directory: Maze

The previous example shows how to use property procedures to access a value declared privately within a .bas module. Only the property procedures can directly access the data. Other parts of the program must use these procedures to manipulate the value indirectly.

This is just one way to hide data inside a module. You can also hide more complex data structures inside modules and provide access routines to allow the rest of the program to interact with the data indirectly. This frees the rest of the program from knowing how the data is stored and how it works.

Example program Maze uses this technique to manage a maze data structure. The maze data is stored in the Maze.bas module. All of the details for loading, storing, and manipulating the maze and the player's current position are hidden inside the module. The rest of the program manipulates the data structure through methods provided by the module.

Program Maze.

How It Works

The main program can access the data only through the public routines defined in Maze.bas. This protects the data from invalid changes by the main program and makes the main program extremely simple. In this program, there are only two public routines in Maze.bas: InitializeMaze and ProcessMoveKey. The entire main program is shown in the following code.

```
Option Explicit

' Initialize the maze and player.
Private Sub Form_Load()
    InitializeMaze Me, picPlayer, _
        App.Path & "\maze.dat"
End Sub

' Process movement keys.
Private Sub Form_KeyDown(KeyCode As Integer, Shift As Integer)
    ProcessMoveKey KeyCode
End Sub
```

The Maze.bas module contains the code that loads the maze, processes user key strokes, and moves the player accordingly. This code is fairly long, and it is not important to the idea of hiding data within a module, so it is not shown here. You can see the complete source code on the CD-ROM.

10. Use Classes and Modules

 ④ ⑤ ⑥

Directory: MazeCls

The previous example shows how to use a .bas module to hide data from the main program. This is very similar to the way classes encapsulate data. Because these methods are so similar, you might wonder when you should use a class and when you should use a .bas module.

Example program MazeCls is very similar to program Maze except it uses a class to hide maze data instead of a .bas file.

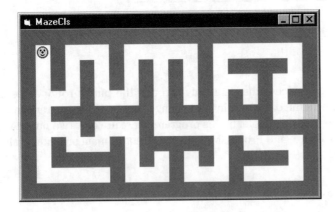

Program MazeCls.

How It Works

A class is very similar to a .bas module with one big exception: A program can create multiple instances of a class. After the class is defined, the program can create any number of objects that are members of that class. There is only a single instance of any given .bas module in a program.

On a more conceptual level, if the program works with things that you consider objects, they should probably be instances of a class. If the objects perform actions, you should give the class methods (subroutines and functions) that make them perform those actions. You should implement properties that describe the state of the objects using property procedures.

On the other hand, if you have a routine that applies to more than one general type of thing, it belongs in a .bas module. For instance, a routine that draws a company logo on a form, picture box, or printer object does not belong to any one of those objects. It probably does not belong to a class you have created, so it belongs in a .bas module. It can take the object on which to draw as a parameter.

You can also use a .bas module when you need only a single instance of something that is object-like. The previous example uses a single instance of a maze object implemented in a .bas file. In this case, there is very little difference between the .bas module and a .cls module that defines a class. If there is a chance that you may later need to create more than one object of this type, however, you can make that simpler by implementing the object with a class.

Example program MazeCls is very similar to program Maze described in the previous example, but it uses a Maze class instead of data hidden in a .bas module. The following code shows the main MazeCls program in its entirety. Only four lines have been changed to refer to a Maze object.

```
Option Explicit

Private TheMaze As Maze

' Initialize the maze and player.
Private Sub Form_Load()
    Set TheMaze = New Maze

    TheMaze.InitializeMaze Me, picPlayer, _
        App.Path & "\maze.dat"
End Sub

' Process movement keys.
Private Sub Form_KeyDown(KeyCode As Integer, Shift As Integer)
    TheMaze.ProcessMoveKey KeyCode
End Sub
```

The only change required to the maze data structure was to move its variables and routines into a class module. Other than that, the code is exactly identical to the code in the .bas module used by program Maze. You can see the complete code on the CD-ROM.

This program could easily use the Maze class to create multiple Maze objects. It could then display more than one maze at the same time. That might not make sense for this program, but other programs do need to manage more than one object of a particular kind. If a program needs to use more than one instance of the same kind of object, or if you think you might want it to later, implement the object in a class. Otherwise, you can keep the object's data in a .bas module.

11. Use Implements

Directory: Impl

The Implements keyword lets you tell Visual Basic that a certain class implements the features defined by another class. This lets the system understand more precisely what objects can and cannot do. This extra information allows Visual Basic to check certain operations at compile time and verify that they are possible. That not only helps you debug your program by providing better error checking, but it also allows the program to run faster because it does not need to worry about whether the operations are possible at run time.

Example program Impl uses this technique to draw circles, squares, ellipses, and rectangles. Click an option button, and then click on the form to draw a shape.

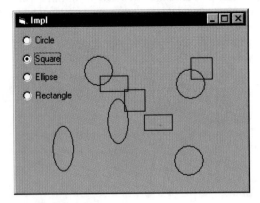

Program Impl.

How It Works

Suppose you create a VisibleShape class that defines public variables ShapeX, ShapeY, and ShapeSize, and a public Draw subroutine, as shown in the following code.

```
Option Explicit


' The object's position and size.
Public ShapeX As Single
Public ShapeY As Single
Public ShapeSize As Single


' Draw the shape.
Public Sub Draw(Canvas As Form)


End Sub
```

Next you can define other classes that implement the features defined by VisibleShape. When you insert the statement Implements VisibleShape in a class, Visual Basic automatically creates a new code section named VisibleShape. It creates entries within that section for routines to implement the public features defined by the VisibleShape class. In this case, it creates property procedures for VisibleShape_ShapeX, VisibleShape_ShapeY, and VisibleShape_ShapeSize. It also creates a subroutine named VisibleShape_Draw.

Using the combo boxes in the Visual Basic code editor, you can select these routines and enter code to implement them. The following code shows how a VisibleCircle class might handle these routines.

```
Option Explicit

Implements VisibleShape

Private ShapeX As Single
Private ShapeY As Single
Private ShapeSize As Single


' Draw the circle.
Private Sub VisibleShape_Draw(Canvas As Form)
    Canvas.Circle (ShapeX, ShapeY), _
        2 * ShapeSize
End Sub


' Save the new ShapeSize value.
Private Property Let VisibleShape_ShapeSize(ByVal RHS As Single)
    ShapeSize = RHS
End Property


' Return the ShapeSize value.
Private Property Get VisibleShape_ShapeSize() As Single
    VisibleShape_ShapeSize = ShapeSize
End Property


' Save the new ShapeX value.
Private Property Let VisibleShape_ShapeX(ByVal RHS As Single)
    ShapeX = RHS
End Property
```

```
' Return the ShapeX value.
Private Property Get VisibleShape_ShapeX() As Single
    VisibleShape_ShapeX = X
End Property


' Save the new ShapeY value.
Private Property Let VisibleShape_ShapeY(ByVal RHS As Single)
    ShapeY = RHS
End Property


' Return the ShapeY value.
Private Property Get VisibleShape_ShapeY() As Single
    VisibleShape_ShapeY = Y
End Property
```

Similarly you can create other classes that implement the VisibleShape features. Then a program can treat any object that implements VisibleShape as if it really were a Visible-Shape object.

When you click on its form, program Impl creates an object of the appropriate type and stores it in its Shapes collection. It then refreshes the form. The form's Paint event handler draws the shapes by invoking the Draw subroutine provided by each of the objects in the Shapes collection.

```
Option Explicit

Private Shapes As Collection

' Create the Shapes collection.
Private Sub Form_Load()
    Set Shapes = New Collection
End Sub

' Create a new shape.
Private Sub Form_MouseDown(Button As Integer, Shift As Integer, _
    X As Single, Y As Single)
Dim new_shape As VisibleShape

    ' Create a shape of the correct type.
    If optCircle.Value Then
        Set new_shape = New VisibleCircle
    ElseIf optSquare.Value Then
        Set new_shape = New VisibleSquare
    ElseIf optEllipse.Value Then
        Set new_shape = New VisibleEllipse
    Else
        Set new_shape = New VisibleRectangle
    End If

    ' Save the shape's center and width.
    new_shape.ShapeX = X
```

```
    new_shape.ShapeY = Y
    new_shape.ShapeSize = 144

    ' Add the shape to the Shapes collection.
    Shapes.Add new_shape

    ' Make the form redraw.
    Refresh
End Sub

' Make the shapes draw themselves.
Private Sub Form_Paint()
Dim visible_shape As VisibleShape

    For Each visible_shape In Shapes
        visible_shape.Draw Me
    Next visible_shape
End Sub
```

Using Implements has three advantages. First, it lets a program treat different kinds of objects as if they were the same. Program Impl treats circles, squares, ellipses, and rectangles as if they were all VisibleShape objects.

Second, giving Visual Basic concrete object types allows it to perform error checking sooner. If the Form_Paint event handler in the previous code tried to invoke the visible_shape object's Redraw subroutine, Visual Basic would know there was a problem at compile time because the VisibleShape class does not have a Redraw subroutine. On the other hand, if you declared visible_shape to be of type Object, Visual Basic would not know what kind of object visible_shape was until run time. It would be unable to tell whether the object has a Redraw subroutine until run time.

Finally, when Visual Basic works with a concrete data type, it can invoke object methods more quickly. The program could store generic objects in the Shapes collection, but it would not be able to access their properties and subroutines as quickly. The following example demonstrates this principle.

12. Use Concrete Object Types

Directory: Concrete

The previous example manipulates more than one kind of object using the same variable. Using Implements allows the program to give Visual Basic more information about the object than it would otherwise have. That allows Visual Basic to use the object more efficiently.

This principle applies more generally to all objects. Using a more specific object type gives Visual Basic more information about the object and allows it to work more efficiently.

Example program Concrete compares the time needed to access a method in two objects. One is declared as a generic Object, and the other is declared as a specific NumberClass object. In one set of tests, using the generic object took 38 times as long as using the specific object.

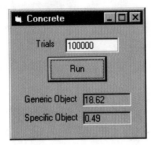

Program Concrete.

How It Works

The following code shows how program Concrete works. The cmdRun_Click event handler declares a variable of type Object and another of type NumberClass. It initializes both to NumberClass objects, sets their Value property a number of times, and displays the results.

```
Option Explicit

' Test the declaration methods.
Private Sub cmdRun_Click()
Dim generic_obj As Object
Dim specific_obj As NumberClass
Dim start_time As Single
Dim trial As Long
Dim num_trials As Long

    Screen.MousePointer = vbHourglass
    lblGeneric.Caption = ""
    lblSpecific.Caption = ""
    DoEvents

    ' Test the generic object.
    num_trials = CLng(txtTrials.Text)
    Set generic_obj = New NumberClass
    start_time = Timer
    For trial = 1 To num_trials
        generic_obj.Value = trial
    Next trial
    lblGeneric.Caption = Format$(Timer - start_time, "0.00")
    DoEvents
```

```
      ' Test the specific object.
      Set specific_obj = New NumberClass
      start_time = Timer
      For trial = 1 To num_trials
          specific_obj.Value = trial
      Next trial
      lblSpecific.Caption = Format$(Timer - start_time, "0.00")

      Screen.MousePointer = vbDefault
  End Sub
```

In Visual Basic 5 or later, you can use the Implements keyword to give Visual Basic some information about an object. For instance, the VisualCircle class might implement the features of the VisibleShape class. Declaring an object of type VisibleShape is more efficient than declaring it to be of type Object. If the object is actually a VisibleCircle, declaring it to be of type VisibleCircle is more efficient still.

13. Track Object Creation and Destruction

Directory: TrackObj

It is often hard to figure out when objects are created and destroyed. When in doubt, stick Debug.Print statements in the object's Initialize and Terminate event handlers to try to see what's happening.

You can also create global variables to keep track of the number of objects created and destroyed. Before the program exits, it should check these counts to make sure they are zero. If a count is greater than zero, some object was created that was not destroyed. That may indicate that a data structure was not properly destroyed and there is a bug in the program.

Example program TrackObj uses this technique to keep track of objects created and destroyed. Enter a number of items. Click the Create Items button to create that many items. Click the Destroy Items button to destroy that many items. The program displays object creation and destruction information in the Debug or Immediate window. When you close the program, it also warns you if objects were created but not destroyed.

Program TrackObj.

How It Works

The following code shows how the MyClass class keeps track of objects created and destroyed. The variable NumMyClass is declared publicly in a .bas module.

```
Option Explicit

' Increment the object count.
Private Sub Class_Initialize()
    NumMyClass = NumMyClass + 1

    Debug.Print "Created MyClass object " & _
        Format$(NumMyClass)
End Sub

' Decrement the object count.
Private Sub Class_Terminate()
    Debug.Print "Destroyed MyClass object " & _
        Format$(NumMyClass)

    NumMyClass = NumMyClass - 1
End Sub
```

The following code shows how program TrackObj verifies that all created objects were destroyed before it exits.

```
' Verify that all items are destroyed.
Private Sub Form_Unload(Cancel As Integer)
    If NumMyClass > 0 Then
        MsgBox "Warning: " & Format$(NumMyClass) & _
            " MyClass items were allocated but not destroyed."
    End If
End Sub
```

Code such as this can make finding corrupt data structures much easier. You may want to comment out the code that maintains the object counts before you create a compiled executable. That code takes very little time, however, so it may be better to just leave it alone. The Debug.Print statements are removed automatically anyway, and when the program unloads, the error message may alert you to a previously undetected problem.

14. Understand Parenthesized Arguments   ④ ⑤ ⑥

Directory: ParenArg

When Visual Basic sees an expression surrounded by parentheses, it evaluates the expression and works with the result. This is obvious in the following code. The program evaluates X + 3, multiplies the result by 2, and assigns the result to Y.

```
Y = (X + 3) * 2
```

This fact is much less obvious when you call a procedure or function with extra parentheses around the parameters. In the following code, the program evaluates X and passes the result to the MySub subroutine.

```
MySub (X)
```

Note that the program does not pass X itself to MySub. It calculates the expression X and passes the result of that expression to MySub. This value is stored internally in a temporary variable that the main program never sees. That means if MySub changes its parameter's value, the main program does not see the change.

Example program ParenArg demonstrates this effect. Enter a value and click the Pass Value button to pass the value itself into subroutine DoubleIt. Click the Pass With Parens button to pass the value into subroutine DoubleIt with extra parentheses. In either case, subroutine DoubleIt multiplies its parameter by two. When you pass the value without parentheses, the value is returned to the main program doubled. When you pass the value with parentheses, the modified value is hidden from the main program.

Program ParenArg.

How It Works

The following code shows how program ParenArg works.

```
Option Explicit

' Pass the value normally.
Private Sub cmdPassValue_Click()
Dim value As Long

    value = CLng(txtValue.Text)
    DoubleIt value
    lblNewValue.Caption = Format$(value)
End Sub

' Pass the value with extra parentheses.
Private Sub cmdPassWithParens_Click()
```

```
Dim value As Long

    value = CLng(txtValue.Text)
    DoubleIt (value)
    lblNewValue.Caption = Format$(value)
End Sub

' Double the value of the parameter.
Private Sub DoubleIt(i As Long)
    i = i * 2
End Sub
```

You should not place extra parentheses around subroutine arguments because they are confusing. If the subroutine should never change its parameter, you should declare the routine using the ByVal keyword. If you normally want the value to change but you want to use one instance where it does not, use a separate variable that can change. That will make the code easier to understand, debug, and maintain.

15. Beware of Foreign Syntax

Directory: CSyntax

Beware of statements that look like commands in other programming languages, such as C or C++. For instance, the following equality statement is valid in C, C++, and Visual Basic.

```
Dim A As Integer
Dim B As Integer

    A = B = 12
```

Even though this statement is legal in all three languages, it means one thing in C and C++ and another in Visual Basic. In C and C++, this statement assigns the value 12 to B and then assigns the value of B to A. This makes A and B both 12.

Example program CSyntax shows the results of this code in Visual Basic. Enter a value and click the Set Value button. The program executes the statement A = B = <the value you specified>. If you enter the value 0, the program sets A to -1 and B to 0. If you enter any other value, the program sets both A and B to 0.

Program CSyntax.

How It Works

The following code shows how program CSyntax performs its duties.

```
Option Explicit

' Set the value.
Private Sub cmdSetValue_Click()
Dim A As Integer
Dim B As Integer

    A = B = CInt(txtValue.Text)
    lblAValue.Caption = Format$(A)
    lblBValue.Caption = Format$(B)
End Sub
```

Visual Basic treats the statement A = B = CInt(txtValue.Text) as if it were written A = (B = CInt(txtValue.Text)). It regards B = CInt(txtValue.Text) as a Boolean expression that is True if B matches the value you enter and False if it does not. Because A and B have just been allocated, they are currently both 0. If you entered 0, the values match so B is True.

The program then assigns the Boolean value to variable A. If the value is True, it sets A to -1. If the value is False, it sets A to 0. In either case, the variable B is never assigned a value so it remains 0.

Beware of statements like this that work in more than one language but that have different meanings.

16. Understand Null Values

④ ⑤ ⑥

Directory: Nulls

The values Null, Empty, vbNullString, and Nothing are similar, but they have slightly different meanings. Example program Nulls shows some of the ways a program can use these values. When it starts, the program calculates and displays the results of some expressions that demonstrate the special features of these values.

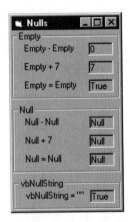

Program Nulls.

How It Works

In general, Empty behaves as if it were an uninitialized value, Null makes expression results Null, and vbNullString acts like an empty string. The exact details are a little more involved. The following sections explain the differences between these values.

Null

Null is a variant subtype like Integer or String. It represents a variant that contains no valid data. This is different from zero, Nothing, Empty, or vbNullString. Most other values when combined with Null produce a Null result. For instance:

```
Null - Null     is Null not 0
Null + 7        is Null not 7
Null = Null     is Null not True
```

You can use IsNull to determine whether an expression is Null:

```
If IsNull(my_variable) Then ...
```

You can use Null to represent a value that is initialized but that does not have a meaningful value.

Empty

This is another variant subtype like Integer or String. It represents a variable that has not yet been initialized. This is different from Null, which represents a value that specifically contains no valid data.

A variant variable that has not yet been initialized has the value Empty. If a program declares a variant, it has the value Empty until the program gives it a different value.

You can use IsEmpty to see if a variant has been initialized. This is convenient for initializing static variables the first time a routine is used.

```
If IsEmpty(my_variant) Then ...
```

When you combine an Empty value with another in an expression, the Empty value is treated as blank for strings or zero for numeric data types. For example, Empty + 7 = 7.

vbNullString

This constant represents an empty string. This is not the same as a blank string "". It is not a string that is blank; it is a string that in some sense does not exist. While this value is not a blank string, a program can treat vbNullString as if it were a blank string for most purposes.

The most important use for vbNullString is in passing null parameters to API functions. For instance, an API function may take the address of a data structure as a parameter. A Visual Basic program can pass the value vbNullString for that argument to make the API function receive the null (0) address instead. How the API function behaves depends on the particular function.

Nothing

Nothing is an object reference that points to no object. When you set an object reference to Nothing, you free that reference. If no other references point to the object, Visual Basic knows the program cannot refer to the object any more, so it automatically destroys the object.

For instance, the following code declares and allocates an object, uses it for a while, and then destroys it by setting the program's only reference to it to Nothing.

```
Dim obj As MyClass

    ' Allocate the object.
    Set obj = New MyClass
```

```
' Work with the object.
    :
' Destroy the object.
Set obj = Nothing
```

It is sometimes important and always a good idea to set object references to Nothing when you are done with them. This lets Visual Basic destroy the objects and reclaim their memory.

Use Is Nothing to determine whether a reference points to nothing, as in the following statement:

```
If obj IsNothing Then ...
```

Program Nulls

The following code shows how program Nulls works.

```
Option Explicit

Private Sub Form_Load()
Dim a_variant As Variant
Dim result As Variant

    ' Empty (an uninitialized variant).
    ' Empty - Empty.
    result = a_variant - a_variant
    lblEmpty1.Caption = Format$(result)
    ' Empty + 7.
    result = a_variant + 7
    lblEmpty2.Caption = Format$(result)
    ' Empty = Empty.
    result = a_variant = a_variant
    lblEmpty3.Caption = Format$(result)

    ' Null (variant set to Null).
    a_variant = Null
    ' Null - Null.
    result = a_variant - a_variant
    If IsNull(result) Then
        lblNull1.Caption = "Null"
    Else
        lblNull1.Caption = Format$(result)
    End If
    ' Null + 7.
    result = a_variant + 7
    If IsNull(result) Then
        lblNull2.Caption = "Null"
    Else
```

```
        lblNull2.Caption = Format$(result)
    End If
    ' Null = Null.
    result = a_variant = a_variant
    If IsNull(result) Then
        lblNull3.Caption = "Null"
    Else
        lblNull3.Caption = Format$(result)
    End If

    ' vbNullString.
    a_variant = vbNullString
    result = a_variant = ""
    lblNullString1.Caption = Format$(result)
End Sub
```

You should learn the differences between these unusual values and use the correct value under different circumstances.

Manipulating Numbers

Many programs perform a lot of numerical calculations. This chapter covers a sampling of useful numeric techniques. It explains such topics as using random numbers, performing simple encryption, taking the roots of numbers, and sorting lists of items.

17. Generate Random Values

Directory: **Random**

Visual Basic's Rnd function returns a random value between 0 and 1. You can use the following formula to generate a random integer value between min_val and max_val inclusive.

```
value = Int((max_val - min_val + 1) * Rnd) + min_val
```

Example program Random uses Rnd to produce random numbers and strings of letters. Click the Randomize button to make the program generate new random lists of numbers and letters.

Program Random.

How It Works

If you use the previous formula to generate a sequence of random numbers, you may be surprised to find that the program produces the same sequence of numbers every time you run it. This happens because Rnd does not really produce a random sequence. Instead, it produces a pseudo-random sequence. It looks random on casual inspection, but it is repeatable and not really completely random.

You can make Rnd produce a new sequence of numbers by using the Randomize statement. Simply execute Randomize whenever you want to randomize the sequence. Usually, it is sufficient to call Randomize once when the program starts.

Example program Random uses the following code to select numbers between 10000 and 99999 so they all have five digits. It also generates random five-letter strings. For each letter, the program picks a random number between 65 and 90, the ASCII values for A and Z, respectively. It then uses Chr$ to convert the numeric value into a letter.

```
Option Explicit

' Initialize the random number generator.
Private Sub Form_Load()
    Randomize
End Sub


Private Sub cmdRandomize_Click()
Const MIN_VAL = 10000
Const MAX_VAL = 99999
Const MIN_LETTER = 65 ' ASCII code for A.
Const MAX_LETTER = 90 ' ASCII code for Z.
Dim row As Integer
Dim col As Integer
Dim txt As String
Dim new_long As Long
Dim new_word As String
```

```
Dim new_letter As String
Dim letter As Integer

    ' Generate the random numbers.
    For row = 1 To 5
        For col = 1 To 5
            new_long = Int(Rnd * (MAX_VAL - MIN_VAL + 1)) + MIN_VAL
            txt = txt & Format$(new_long) & " "
        Next col
        txt = txt & vbCrLf
    Next row
    lblNumbers.Caption = txt

    ' Generate the random words.
    txt = ""
    For row = 1 To 5
        For col = 1 To 5
            new_word = ""
            For letter = 1 To 5
                new_letter = _
                    Chr$(Int(Rnd * (MAX_LETTER - MIN_LETTER + 1)) _
                    + MIN_LETTER)
                new_word = new_word & new_letter
            Next letter
            txt = txt & new_word & " "
        Next col
        txt = txt & vbCrLf
    Next row
    lblLetters.Caption = txt
End Sub
```

Using similar code, you can write programs that generate random numbers between any two values. Be sure to call Randomize to initialize the random number generator before you use Rnd.

18. Seed Rnd

Directory: SeedRnd

Visual Basic's random number generator uses an internal state to keep track of where it is in its sequence of pseudo-random values. You can *seed* the random number generator to set that internal state explicitly.

Example program SeedRnd shows how this works. Enter a seed value in the text box, and click the Randomize button. The program generates a sequence of random numbers. If you enter the same seed and click the button again, the program generates the same numbers. If you enter a different seed, the program produces different numbers.

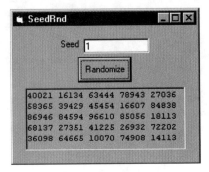

Program SeedRnd.

How It Works

To set the random number generator's state, invoke the Rnd function, passing it a negative value as a parameter. Then call Randomize, passing it the seed value.

```
Rnd -1
Randomize 12345
```

Whenever you reset the random number generator using the same seed value, Rnd produces the same sequence of random numbers. This is convenient for programs that need to use a repeatable sequence of "random" values.

For instance, a program might seed the generator with the value 12345 and then use the numbers produced by Rnd to encode the text in a file. Later, another program could seed the random number generator using the same value 12345 and use the values produced by Rnd to decode the file.

Note that the random number generator is not guaranteed to produce the same values for all versions of Visual Basic. Microsoft could change how Rnd works between versions. In other words, Rnd in Visual Basic 5 may produce a different series of numbers than Rnd in Visual Basic 7, even when both use the same seed. If you need a sequence of numbers that remains consistent across Visual Basic versions, you may want to create your own pseudo-random number generator.

19. Cipher Text

Directory: Cipher

You can use Visual Basic's random number generator to make a simple cipher. First, convert a text password into a number and use that number as a seed for the Rnd function. Use the values produced by Rnd to encipher the text.

To decipher text, another program uses the same password to seed Rnd. It then uses the values produced by Rnd to decipher the text.

Example program Cipher uses this technique to encipher and decipher text. Enter some text in the left TextBox. Enter a password and click the Encipher button.

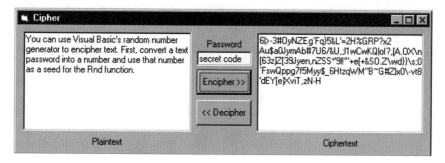

Program Cipher.

After you have enciphered some text, enter the correct password and click the Decipher button to make the code produce the original message. If you enter the wrong password, the program will not use the correct value for Rnd's seed. The numbers produced by Rnd will not match those used to encipher the text, so the program will be unable to decipher it.

Figure 2.1 shows program Cipher using the password "secret codes" to decipher text that was enciphered using the password "secret code." Although these passwords differ by only one character, the result is completely illegible.

How It Works

The following code shows how program Cipher converts a text password into a numeric value for use as Rnd's seed. This function uses two shift values to add the byte value of each letter in the password into a numeric value. It shifts each letter's byte value by these amounts and adds the letter to the numeric value using Xor. It then increases the shift values by 7 bits and 13 bits, respectively. This system makes small changes to the password cause large changes in the numeric value.

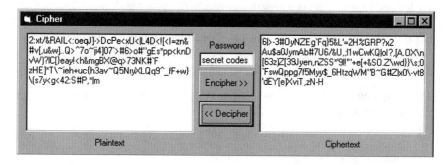

Figure 2.1   With the wrong password, program Cipher produces gibberish.

For instance, the numeric value corresponding to the password SECRET is 46062224, and the numeric value for the password SECRES is 42064528. These passwords are almost the same, but the numeric values are very different. This means that even someone who knows part of the password will be unable to duplicate the correct numeric value and use it to decipher a message.

```
Private Function NumericPassword(ByVal password As String) As Long
Dim value As Long
Dim ch As Long
Dim shift1 As Long
Dim shift2 As Long
Dim i As Integer
Dim str_len As Integer

    str_len = Len(password)
    For i = 1 To str_len
        ' Add the next letter.
        ch = Asc(Mid$(password, i, 1))
        value = value Xor (ch * 2 ^ shift1)
        value = value Xor (ch * 2 ^ shift2)

        ' Change the shift offsets.
        shift1 = (shift1 + 7) Mod 19
        shift2 = (shift2 + 13) Mod 23
    Next i
    NumericPassword = value
End Function
```

After it generates a numeric password value and uses it to seed Rnd, the program considers each letter in the message text. There are 95 printable ASCII characters with values between 32 (space) and 126 (~). The program generates a random number between 0 and 94 and adds that value to the message letter. If the result is greater than 126, the program subtracts 95, so the result is the ASCII code of a printable character. This result is the ASCII code for the enciphered character. The program repeats this process for each letter in the message.

To decipher a message, the program reverses the process. It seeds the random number generator and generates random numbers exactly as before. Instead of adding the number to each letter, however, the program subtracts it. If the result is less than the smallest printable ASCII value 32, the program adds 95 so it is again a printable ASCII value. The result is the originally enciphered character.

The following code shows how program Cipher uses this technique to encipher and decipher text messages.

```
Private Const MIN_ASC = 32      ' Space.
Private Const MAX_ASC = 126     ' ~.
Private Const NUM_ASC = MAX_ASC - MIN_ASC + 1
```

```vb
' Encipher the text using the password.
Private Sub Encipher(ByVal password As String, _
    ByVal from_text As String, to_text As String)
Dim str_len As Integer
Dim i As Integer
Dim ch As Integer

    ' Initialize the random number generator.
    Rnd -1
    Randomize NumericPassword(password)

    ' Encipher the string.
    str_len = Len(from_text)
    For i = 1 To str_len
        ch = Asc(Mid$(from_text, i, 1))

        ' Ignore nonprinting characters.
        If ch >= MIN_ASC And ch <= MAX_ASC Then
            ch = ch + Int(NUM_ASC * Rnd)
            If ch > MAX_ASC Then ch = ch - NUM_ASC
            to_text = to_text & Chr$(ch)
        End If
    Next i
End Sub


' Decipher the text using the password.
Private Sub Decipher(ByVal password As String, _
    ByVal from_text As String, to_text As String)
Dim str_len As Integer
Dim i As Integer
Dim ch As Integer

    ' Initialize the random number generator.
    Rnd -1
    Randomize NumericPassword(password)

    ' Decipher the string.
    str_len = Len(from_text)
    For i = 1 To str_len
        ch = Asc(Mid$(from_text, i, 1))

        ' Ignore non-printing characters.
        If ch >= MIN_ASC And ch <= MAX_ASC Then
            ch = ch - Int(NUM_ASC * Rnd)
            If ch < MIN_ASC Then ch = ch + NUM_ASC
            to_text = to_text & Chr$(ch)
        End If
    Next i
End Sub
```

Note that this technique for enciphering messages is fairly weak. It will probably stop casual hackers and eavesdroppers, but it will not stop a skilled and determined attacker. If you have important data to protect, use a more powerful method. An excellent source of information on more powerful cryptographic techniques is *Applied Cryptography* by Bruce Schneier (John Wiley & Sons, 1996).

20. Randomize a List   ④ ⑤ ⑥

Directory: RndList

Some programs need to display a list of items in a random order. For instance, a tip-of-the-day program might display one piece of advice every time it starts. To display the tips in random order, it would randomize the list of tips and save them in a file. It would then take the tips from the file and display them in their randomized order.

Example program RndList displays a randomized list of animals. Each time you click the Randomize button, the program randomizes the list again.

Program RndList.

How It Works

One method to randomize a list is to consider each position in the list. For each position, randomly select an item from the remaining positions. Then swap that item into position, as shown in the following code.

```
Private Sub RandomizeArray(items() As String)
Dim min_index As Long
Dim max_index As Long
Dim cur_index As Long
Dim new_index As Long
Dim tmp_value As String
```

```
        min_index = LBound(items)
        max_index = UBound(items)
        For cur_index = min_index To max_index - 1
            ' Pick an item to put in position cur_index.
            new_index = Int(Rnd * _
                (max_index - cur_index + 1) + cur_index)

            ' Swap the items in positions new_index
            ' and cur_index.
            tmp_value = items(new_index)
            items(new_index) = items(cur_index)
            items(cur_index) = tmp_value
        Next cur_index
    End Sub
```

It can be shown that every item in the list has an equal chance to end up in any particular position in the reordered list. That means this algorithm does a good job of randomizing the list, assuming Rnd works well. It also means applying the routine more than once does not make the list any more random. Unlike shuffling a deck of cards, applying the routine once is good enough.

21. Randomize a Two-Dimensional Array ④ ⑤ ⑥

Directory: Rnd2D

Some programs need to randomize the items in a multidimensional array. You can do this by extending the technique for randomizing a one-dimensional array. Pretend the array is one-dimensional. If it has 5 rows and 10 columns, pretend it is a one-dimensional array with 50 entries.

Example program Rnd2D uses this method to randomize a two-dimensional array. When you click the Randomize button, the program randomizes its array and displays the results.

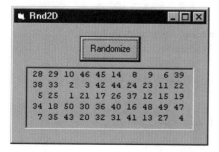

Program Rnd2D.

How It Works

For each position in the array, the program randomly selects an item in the remaining positions. It then swaps the two items. The only real difference between program Rnd2D and program RndList is that this program's array has two dimensions. Before swapping the items, the program needs to convert the one-dimensional randomly selected indexes into rows and columns. If the array's lower bounds are 1, the program can use these formulas to make the conversions:

```
row = (index - 1) \ max_col + 1
col = (index - 1) Mod max_col + 1
```

The following code shows how program Rnd2D randomizes its two-dimensional array.

```
Private Sub RandomizeArray(items() As String)
Dim max_row As Long
Dim max_col As Long
Dim min_index As Long
Dim max_index As Long
Dim cur_index As Long
Dim cur_row As Long
Dim cur_col As Long
Dim new_index As Long
Dim new_row As Long
Dim new_col As Long
Dim tmp_value As String

    max_row = UBound(items, 1)
    max_col = UBound(items, 2)

    min_index = 1
    max_index = max_row * max_col
    For cur_index = min_index To max_index - 1
        ' Pick an item to put in position cur_index.
        new_index = Int(Rnd * _
            (max_index - cur_index + 1) + cur_index)

        ' Calculate the corresponding rows and columns.
        cur_row = (cur_index - 1) \ max_col + 1
        cur_col = (cur_index - 1) Mod max_col + 1
        new_row = (new_index - 1) \ max_col + 1
        new_col = (new_index - 1) Mod max_col + 1

        ' Swap the items in positions new_index
        ' and cur_index.
        tmp_value = items(new_row, new_col)
        items(new_row, new_col) = items(cur_row, cur_col)
        items(cur_row, cur_col) = tmp_value
```

```
      Next cur_index
   End Sub
```

You can extend this idea further to randomize arrays with three or even more dimensions.

22. Sort a List

Directory: SortList

Many programs need to sort data. Almost any kind of information is more meaningful when it is sorted in some way. Sorting the values makes it easier for users to find a particular value, to see what the values' minimum and maximum values are, and to see how widely the values differ.

Example program SortList displays a sorted list of numbers. Click the Randomize button to randomize the list. Click the Sort button to make the program sort the list again.

Program SortList.

How It Works

There are many different ways to sort a list. One algorithm that works very well under most circumstances is *quicksort*. The basic idea behind quicksort is to divide the list to be sorted into two sublists. The quicksort subroutine moves all the small items into the first sublist and all the big items into the second sublist. It then recursively calls itself to sort the sublists.

The following code shows the details. The parameter list is the array to be sorted. The min and max values give the indexes of the items in the array that need sorting.

The routine begins by checking to see if there are fewer than two items to be sorted. If so, the list is already sorted, so the subroutine exits. For instance, if min and max include only one item, that item does not need to be sorted.

Next the routine selects a random dividing item from the array. It then looks through the array, moving items that are smaller than this dividing item into the first half of the array and moving items that are bigger into the second half of the array. This part is a bit tricky, so you may want to step through the code a few times in the debugger to see how it works.

When it has finished separating the large and small items, the subroutine recursively invokes itself to sort the two halves of the array.

```
Private Sub QuickSort(list() As String, _
    ByVal min As Integer, ByVal max As Integer)
Dim med_value As String
Dim hi As Integer
Dim lo As Integer
Dim i As Integer

    ' If the list has no more than CutOff elements,
    ' finish it off with SelectionSort.
    If max <= min Then Exit Sub

    ' Pick the dividing value.
    i = Int((max - min + 1) * Rnd + min)
    med_value = list(i)

    ' Swap it to the front.
    list(i) = list(min)

    lo = min
    hi = max
    Do
        ' Look down from hi for a value < med_value.
        Do While list(hi) >= med_value
            hi = hi - 1
            If hi <= lo Then Exit Do
        Loop
        If hi <= lo Then
            list(lo) = med_value
            Exit Do
        End If

        ' Swap the lo and hi values.
        list(lo) = list(hi)

        ' Look up from lo for a value >= med_value.
        lo = lo + 1
        Do While list(lo) < med_value
            lo = lo + 1
            If lo >= hi Then Exit Do
        Loop
        If lo >= hi Then
            lo = hi
            list(hi) = med_value
```

```
            Exit Do
        End If

        ' Swap the lo and hi values.
        list(hi) = list(lo)
    Loop

        ' Sort the two sublists.
        QuickSort list(), min, lo - 1
        QuickSort list(), lo + 1, max
    End Sub
```

The quicksort subroutine calls itself recursively to divide lists into smaller and smaller sublists. Eventually, the sublists shrink until they contain zero or one item. At that point, the sublists are sorted and the algorithm is finished. For more information on sorting algorithms, consult *Ready-to-Run Visual Basic Algorithms, Second Edition* by Rod Stephens (John Wiley & Sons, 1998).

23. Remove Duplicates from a List ☆ ☆ ④ ⑤ ⑥

Directory: NoDups

The previous section shows how to sort a list of items. Once you have the list sorted, it is easy to remove any duplicate items. Simply look through the list, copying items to the beginning of the array. When you find an item that is the same as the previous item, do not copy it.

Example program NoDups uses this technique to remove duplicates from a list. When you click the Randomize button, the program randomly generates 50 items with values between 10 and 50. Because there are 50 items and they can take only 41 values, there are guaranteed to be some duplicates.

Next click the Remove Duplicates button to make the program sort the list and remove the duplicate values.

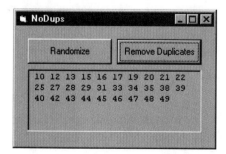

Program NoDups.

How It Works

Program NoDups begins by sorting the array using quicksort. This is the same quicksort algorithm used by the previous example so it is not reproduced here. To see the quicksort code, look in the previous section.

The program then examines each item in the list. The variable look_here indicates the item it is considering. The variable move_here holds the position where the item will be moved if it is not a duplicate. The program compares each item to the previous one. If it is not a duplicate, the program copies the item into position move_here and increments move_here.

```
Private Sub RemoveDuplicates(list() As String)
Dim look_here As Integer
Dim move_here As Integer

    ' Sort the list.
    QuickSort list, LBound(list), UBound(list)

    ' Remove any duplicates. Start by comparing
    ' the second item to the first.
    move_here = LBound(list) + 1
    For look_here = LBound(list) + 1 To UBound(list)
        If list(look_here) <> list(look_here - 1) Then
            ' This is not a duplicate. Copy it.
            list(move_here) = list(look_here)
            move_here = move_here + 1
        End If
    Next look_here

    ' Remove unnecessary entries from the array.
    ReDim Preserve list(LBound(list) To move_here - 1)
End Sub
```

Sorting the numbers may seem like extra work because it does not directly remove duplicate items from the list. What it does is place duplicate items next to each other so they are easy to identify. Without that step, finding and removing them takes much longer.

24. Take Numeric Roots

Directory: Roots

Visual Basic's Sqrt function returns the square root of a number, but Visual Basic has no function for taking other roots, such as cubed roots or fractional roots.

Example program Roots shows one technique for calculating unusual roots. Enter a number and root, and click the Compute button. The program displays the root and the number raised to the root's power to verify that the root is correct.

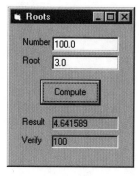

Program Roots.

How It Works

The Rth root of a number is the same as the number to the 1/R power. This fact lets a program use Visual Basic's exponentiation function to calculate unusual roots. For instance, the cubed root of 100 is given by the formula 100 ^ (1/3).

Note that the number and root do not need to be integers but there are some restrictions on the sign of the values. For instance, the root cannot be zero because the program must calculate 1/root, and the number must be positive.

Handling Text

Many programs perform extensive string processing. This chapter demonstrates techniques that make text manipulation easier. It explains such topics as providing a find and replace dialog, finding the last occurrence of a string within another string, and breaking a delimited string into tokens.

---

25. Search a TextBox

Directory: SrchText

Commercial word processors provide advanced find and replace capabilities. You can, too, using a customized dialog box.

Example program SrchText provides a Find dialog that allows the user to search for text, replace specific instances of the text, or replace every occurrence of the text. The user can also specify whether the search should be case sensitive and whether it should match only whole words.

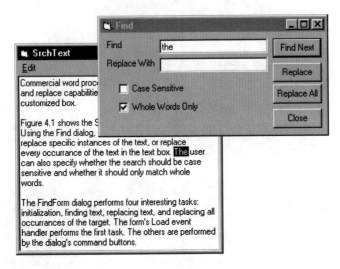

Program SrchText.

How It Works

The find dialog performs four interesting tasks: initializing, finding text, replacing text, and replacing all occurrences of the target. The form's Load event handler performs the first task. The others are performed by the dialog's command buttons. These tasks are described in the following sections.

Initialization

After it finds the target text, the dialog selects it in the client text box on the main form. Unfortunately, a text box does not display its selection unless its form has the input focus. To make the selection visible, the dialog gives the focus back to the main form.

Normally that would make the Find dialog fall behind the main form and disappear. The dialog's Load event handler prevents this by using the SetWindowPos API function to make itself a topmost window. That keeps it on top of other windows even when it does not have the focus.

The Load event handler also determines whether the user selected text before invoking the dialog. If so, the dialog copies the selected text into its Find text box.

```
' Make the dialog stay on top of all other windows.
' If text is selected in the client TextBox,
' use it as the default selection text.
Private Sub Form_Load()
    SetWindowPos hWnd, _
        HWND_TOPMOST, 0, 0, 0, 0, _
        SWP_NOMOVE + SWP_NOSIZE

    ' If text is selected in the client TextBox,
```

```
' use it as the default selection text.
If ClientTextBox.SelLength > 0 Then
    txtFind.Text = Trim$(ClientTextBox.SelText)
    ClientTextBox.SelLength = Len(txtFind.Text)
End If

Me.Show
txtFind.SetFocus
End Sub
```

Finding Text

Subroutine cmdFindNext_Click finds the next occurrence of the target text. It begins by creating local copies of the target text and the text to search. It then determines whether the Case Sensitive check box is selected. If it is, the routine sets its compare variable to 0. If the check box is not selected, it sets compare to 1. These values are passed to the InStr function later to indicate whether the search should be case sensitive.

The routine sets the pos variable to the client text box's current insertion point. It then checks to see if the currently selected text is the same as the target. If it is, the user has already seen this occurrence so the routine skips it.

Next the routine uses InStr to search for the target text. It uses the compare variable to tell InStr whether to perform a case-sensitive search.

If the Whole Words Only check box is selected, the routine calls the IsWholeWord function to see if this occurrence of the target text is a separate word and not part of a larger word. If the occurrence passes this test, the routine selects it and returns the input focus to the main form.

If the occurrence is unsatisfactory, the routine skips it and tries again. The subroutine continues looking for an acceptable match until it finds one or until it has searched the whole string unsuccessfully.

The IsWholeWord function simply examines the characters before and after the target text and returns True if those characters are not letters or numbers.

```
' Find the next occurrence of the text.
Private Sub cmdFindNext_Click()
Dim pos As Integer
Dim target As String
Dim target_len As Integer
Dim client_text As String
Dim client_text_len As Integer
Dim wrapped As Boolean
Dim compare As Integer
Dim value_ok As Boolean

    client_text = ClientTextBox.Text
    target = txtFind.Text
    client_text_len = Len(client_text)
```

```vb
        target_len = Len(target)
        ' See if the comparison should be case sensitive.
        If chkCaseSensitive.Value = vbChecked Then
            compare = 0 ' Case sensitive.
        Else
            compare = 1 ' Case insensitive.
        End If


        ' Start at the current selection point.
        pos = ClientTextBox.SelStart + 1

        ' If the target is there and selected, skip it.
        If LCase$(Trim$(ClientTextBox.SelText)) = LCase$(target) Then _
            pos = pos + target_len

        ' Find the target text.
        Do
            pos = InStr(pos, client_text, target, compare)
            If pos > 0 Then
                ' We found it. See if it satisfies any
                ' whole word requirement.
                If chkWholeWordsOnly.Value = vbChecked Then
                    value_ok = IsWholeWord( _
                        client_text, pos, _
                        client_text_len, target_len)
                Else
                    value_ok = True
                End If

                If value_ok Then
                    ClientTextBox.SelStart = pos - 1
                    ClientTextBox.SelLength = target_len
                    ClientTextBox.SetFocus
                    Exit Do
                Else
                    pos = pos + 1
                End If
            ElseIf wrapped Then
                ' We did not find it, and we have
                ' already tried from the beginning.
                ' Give up.
                MsgBox "Done."
                Exit Do
            Else
                ' Try again, starting from the beginning.
                pos = 1
                wrapped = True
            End If
        Loop
End Sub
```

```vb
' Return true if this occurrence of the target is
' surrounded by characters that are not letters
' or numbers.
Private Function IsWholeWord(ByVal client_text As String, _
    ByVal pos As Integer, ByVal client_text_len As Integer, _
    ByVal target_len As Integer) As Boolean
Dim ch As String

    ' Assume this is not a whole word.
    IsWholeWord = False

    ' See if the previous character is OK.
    If pos > 1 Then
        ' If the previous character is a letter
        ' or number, this is not a whole word.
        ch = Mid$(client_text, pos - 1, 1)

        If ( _
            (ch >= "A" And ch <= "Z") Or _
            (ch >= "a" And ch <= "z") Or _
            (ch >= "0" And ch <= "9")) _
                Then Exit Function
    End If

    ' See if the following character is OK.
    If pos + target_len < client_text_len Then
        ' If the following character is a letter
        ' or number, this is not a whole word.
        ch = Mid$(client_text, pos + target_len, 1)

        If ( _
            (ch >= "A" And ch <= "Z") Or _
            (ch >= "a" And ch <= "z") Or _
            (ch >= "0" And ch <= "9")) _
                Then Exit Function
    End If

    ' This is a whole word.
    IsWholeWord = True
End Function
```

Replacing Text

Replacing text is relatively simple. The dialog simply replaces the currently selected text with the replacement value.

```vb
' Replace the currently selected text with the
' text in txtReplace and move to the next selection.
Private Sub cmdReplace_Click()
```

```
    ' Replace the text.
    ClientTextBox.SelText = txtReplace.Text

    ' Move to the next selection.
    cmdFindNext_Click
End Sub
```

Replacing All

The code that replaces all occurrences of the target text works with a string variable containing a duplicate of the text in the client text box. It starts from the beginning of the string and searches it much as the cmdFindNext_Click event handler does. Whenever it finds an acceptable occurrence of the target, the routine replaces it with the new text.

```
' Replace all occurrences of the text. This routine
' works on a copy of the text and then replaces all
' of the control's text when it is done.
Private Sub cmdReplaceAll_Click()
Dim pos As Integer
Dim target As String
Dim target_len As Integer
Dim client_text As String
Dim replacement_text As String
Dim replacement_len As Integer
Dim value_ok As Boolean
Dim end_ch As String
Dim num_replacements As Integer
Dim orig_start As Integer
Dim compare As Integer

    client_text = ClientTextBox.Text
    replacement_text = txtReplace.Text
    replacement_len = Len(replacement_text)
    target = txtFind.Text
    target_len = Len(target)

    ' See if the comparison should be case sensitive.
    If chkCaseSensitive.Value = vbChecked Then
        compare = 0 ' Case sensitive.
    Else
        compare = 1 ' Case insensitive.
    End If

    ' Record the initial start position.
    orig_start = ClientTextBox.SelStart

    ' Start at the beginning.
    pos = 1

    ' Find the target text.
```

```
    Do
        pos = InStr(pos, client_text, target, compare)

        ' If there are no more occurrences, we're done.
        If pos = 0 Then Exit Do

        ' See if this selection satisfies any
        ' whole word requirement.
        If chkWholeWordsOnly.Value = vbChecked Then
            value_ok = IsWholeWord( _
                client_text, pos, _
                client_text_len, target_len)
        Else
            value_ok = True
        End If

        ' If we have a match, make the replacement.
        If value_ok Then
            client_text = _
                Left$(client_text, pos - 1) & _
                replacement_text & _
                Mid$(client_text, pos + target_len)
            pos = pos + replacement_len
            num_replacements = num_replacements + 1

            ' If the replacement is before the
            ' original start position, update that
            ' position.
            If pos <= orig_start Then
                orig_start = orig_start - _
                    target_len + replacement_len
            End If
        Else
            pos = pos + 1
        End If
    Loop

    ' Present the new text.
    ClientTextBox.Text = client_text

    If num_replacements = 1 Then
        MsgBox Format$(num_replacements) & " replacement."
    Else
        MsgBox Format$(num_replacements) & " replacements."
    End If

    ' Restore the selection position and set focus
    ' to the client TextBox.
    ClientTextBox.SelStart = orig_start
    ClientTextBox.SetFocus
End Sub
```

Taken individually, the tasks performed by the Find and Replace dialog are relatively simple. Together they perform a complex task that makes word processing applications more powerful and professional.

26. Find Last Occurrences

Directory: FindLast

The InStr function returns the position of the next occurrence of a target string within another string starting from a specific position. Visual Basic 6 provides the InstrRev function for finding the last occurrence of a string before a specified position. Although this function does not exist in Visual Basic 4 or 5, it is relatively easy to implement.

Example program FindLast demonstrates this routine. Enter some source text and a target string. Click the source text to indicate where you want the search to begin. Then press the Enter key or click the Find Last button. The program locates the last occurrence of the target before the position where you clicked and selects the target it found.

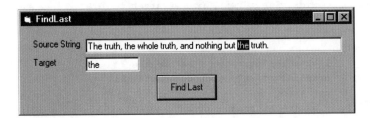

Program FindLast.

How It Works

The FindLast function shown in the follow code uses InStr to search for the target string. When it finds the target, the function updates its return value to indicate that occurrence's position in the string. It continues searching from that point until it fails to find the target or it finds an occurrence that comes after the indicated start position. At that point, the function's return value indicates the position of the previous occurrence. That is the last occurrence at or before the starting position.

```
' Return the position of the last occurrence of the
' text at or before before start_pos. Return 0 if
' the target text is not found.
Private Function FindLast(ByVal source_text As String, _
    ByVal target_text As String, ByVal start_pos) As Integer
Dim pos As Integer

    pos = 0
    Do
```

```
        FindLast = pos
        pos = InStr(pos + 1, source_text, _
            target_text)
    Loop While (pos <= start_pos) And (pos > 0)
End Function
```

27. Tokenize Strings

Directory: Tokens

Sometimes it is convenient to store several values in one string separated by delimiters. For instance, a form's Load event handler could store the form's original Left, Top, Width, and Height property values in its Tag property, separated by semi-colons. The program could break the values apart later and use them to return the form to its original position.

Example program Tokens shows how a program can separate tokens. Enter a source string and a delimiter. Then click the Get Tokens button to make the program separate and display the tokens.

Program Tokens.

How It Works

The GetToken function shown in the following code breaks the tokens out of a tokenized string. Initially, the program passes the text string and the delimiter string to the function. GetToken returns the first token through its token parameter.

To retrieve other tokens from the same string, the program passes GetToken a blank source string. When it receives a blank string, GetToken uses whatever value is left over from the previous call.

GetToken returns True if it is able to find a token. It returns False if it has already returned all of the tokens in the source string.

```
Public Function GetToken(ByVal new_txt As String, _
    ByVal delimiter As String, token As String) As Boolean
```

```
Static txt As String
Dim pos As Integer

    ' Save new text for next time.
    If Len(new_txt) > 0 Then txt = new_txt

    ' If txt is empty, there are no more tokens.
    If Len(txt) = 0 Then
        GetToken = False
    Else
        GetToken = True

        ' Find the next delimiter.
        pos = InStr(txt, delimiter)
        If pos < 1 Then
            ' The delimiter was not found. Return
            ' the rest of the string as the token.
            token = txt
            txt = ""
        Else
            ' The delimiter was not found. Return
            ' the next token.
            token = Left$(txt, pos - 1)
            txt = Mid$(txt, pos + Len(delimiter))
        End If
    End If
End Function
```

Program Tokens uses the following code to find and display tokens.

```
Private Sub cmdGetTokens_Click()
Dim txt As String
Dim token As String
Dim delimiter As String

    delimiter = txtDelimiter.Text
    If GetToken(txtTokens.Text, delimiter, token) _
        Then txt = token

    Do While GetToken("", delimiter, token)
        txt = txt & vbCrLf & token
    Loop

    MsgBox txt
End Sub
```

Note that the delimiter does not need to be a single character. It can include several characters or even words.

28. Parse Commands

Directory: ParseCmd

The previous example shows how to read tokens from a delimited string. A program can use this technique to parse commands. Example program ParseCmd demonstrates this technique. Enter a command string of the format CommandName(arg1, arg2, ...), and click the Parse Command button. The program displays the command's name and its arguments.

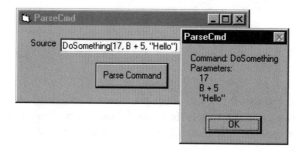

Program ParseCmd.

How It Works

Program ParseCmd uses the GetToken function described in the previous section. To see the GetToken source code, look in that section.

ParseCmd uses three different delimiters to parse a command string of the form CommandName(arg1, arg2, ...). First, it searches for an open parenthesis to see where the command name ends. It then searches for a close parenthesis to see where the argument list ends. It looks for commas to tell where one parameter ends and the next begins.

```
Private Sub cmdParseCommand_Click()
Dim command As String
Dim parameters As String
Dim txt As String
Dim token As String

    command = Trim$(txtcommand.Text)

    ' Find the command delimited by "(".
    If Not GetToken(command, "(", token) Then
        Beep
        Exit Sub
    End If
    txt = "Command: " & token & vbCrLf & _
        "Parameters: " & vbCrLf
```

```
    ' Find the parameters delimited by ")".
    If Not GetToken("", ")", parameters) Then
        Beep
        Exit Sub
    End If

    ' Break the parameters apart delimited by ",".
    If GetToken(parameters, ",", token) Then _
        txt = txt & "      " & token & vbCrLf

    Do While GetToken("", ",", token)
        txt = txt & "      " & token & vbCrLf
    Loop

    MsgBox txt
End Sub
```

This technique is simple but powerful. It lets a program parse command expressions that are quite complex. Its main restriction is that none of the parts of a command can contain the delimiters. For instance, a command parameter cannot be a string that contains a closing parenthesis.

29. Replace Text Occurrences

Directory: ReplText

Visual Basic 6 provides the Replace function to replace occurrences of one string within another, but Visual Basic 4 and 5 have no such function. Fortunately, you can implement this function using Visual Basic code.

Example program ReplText demonstrates this feature. Enter some text, a substring to replace, and a new value for it. Then click the Substitute button to make the program perform the replacements.

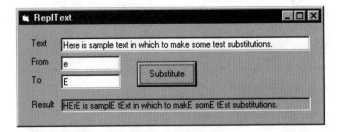

Program ReplText.

How It Works

The ReplaceText function shown in the following code searches for occurrences of the string from_str. When it finds one, it replaces it with the value to_str. It continues its search after the newly inserted text. This prevents an infinite loop if to_str contains from_str. For instance, if from_str is E and to_str is EEE, the program would enter an infinite loop if it did not skip newly inserted text.

```
Public Function ReplaceText(ByVal txt As String, _
    ByVal from_str As String, ByVal to_str As String) As String
Dim from_str_len As Integer
Dim to_str_len As Integer
Dim pos As Integer

    from_str_len = Len(from_str)
    to_str_len = Len(to_str)
    pos = 1
    Do
        ' Find from_str starting at position pos.
        pos = InStr(pos, txt, from_str)

        ' If we didn't find from_str, we're done.
        If pos = 0 Then Exit Do

        ' Make the replacement.
        txt = Left$(txt, pos - 1) & _
            to_str & _
            Mid$(txt, pos + from_str_len)

        ' Skip the new text in the search.
        pos = pos + to_str_len
    Loop
    ReplaceText = txt
End Function
```

The ReplaceText function can also remove text from a string. Simply pass the function an empty string as its final argument.

30. Make a TextBox Capitalize Input

☆ ☆

Directory: SetCase

Using a TextBox control's KeyPress event handler, you can capitalize most text entered by the user, as shown in the following code.

```
Private Sub txtUseKeyPress_KeyPress(KeyAscii As Integer)
    KeyAscii = Asc(UCase$(Chr$(KeyAscii)))
End Sub
```

This code handles text entered normally by the user, but it cannot handle some events. If the user presses Ctrl-V, the system will paste whatever text is in the clipboard into the TextBox without triggering the KeyPress event. If that text contains lowercase letters, they appear in the TextBox. The user can also right-click on the TextBox and use its context menu to paste text into the TextBox.

Similar problems arise if you try to use the KeyPress event handler and the LCase$ function to convert text into lowercase.

You can handle some of these problems using the TextBox's Change event, but that method is cumbersome and tricky. A much simpler solution is to use API functions to tell Windows that the TextBox's input should automatically be converted into uppercase.

Example program SetCase takes this approach. Enter text in the text boxes within the frames to see how the program handles capitalization. Select text from the top text box and copy and paste it into the other text boxes.

Program SetCase.

How It Works

The SetUppercase subroutine shown in the following code uses API functions to make a TextBox automatically convert text into uppercase. First, the routine uses GetWindowLong to retrieve the TextBox's current style value. It uses a bitwise Or to combine this value with the value ES_UPPERCASE. That sets the bit representing uppercase conversion in the style. Finally, the routine uses SetWindowLong to update the TextBox's style.

```
Private Sub SetUppercase(txt As TextBox)
Dim style As Long

    style = GetWindowLong(txt.hWnd, GWL_STYLE)
    style = style Or ES_UPPERCASE
    SetWindowLong txt.hWnd, GWL_STYLE, style
End Sub
```

Subroutine SetLowercase is similar except it uses the value ES_LOWERCASE instead of ES_UPPERCASE. Subroutine SetNormalcase makes the TextBox leave input character's case unchanged. You can see the code for these routines on the CD-ROM that accompanies this book.

31. See If a String Is Blank

Directory: IsBlank

This may seem like a strange example. After all, any Visual Basic programmer knows you can tell if a string is blank by using the following code:

```
If my_string = "" Then ...
```

There are several other methods that also work, and some are considerably faster than others. Example program IsBlank compares these methods. Enter the number of times you want the program to perform its tests, and click the Run button. Because all of these methods are fast, you will need to run the tests many times to get a meaningful result.

Program IsBlank.

How It Works

The following code shows four different methods for testing whether the string test_string is blank.

```
Dim test_string As String
Dim blank_string As String
Dim is_blank As Boolean

    ' Initialize blank_string to a blank string.
    blank_string = ""
```

```
' Initialize test_string to some value.
    :

' Run the tests.
is_blank = (test_string = "")
is_blank = (test_string = blank_string)
is_blank = (Len(test_string) = 0)
is_blank = (test_string = vbNullString)
```

When you run this program, you will find that the test Len(test_string) = 0 is the fastest by a substantial margin. All of these methods are quite fast, however. Unless a program tests a huge number of strings to see if they are blank, the overall impact on performance will be small.

Formatting Output

T he way values are formatted can make a big difference in their usefulness. For instance, of the following two lists of expenses, the one on the right is much easier to read. In the right list, it is easier to find the most expensive item, and it is much easier to verify the total.

ITEM	COST	ITEM	COST
Paper	36.17	Paper	36.17
Printer	217	Printer	217.00
Toner	63.7	Toner	63.70
Monitor	427.89	Monitor	427.89
CPU	762	CPU	762.00
Modem	27.5	Modem	27.50
Tax	126.58	Tax	126.58
Total	1660.84	Total	1660.84

This chapter describes different ways to format output. It explains how to justify text output and convert between various data types before presenting information to the user. It also tells how to use the clipboard to make data available to other programs.

32. Format Numbers

④ ⑤ ⑥

Directory: FmtNum

Sometimes an international application might need to format a number for a different region of the world. It might need to display a number as 12,345.6 at some times and as 12.345,6 at others.

Example program FmtNum formats numeric text. Enter the decimal and thousands separators, the number of digits after the decimal point, and the number of digits per "thousands" grouping. Then enter a numeric string, and click the Format button to make the program display the formatted result.

Program FmtNum.

How It Works

A program can use the GetNumberFormat API function to format numbers. The NUMBERFMT user-defined type specifies the number of digits after the decimal point, the number of digits in groupings, the decimal separator, and the grouping separator. For instance, typically in the United States the number of digits in a group is three, so digits are separated into thousands, millions, and so forth. The decimal separator is a period, and the group separator is a comma. This results in a format such as 12,345.67.

The FormatNumber function shown in the following code formats numeric strings. It first initializes the values in a NUMBERFMT structure and then invokes GetNumberFormat to format the text.

```
Private Type NUMBERFMT
    NumDigits As Long
    LeadingZero As Long
    Grouping As Long
```

```
        lpDecimalSep As String
        lpThousandSep As String
        NegativeOrder As Long
    End Type


    ' Format a numeric string.
    Private Function FormatNumber(ByVal numeric_string As String, _
        ByVal decimal_separator As String, _
        ByVal thousands_separator As String, _
        ByVal num_digits As Integer, _
        ByVal num_per_group As Integer) As String
    Dim fmt As NUMBERFMT
    Dim buf As String * 40
    Dim buflen As Integer

        ' Prepare the NUMBERFMT structure.
        With fmt
            .NumDigits = num_digits
            .LeadingZero = 0
            .Grouping = num_per_group
            .lpDecimalSep = decimal_separator
            .lpThousandSep = thousands_separator
            .NegativeOrder = 0
        End With

        ' Format the text.
        buflen = GetNumberFormat(0, 0, _
            numeric_string, fmt, buf, Len(buf))

        ' Truncate the result buffer at the correct length.
        FormatNumber = Left$(buf, buflen)
    End Function
```

Program FmtNum uses the FormatNumber function to produce its formatted output.

33. Change Case

Directory: ChngCase

Visual Basic's LCase$ and UCase$ functions convert text into lowercase and uppercase, respectively. These functions can be handy for comparing two text strings in a case-insensitive way. The following code shows how a program can determine whether two strings contain the same text, ignoring case.

```
If LCase$(first_string) = LCase$(second_string) Then
    ' The strings are equal.
        :
```

Occasionally, it is convenient to be able to capitalize the first letter in each word in a string. Text where the first letter of each word is capitalized is in *propercase*.

Visual Basic's StrConv function can convert text to propercase. StrConv defines words to be separated by spaces so the result is not always exactly what you might want. For instance, the text "mrs. o'malley from i.b.m." becomes "Mrs. O'malley From I.b.m.," which is not quite right. Using Visual Basic's string processing statements, you can write a ProperCase function that does a better job of handling this situation.

Example program ChngCase demonstrates the LCase$, UCase$, StrConv, and Proper-Case functions. Enter some text, and the program automatically performs the conversions and displays the results.

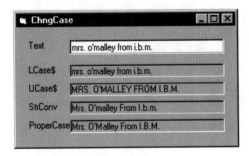

Program ChngCase.

How It Works

The ProperCase function shown in following code capitalizes any letter that follows a nonletter. This gives the result "Mrs. O'Malley From I.B.M."

```
' Capitalize letters that follow nonletters.
Function ProperCase(ByVal txt As String) As String
Dim need_cap As Boolean
Dim i As Integer
Dim ch As String

    txt = LCase(txt)
    need_cap = True
    For i = 1 To Len(txt)
        ch = Mid$(txt, i, 1)
        If ch >= "a" And ch <= "z" Then
            If need_cap Then
                Mid$(txt, i, 1) = UCase(ch)
                need_cap = False
            End If
        Else
            need_cap = True
        End If
```

```
        Next i
        ProperCase = txt
    End Function
```

This function works fairly well for proper names, but it is not always perfect. It converts the string "don't feed mrs. o'malley's cow" into "Don'T Feed Mrs. O'Malley'S Cow." To handle this situation, you would need to modify the code to properly handle such special cases as contractions.

34. Convert Values

Directory: Convert

Visual Basic provides a variety of data type conversion functions including CCur, CInt, CLng, CSng, and so forth. If their inputs are invalid, however, these functions fail. For instance, if the string item_cost is blank, converting it into a currency value using CCur generates an error. If the program does not protect itself from these errors, it crashes.

Example program Convert demonstrates a convenient method for converting text into currency, single, integer, and Boolean values without crashing. If you enter invalid values such as a blank string, the program displays reasonable default values.

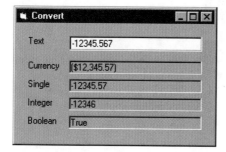

Program Convert.

How It Works

Problems with invalid inputs are easy to catch using the On Error Resume Next statement. If the program encounters an error during the conversion, it can use some reasonable default value for the converted data type.

The following code shows a function that takes any kind of data as input and returns a currency value. If the input makes no sense, the function returns the default value 0.

```
' Convert a value into currency format. If the
' value does not make sense, return 0.
Public Function CurrencyValue(ByVal txt As Variant) As Currency
```

```
      On Error Resume Next
      CurrencyValue = CCur(txt)
      If Err.Number <> 0 Then CurrencyValue = 0
   End Function
```

The Convert program uses this function and several others to convert text input into currency, single, integer, and Boolean values. The other functions are similar to function CurrencyValue so they are not shown here. You can see the complete source code on the CD-ROM that accompanies this book.

35. Justify Output with a Monospaced Font

Directory: Justify

Few programmers realize that they can use Visual Basic's Format$ function to right or left justify strings. Example program Justify uses Format$ to display four columns of justified data. The Number and ID columns are right justified. The name column is left justified. The Total column is justified to line up the decimal points of its values.

```
Number   ID   Name          Total
     1   635  Alice       $668.49
     2   522  Bob       ($4,208.74)
     3   272  Cindy     $5,494.80
     4    13  David     $5,214.47
     5   733  Eustace   $4,180.76
     6    41  Fred      ($1,719.34)
     7   776  Gina      $5,809.60
     8   336  Harold    $9,239.06
     9   784  Ivy       ($8,875.25)
    10   855  Jim       ($2,719.62)
```

Program Justify.

How It Works

A format specifier that contains a series of @ symbols produces a string the length of the format specifier with any necessary blanks added to the left end. If the format specifier begins with an exclamation mark (!), the extra spaces are added at the right. For instance, the following text shows a statement executed in the Debug window and its output.

```
Debug.Print "[" & Format$("ABC", "!@@@@@@") & "]" & _
     vbCrLf & "[" & Format$("ABC", "@@@@@@") & "]"
[ABC   ]
[   ABC]
```

A program can use these format specifiers to produce multiple lines of text that are right or left justified. To produce internally aligned text, such as the Total column generated by program Justify, the program can justify the left and right halves of the values separately and then concatenate them.

The Justify program uses the following code to display its four justified columns of data.

```
Option Explicit

Private NumItems As Integer
Private ID() As Integer
Private Names() As String
Private Total() As Single

' Draw some justified text.
Private Sub Form_Load()
Dim i As Integer
Dim total_string As String

    ' Make the form redraw itself.
    AutoRedraw = True

    ' Use a monospaced font.
    Font.Name = "Courier New"

    ' Make some data.
        :

    ' Display the data.
    CurrentY = 240
    CurrentX = 240
    Print _
        Format$("Number", "@@@@@@") & "   " & _
        Format$("ID", "@@@@") & "   " & _
        Format$("Name", "!@@@@@@@@") & "   " & _
        Format$("Total", "@@@@@@@@@@@@")

    For i = 1 To 10
        CurrentX = 240

        ' Use currency format for Total.
        total_string = Format$(Total(i), "Currency")

        ' If Total is negative, give it one extra
        ' leading space so the decimal lines up.
        If Total(i) < 0 Then
            total_string = Format$(total_string, "@@@@@@@@@@@@")
        Else
            total_string = Format$(total_string, "@@@@@@@@@@@")
        End If
```

```
        Print _
            Format$(i, "@@@@@@") & "   " & _
            Format$(ID(i), "@@@@") & "   " & _
            Format$(Names(i), "!@@@@@@@@") & "   " & _
            total_string
    Next i
End Sub
```

Note that this code displays its values in the monospaced font Courier New. In proportionally spaced fonts such as Times New Roman or Arial, space characters are much thinner than other characters. Right justifying strings by adding spaces on the left will not work well.

For left justified words, this is usually not a problem because it rarely matters if the letters in the words line up correctly. The digits in many proportional fonts have the same width, so left justified numeric columns are also not a problem. For right justified numeric columns, however, the results can be unsightly.

36.   Justify Output with a Proportional Font

Directory: Justify2

The previous example shows how to justify text using format specifiers. That example depends on the form's use of a monospaced font. If the font is proportional, the text will probably not line up properly. Even though the strings may all have the same length in characters, the different character sizes will almost surely make the columns line up poorly.

Example program Justify2 demonstrates another technique for aligning text. It displays four columns of justified text using a proportionally spaced font.

```
 Justify2                    _ □ ✕

Number   ID   Name         Total
     1  830   Alice      $4,444.11
     2  326   Bob       ($7,728.03)
     3  642   Cindy     ($3,678.78)
     4  702   David      $5,152.21
     5  636   Eustace    $6,120.45
     6   67   Fred      ($1,762.07)
     7  681   Gina       $7,925.07
     8  369   Harold    ($9,221.63)
     9  453   Ivy        $7,478.49
    10  809   Jim        $6,964.21
```

Program Justify2.

How It Works

Program Justify2 aligns text by calculating each item's position based on its size and desired alignment. To right justify text, the program subtracts the width of the text from the X coordinate where the text should be aligned. It then prints the text at that position.

The LeftJustify and RightJustify routines that follow display text left and right aligned. The AlignCurrency routine positions the text so its decimal point has the indicated X coordinate.

```
' Display text left justified at the position.
Private Sub LeftJustify(ByVal txt As String, _
    ByVal X As Single, ByVal Y As Single)

    CurrentX = X
    CurrentY = Y
    Print txt
End Sub


' Display text right justified at the position.
Private Sub RightJustify(ByVal txt As String, _
    ByVal X As Single, ByVal Y As Single)

    CurrentX = X - TextWidth(txt)
    CurrentY = Y
    Print txt
End Sub


' Display text with the decimal aligned at
' the X position. If the text contains no decimal,
' right justify it as if it were followed by ".00".
Private Sub AlignCurrency(ByVal txt As String, _
    ByVal X As Single, ByVal Y As Single)
Dim pos As Integer
Dim before_decimal As String

    pos = InStr(txt, ".")
    If pos = 0 Then
        ' There is no decimal.
        CurrentX = X + TextWidth(".00") _
            - TextWidth(txt)
    Else
        ' There is a decimal.
        before_decimal = Left$(txt, pos - 1)
        CurrentX = X - TextWidth(before_decimal)
    End If
    CurrentY = Y
    Print txt
End Sub
```

In many proportional fonts, digits are rather narrow, making columns of numeric values seem cramped. In some cases, it may be better to use a monospaced font for numbers to make them more legible.

37. Track the Clipboard

☆ ☆
④ ⑤ ⑥

Directory: ShowClip

The clipboard allows a program to exchange data with other programs. Example program ShowClip shows how a program can retrieve data from the clipboard. Every second the program checks the clipboard for data. The program lists the kinds of data available. If this includes text or bitmap data, the program also displays the data.

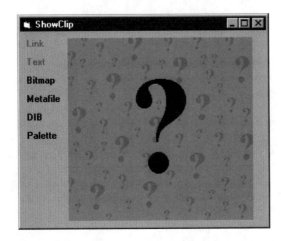

Program ShowClip.

How It Works

The Clipboard object's GetFormat function lets a program determine if there is data available in the clipboard in a certain format. For instance, the call Clipboard.GetFormat(vbCFBitmap) returns True if the clipboard can return data in the bitmap format.

Once a program has determined that data is available in a particular format, it can retrieve that data. If the Clipboard object contains text data, the program can retrieve it using Clipboard.GetText. To retrieve other forms of data, the program should use the GetData function.

Program ShowClip uses a timer control with Interval set to 1000, so it updates itself once each second. When the timer triggers, the program uses the following code to display the clipboard's contents.

The program contains an array of label controls named lblFormat. These controls list the names of the data formats that might be available on the clipboard. The event handler uses the GetFormat function to see which formats are available, and it enables the corresponding labels.

The event handler then checks specifically for text data. If text is available, the routine loads it into its text box and makes the text box visible.

Similarly, the routine determines whether bitmap data is available. If it is, the routine displays it in a picture box and makes the picture box visible.

```
' See which formats are available and display the data.
Private Sub tmrCheckClip_Timer()
Dim i As Integer

    For i = 0 To lblFormat.UBound
        If Clipboard.GetFormat(FormatValue(i)) Then
            lblFormat(i).ForeColor = vbBlack
        Else
            lblFormat(i).ForeColor = &H808080
        End If
    Next i

    ' Check for text.
    If Clipboard.GetFormat(vbCFText) Then
        On Error Resume Next
        txtClipboardText.Text = Clipboard.GetText
        On Error GoTo 0
        txtClipboardText.Visible = True
    Else
        txtClipboardText.Visible = False
    End If

    ' Check for a bitmap.
    If Clipboard.GetFormat(vbCFBitmap) Then
        On Error Resume Next
        picClipboardBitmap.Picture = Clipboard.GetData(vbCFBitmap)
        On Error GoTo 0
        picClipboardBitmap.Visible = True
    Else
        picClipboardBitmap.Visible = False
    End If
End Sub
```

A program can use the Clipboard object's SetText and SetData methods to put data on the clipboard. Before doing so, it should use the Clear method to remove any existing data from the clipboard.

☆ ☆ ☆
④ ⑤ ⑥

38. Copy, Cut, and Paste Pictures

Directory: ClipPic

Copying and pasting text from the clipboard is easy using the Clipboard object's Get-Text and SetText methods. Manipulating parts of images is a little more complicated.

Example program ClipPic shows how a program can copy, cut, and paste parts of an image. Click and drag on one of the pictures to select an area. Then right-click to select Cut or Copy from the picture's context menu, or press the Ctrl-X or Ctrl-C keys. Next click somewhere on either picture. Select the context menu's Paste command, or press Ctrl-V to make the program copy the part of the image you selected to the new location.

Program ClipPic.

How It Works

The Clipboard object's SetData and GetData functions let a program store and retrieve image data from the clipboard. Unfortunately, these routines work only with complete pictures, not with parts of them.

To work around this restriction, program ClipPic uses a hidden picture box named picTemp for temporary work space. To copy part of a picture to the clipboard, the program first uses the PaintPicture method to copy that part of the picture into picTemp. It then copies picTemp's entire picture to the clipboard.

Similarly, to retrieve an image from the clipboard and place it on part of a picture, the program first copies the clipboard data onto picTemp. It then uses PaintPicture to copy picTemp's image onto part of the destination picture.

The following code shows how program ClipPic copies, cuts, and pastes images. When these routines are called, the values X1, X2, Y1, and Y2 bound the region selected by the user. The variable Selpic indicates the index of the picture box the user is currently using to copy, cut, or paste.

```
Option Explicit

Private Dragging As Boolean
Private X1(0 To 1) As Single
Private Y1(0 To 1) As Single
Private X2(0 To 1) As Single
Private Y2(0 To 1) As Single

Private SelPic As Integer

' Copy the selected region to the clipboard.
Private Sub mnuCopy_Click()
    ' Make sure X1 <= X2 and Y1 <= Y2.
    OrderCorners

    ' Copy the selected area into picTemp.
    picTemp.Width = X2(SelPic) - X1(SelPic) + 1
    picTemp.Height = Y2(SelPic) - Y1(SelPic) + 1
    picTemp.PaintPicture _
        picCanvas(SelPic).Picture, _
        0, 0, X2(SelPic) - X1(SelPic) + 1, _
        Y2(SelPic) - Y1(SelPic) + 1, _
        X1(SelPic), Y1(SelPic), X2(SelPic) - X1(SelPic) + 1, _
        Y2(SelPic) - Y1(SelPic) + 1

    ' Copy to the clipboard.
    Clipboard.Clear
    Clipboard.SetData picTemp.Image, vbCFBitmap
End Sub

' Copy the selected region to the clipboard and
' erase the selected area.
Private Sub mnuCut_Click()
    ' Copy the picture to the clipboard.
    mnuCopy_Click

    ' Erase this part of the image.
    picCanvas(SelPic).Line _
        (X1(SelPic), Y1(SelPic))-(X2(SelPic), Y2(SelPic)), _
        picCanvas(SelPic).BackColor, BF
End Sub

' Paste whatever is in the clipboard at (X1, Y1).
Private Sub mnuPaste_Click()
    ' Make sure an image exists. This will happen
```

```
    ' if the clipboard does not contain a bitmap
    ' and the user presses ^V.
    If Not Clipboard.GetFormat(vbCFBitmap) Then Exit Sub

    ' Make sure X1 <= X2 and Y1 <= Y2.
    OrderCorners

    picTemp.AutoSize = True
    picTemp.Picture = Clipboard.GetData(vbCFBitmap)
    picTemp.AutoSize = False

    picCanvas(SelPic).PaintPicture _
        picTemp.Picture, _
        X1(SelPic), Y1(SelPic), _
        picTemp.ScaleWidth, picTemp.ScaleHeight, _
        0, 0, picTemp.ScaleWidth, picTemp.ScaleHeight

    ' Make the picture part of the background.
    picCanvas(SelPic).Picture = picCanvas(SelPic).Image
End Sub

' Make sure X1 <= X2 and Y1 <= Y2.
Private Sub OrderCorners()
Dim tmp As Single

    If X1(SelPic) > X2(SelPic) Then
        tmp = X1(SelPic)
        X1(SelPic) = X2(SelPic)
        X2(SelPic) = tmp
    End If
    If Y1(SelPic) > Y2(SelPic) Then
        tmp = Y1(SelPic)
        Y1(SelPic) = Y2(SelPic)
        Y2(SelPic) = tmp
    End If
End Sub
```

How the program allows the user to select this region is explained in Example 118, *Let the User Select Areas*, so it is not described here. For more information, read that example in Chapter 13, "Generating Graphics."

39. Display an Integer in Binary

Directory: Bases

Sometimes it is useful to view a number in its hexadecimal or binary form. The Hex$ command converts a number into hexadecimal, but Visual Basic does not contain a function that displays binary values.

Program Bases displays a number's decimal, hexadecimal, and binary representations. Enter a value in any of the text boxes, and the program will show you the value's other representations.

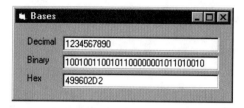

Program Bases.

How It Works

The binary representation of a number is a string of 0s and 1s. The bits in a binary value represent powers of 2. The rightmost bit, called the least significant bit or LSB, determines whether the number includes the value $2^0 = 1$. The next bit determines whether the value includes $2^1 = 2$. The following bits represent the values 2^2, 2^3, and so forth. For instance, 11010 represents the value $0 * 2^0 + 1 * 2^1 + 0 * 2^2 + 1 * 2^3 + 1 * 2^4 = 2 + 8 + 16 = 26$.

The following code uses the And operator to combine a number to the value 1. The And operator performs a bitwise comparison of two numbers. A bit in the result is 1 if both of the numbers being combined have the value 1 in that bit position. The decimal value 1 has every bit set to 0 except for its LSB, which is 1. When the routine combines a number with the value 1 using the And operator, the result has an LSB of 1 if the number also has an LSB of 1. If the number's LSB is 0, the result has an LSB of 0. All the other bits in the result are 0. That means the result is the decimal value 0 if the number has a LSB of 0.

In Visual Basic, a value that is 0 is considered False as a Boolean expression. Putting all this together, the routine uses the And operator to decide whether the number has an LSB of 1. If so, it adds the character "1" to its output string. If the LSB is 0, the routine adds the character "0" to its output string.

The routine next divides the number by 2 using integer division. This essentially slides the number's bits one position to the right. For instance, the value 11010 becomes 1101. This moves the second least significant bit into the LSB position. The routine then repeats its comparison to learn the value of that bit. It continues this process until all the bits in the number have been processed and the number is 0.

```
' Return a binary representation of a long integer.
Function LongToBinary(ByVal long_value As Long) As String
Dim txt As String
Dim i As Integer

    Do While long_value >= 1
        ' See if the least significant bit is 1.
        If long_value And 1 Then
```

```
                txt = "1" & txt
            Else
                txt = "0" & txt
            End If


            ' Remove the least significant bit.
            long_value = long_value \ 2
        Loop
        LongToBinary = txt
    End Function
```

Initializing a variable using a binary text representation is somewhat easier. The following routine examines each bit in the binary representation. It uses the variable bit_value to keep track of the value represented by each bit. When it finds a bit with value 1, it adds bit_value to the result it is calculating. Each time it considers a new bit, it multiplies bit_value by 2 so it contains the amount represented by the next bit.

```
    ' Return the long integer corresponding to a binary text representation.
    Function BinaryToLong(ByVal txt As String) As Long
    Dim long_value As Long
    Dim bit_value As Long
    Dim i As Integer

        ' bit_value is the value of the bit we are considering.
        ' We start with the LSB, which has value 1.
        bit_value = 1

        ' Examine the bits in the string starting with the LSB.
        For i = Len(txt) To 1 Step -1
            ' See if this bit is 1.
            If Mid$(txt, i, 1) = "1" Then
                ' It is. Add in the new bit.
                long_value = long_value + bit_value
            End If

            ' Prepare for the next bit.
            bit_value = bit_value * 2
        Next i

        BinaryToLong = long_value
    End Function
```

Program Bases uses this code to convert values between decimal and binary representations. It uses CLng to convert hexadecimal text values into long integers, as shown in the following code fragment.

```
    num = CLng("&H" & txtHex.Text)
```

The program uses Visual Basic's Hex$ function to display hexadecimal values.

CHAPTER 5

Tackling Timers

Visual Basic's Timer control lets a program perform periodic tasks. For instance, a program can use a Timer to check a directory once each minute to see if a particular file has been deleted.

Using Timer controls is fairly easy. The two properties, Interval and Enabled, determine the control's behavior. If Enabled is False, the control does nothing. When the control is enabled, its Interval property determines the approximate length of time between the control's Timer events in milliseconds. For instance, if Interval is 1000 and Enabled is True, then the control raises a Timer event every 1000 milliseconds, or every second.

There are two minor twists to this simple control. First, if the Interval property is set to 0, the control does not raise Timer events even if Enabled is True. Second, if a program changes a Timer control's Interval property while the Timer is enabled, its next Timer event may fire after the old interval has elapsed instead of after the new one. To make the Timer cancel any pending events and start using the new Interval value, the program should disable and reenable the control.

```
tmrCheckFile.Interval = 1000    ' Set the new Interval.
tmrCheckFile.Enabled = False    ' Disable the Timer.
tmrCheckFile.Enabled = True     ' Reenable the Timer.
```

The rest of this chapter describes several useful techniques for working with Timer controls.

40. Make a Blinking Label ④ ⑤ ⑥

Directory: BlinkLbl

To implement a blinking label, a program can change a Label control's ForeColor and BackColor properties when the Timer event fires. Example program BlinkLbl uses this method to create three labels that blink in different colors.

Program BlinkLbl.

How It Works

The following code shows how program BlinkLbl works.

```
Option Explicit

' The colors used by the controls. ForeColors(i, j)
' is the ForeColor value for lblBlink control number i.
' The value j switches between 0 and 1 to make the
' control blink.
Private ForeColors(0 To 2, 0 To 1) As Long
Private BackColors(0 To 2, 0 To 1) As Long

' Initialize blink colors.
Private Sub Form_Load()
    ' Blink between black/gray and gray/gray.
    ForeColors(0, 0) = vbBlack
    ForeColors(0, 1) = BackColor
    BackColors(0, 0) = BackColor
    BackColors(0, 1) = BackColor

    ' Blink between red/gray and gray/gray.
    ForeColors(1, 0) = vbRed
    ForeColors(1, 1) = BackColor
    BackColors(1, 0) = BackColor
    BackColors(1, 1) = BackColor

    ' Blink between white/gray and black/gray.
    ForeColors(2, 0) = vbWhite
```

```
ForeColors(2, 1) = vbBlack
BackColors(2, 0) = BackColor
BackColors(2, 1) = BackColor

    ' Trigger the Timer's event handler to set the
    ' initial colors.
    tmrBlink_Timer

    ' Enable the timer.
    tmrBlink.Interval = 500
    tmrBlink.Enabled = True
End Sub

' Set the labels' colors appropriately.
Private Sub tmrBlink_Timer()
Static state As Integer

Dim fore_color As Long
Dim i As Integer

    ' Toggle the state.
    state = 1 - state

    ' Set the colors.
    For i = 0 To 2
        lblBlink(i).ForeColor = ForeColors(i, state)
        lblBlink(i).BackColor = BackColors(i, state)
    Next i
End Sub
```

Keep in mind that blinking labels draw the user's eye very strongly. They can be extremely annoying if they are overused or if they blink too quickly. A program should use them only to draw the user's attention to very important items.

41. Make Text Blink in a PictureBox ④ ⑤ ⑥

Directory: BlinkTxt

Just as a program can make a label blink, it can make text drawn on a PictureBox or Form blink. Example program BlinkTxt demonstrates this technique by making the text URGENT blink in a list of jobs.

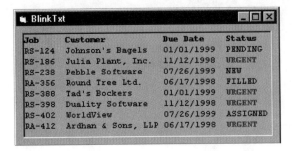

Program BlinkTxt.

How It Works

When the Timer event occurs, the program redraws any text that should blink using the Form's or PictureBox's Print method.

When it starts, program BlinkTxt saves the locations where the string URGENT appears on its PictureBox. When the Timer event occurs, the program redraws the text using different colors.

```
Option Explicit

' Positions of the text that blinks.
Private Xpos As New Collection
Private Ypos As New Collection

' The target text to blink.
Private Const TARGET = "URGENT"

Private Sub Form_Load()
    ' Use a fixed width font so things line up.
    picJobs.Font.Name = "Courier New"

    ' Print a header.
    picJobs.Font.Bold = True
    PrintJob "Job       Customer          Due Date     Status"
    picJobs.Font.Bold = False

    ' Print some job information.
    PrintJob "RS-124    Johnson's Bagels   01/01/1999   PENDING"
    PrintJob "RS-186    Julia Plant, Inc.  11/12/1998   URGENT"
    PrintJob "RS-238    Pebble Software    07/26/1999   NEW"
    PrintJob "RA-356    Round Tree Ltd.    06/17/1998   FILLED"
    PrintJob "RS-388    Tad's Bockers      01/01/1999   URGENT"
    PrintJob "RS-398    Duality Software   11/12/1998   URGENT"
    PrintJob "RS-402    WorldView          07/26/1999   ASSIGNED"
    PrintJob "RA-412    Ardhan & Sons, LLP 06/17/1998   URGENT"
```

```
    ' Start the timer.
    tmrBlink.Interval = 500
    tmrBlink.Enabled = True
End Sub

' Print a line. Search for the string TARGET in
' the status. If we find it, save its position
' for blinking later.
Private Sub PrintJob(txt As String)
Dim pos As Integer

    ' Search for URGENT.
    pos = InStr(txt, TARGET)
    If pos = 0 Then
        ' Print the string.
        picJobs.Print txt
    Else
        ' Print the first part of the string. Note
        ' the carriage return to stop the
        ' PictureBox from moving to the next line.
        txt = Left$(txt, pos - 1)
        picJobs.Print txt;

        ' Save URGENT's position.
        Xpos.Add picJobs.CurrentX
        Ypos.Add picJobs.CurrentY

        ' Print the target.
        picJobs.Font.Bold = True
        picJobs.Print TARGET
        picJobs.Font.Bold = False
    End If
End Sub
```

Again, remember that blinking is very eye-catching and can be quite annoying. Use it only when it is extremely important that you catch the user's attention immediately.

42. Make a Program Countdown ④ ⑤ ⑥

Directory: CountDwn

Sometimes it is useful to display the time remaining until some event, rather than the current time. Program CountDwn does this to count down from two hours until it reaches zero.

Program CountDwn.

How It Works

To implement a countdown using a Timer control, a program subtracts the current time from a desired alarm time whenever it receives a Timer event. When the difference in time reaches zero, the program has finished the countdown.

The following code shows how program CountDwn works.

```
Option Explicit

' Count down to this time.
Private AlarmTime As Date

Private Sub Form_Load()
    ' Count down until two hours from now.
    AlarmTime = DateAdd("h", 2, Now)

    ' Start the timer.
    tmrCountdown.Interval = 1000
    tmrCountdown.Enabled = True
End Sub

' Update the countdown display.
Private Sub tmrCountdown_Timer()
Dim time_left As Single

    ' See how much time is left.
    time_left = AlarmTime - Now

    ' See if the time has expired.
    If time_left <= 0 Then
        ' If so, say so and stop the countdown.
        tmrCountdown.Enabled = False
        lblCountdown.Caption = "DONE"
        lblCountdown.ForeColor = vbWhite
        lblCountdown.BackColor = vbRed
        Beep
    Else
        ' If not, display the time remaining.
        lblCountdown.Caption = _
            Format$(time_left, "h:mm:ss")
```

```
        End If
End Sub
```

To make the alarm more attention-grabbing, you could combine this technique with the one described in the previous sections. After the countdown finishes, the program would display a blinking label or text to catch the user's attention.

43. Display a Digital Clock ④ ⑤ ⑥

Directory: Clock

Even though Timer controls do not keep time, a program can use a Timer to decide when it should update a clock display. Example program Clock uses this approach to display a digital clock.

Program Clock.

How It Works

Program Clock updates its clock display when it receives a Timer event. These events are not guaranteed to fire exactly on time. If the Timer's Interval property is set to 1000 (1 second), the event may sometimes fire a little late. That may make the control occasionally skip a second. To prevent this, program Clock sets its Timer control's Interval property to 250 (one-quarter second). That ensures that the clock is always correct to within roughly one-quarter second.

```
Option Explicit

Private Sub Form_Load()
    ' Enable the timer. Update every 1/4 second.
    tmrClock.Interval = 250
    tmrClock.Enabled = True

    ' Invoke the timer to display the initial time.
    tmrClock_Timer
End Sub

Private Sub Form_Resize()
    ' Make the label fill the form.
    lblClock.Move 0, 0, ScaleWidth, ScaleHeight
End Sub
```

```
' Display the current time.
Private Sub tmrClock_Timer()
Static last_time As Date
Dim time_now As Date

    ' See what time it is.
    time_now = Time

    ' If this time is already displayed, do nothing.
    If time_now = last_time Then Exit Sub

    ' Display the new time.
    lblClock.Caption = Format$(time_now, "Long Time")

    ' Update the last time displayed.
    last_time = time_now
End Sub
```

Using similar Timer code, you can write a program that displays an analog clock. The only difference in the two programs would be in the ways they display the time.

44. Trigger Alarms

Directory: Alarms

The Timer control is designed to generate Timer events at specified intervals. The Interval property can take values between 0 and roughly 65,000, so the control can generate events at most 65,000 milliseconds, or 65 seconds, apart. Even with this restriction, a program can use a Timer control to manage greater intervals or irregular intervals. Example program Alarms uses a Timer control to generate alarms every 5 minutes at 0, 5, 10, ..., 55 minutes after the hour.

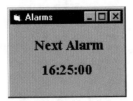

Program Alarms.

How It Works

The basic idea is for the program to store the next time it should raise an alarm. When it receives a Timer event, the program checks to see if that alarm time has arrived. If so, the program takes action and then calculates the next time it should raise an alarm.

The following code shows how program Alarms works. The tmrAlarm_Timer event handler determines whether the next alarm time has arrived. If it has, the program beeps and calculates the next alarm time using the NextAlarmTime subroutine.

If the alarm time has not arrived, the program calculates the number of seconds left until that time. If this is less than 60 seconds, the program sets the Timer control's Interval property to wait for the needed amount of time.

If it is more than 60 seconds until the next alarm time, the program sets the Interval property to 60,000 so the control waits for 1 minute. When it receives the next Timer event, the program repeats the process.

```
Option Explicit

' Fire the timer to calculate the first alarm time.
Private Sub Form_Load()
    tmrAlarm_Timer
End Sub

' See if it is time for the alarm.
Private Sub tmrAlarm_Timer()
Static next_alarm As Date
Dim secs_to_go As Single

    ' See if we have initialized next_alarm.
    If next_alarm = 0 Then
        ' Initialize next_alarm.
        next_alarm = NextAlarmTime
        lblNextAlarm.Caption = Format$(next_alarm, "hh:mm:ss")
    End If

    ' See how many milliseconds until the next
    ' alarm time.
    secs_to_go = DateDiff("s", Now, next_alarm)

    ' Stop the timer to clear previous alarms.
    tmrAlarm.Enabled = False

    ' Set the timer's Interval.
    If secs_to_go < 1 Then
        ' Fire the alarm.
        ' Do something more interesting here.
        Beep

        ' Reinitialize next_alarm.
        next_alarm = NextAlarmTime
        lblNextAlarm.Caption = Format$(next_alarm, "hh:mm:ss")
    ElseIf secs_to_go < 60 Then
        tmrAlarm.Interval = secs_to_go * 1000
    Else
        tmrAlarm.Interval = 60000
```

```
        End If

        ' Restart the timer.
        tmrAlarm.Enabled = True
End Sub

' Return the next time that is a multiple of
' 5 minutes after the hour.
Private Function NextAlarmTime() As Date
' The number of minutes between alarms.
Const ALARM_INTERVAL = 5

Dim time_now As Date
Dim h As Integer
Dim m As Integer
Dim seconds As Long
Dim next_m As Integer

        ' Get the current time.
        time_now = Now

        ' Get the hour and minutes.
        h = DatePart("h", time_now)
        m = DatePart("n", time_now)

        ' Calculate the next multiple of ALARM_INTERVAL.
        next_m = ((m \ ALARM_INTERVAL) + 1) * ALARM_INTERVAL

        NextAlarmTime = DateAdd("n", h * 60 + next_m, Date)
End Function
```

Program Alarms simply beeps. A more useful program might check directories for files, verify network connections, or download stock quotes from the Internet.

45. Make a Long Waiting Timer

Directory: LongTmr

The Timer control's Interval property can be no larger than roughly 65,000, so a Timer control alone cannot wait for intervals longer than approximately 65 seconds. The previous section shows how to use a Timer control to wait for a time further in the future. This method is effective, but it requires a small amount of extra overhead for the Timer event to fire every minute until the alarm time arrives.

A program can use API functions to create timers that can wait much longer. Example program LongTmr uses this technique. Enter an interval in seconds, and click the Start button. The program sets a time for the indicated interval and changes the button's caption to Stop. Each time the timer fires, the program increments its displayed count. Click the Stop button to stop the timer.

Program LongTmr.

How It Works

The following code shows how program LongTmr controls its timer. To create a timer, it calls the SetTimer API function, passing it the address of the function the system should invoke when the timer expires. Because the AddressOf operator was not introduced until Visual Basic 5, this does not work in earlier versions of Visual Basic.

```
Option Explicit

Private TimerID As Long

' The API timer has fired. Do something.
Public Sub TimerFired()
Static i As Integer

    i = i + 1
    LongTmrForm.lblTimer.Caption = Format$(i)
End Sub

' Start or stop the timer. See also Form_Unload.
Private Sub cmdStart_Click()
Static running As Boolean
Dim pause As Long

    If running Then
        ' Stop the timer.
        KillTimer 0, TimerID
        cmdStart.Caption = "Start"
        lblRunning.Caption = "Stopped"
    Else
        ' Start the timer.
        pause = CSng(txtPause.Text) * 1000
        TimerID = SetTimer(0, 0, pause, _
            AddressOf TimerCallback)
```

```
            cmdStart.Caption = "Stop"
            lblRunning.Caption = "Running"
        End If
        running = Not running
    End Sub


    ' Save this form as the one to notify when the
    ' API timer fires.
    Private Sub Form_Load()
        Set TimerForm = Me
    End Sub


    ' Kill the timer if it is running.
    Private Sub Form_Unload(Cancel As Integer)
        If TimerID <> 0 Then KillTimer 0, TimerID
    End Sub
```

The following code is contained in the file LongTmr.bas. It contains API function declarations for SetTimer and KillTimer. It also contains the TimerCallback subroutine invoked by the system when the timer fires. This subroutine calls the TimerFired method defined by the form.

```
    Declare Function SetTimer Lib "user32" (ByVal hwnd As Long, _
        ByVal nIDEvent As Long, ByVal uElapse As Long, _
        ByVal lpTimerFunc As Long) As Long
    Declare Function KillTimer Lib "user32" (ByVal hwnd As Long, _
        ByVal nIDEvent As Long) As Long


    ' We invoke this form's TimerFired subroutine
    ' when the timer fires.
    Public TimerForm As Form


    ' This is the timer callback function executed
    ' when the timer expires.
    Public Sub TimerCallback(hwnd As Long, msg As Long, _
        idTimer As Long, dwTime As Long)

        TimerForm.TimerFired
    End Sub
```

Using the SetTimer and KillTimer API functions, a program can make a timer that waits up to roughly 23 days.

46. Scroll Text

Directory: ScrTxt

An ActiveX control can use a Timer to make text that scrolls. Example program ScrTxt uses a Timer to make text scroll from right to left across a label. Because this program uses a custom ActiveX control, it works only in Visual Basic 5 and later.

Program ScrTxt.

How It Works

To make a scrolling text control, add a Timer to the UserControl object. Whenever the Timer event occurs, erase the UserControl and redraw the text moved slightly.

The following code shows the key pieces of the TextScroller ActiveX control used by program ScrTxt. The key properties that manage the control's appearance are Text, Interval, Distance, and ScrollUntilGone. Text is the text displayed by the control. Interval is the length of time between the control's redrawing of the text. This property is mapped directly to the Timer control's Interval property. Distance determines how far the text is moved each time it is redrawn. ScrollUntilGone is a Boolean value that indicates whether the control should scroll the text until it has moved completely out of the control. If this value is False, the control stops when the beginning of the text reaches the control's left edge.

Two other variables control the text's position. CurX indicates the text's current position. MinX gives the smallest value the program will use for CurX. When CurX reaches MinX, the control stops moving the text.

```
Option Explicit

'Property Variables:
Dim m_ScrollUntilGone As Boolean
Dim m_Text As String
Dim m_Distance As Integer
```

```vb
'Event Declarations:
' Fires when all of the text has scrolled
' off the control.
Event ScrollingDone()

Private CurX As Single
Private MinX As Single

'WARNING! DO NOT REMOVE OR MODIFY THE FOLLOWING COMMENTED LINES!
'MappingInfo=tmrScroll,tmrScroll,-1,Interval
Public Property Get Interval() As Long
    Interval = tmrScroll.Interval
End Property

Public Property Let Interval(ByVal New_Interval As Long)
    tmrScroll.Interval() = New_Interval
    PropertyChanged "Interval"
End Property

' Move the text a little bit.
Private Sub tmrScroll_Timer()
    If Not Ambient.UserMode Then Exit Sub

    Cls
    CurrentY = 0
    CurrentX = CurX
    Print m_Text

        ' See if it's time to stop.
    If CurX <= MinX Then
        Enabled = False
        RaiseEvent ScrollingDone
    End If

        ' Move CurX for the next time.
    CurX = CurX - m_Distance
    If CurX < MinX Then CurX = MinX
End Sub

'WARNING! DO NOT REMOVE OR MODIFY THE FOLLOWING COMMENTED LINES!
'MappingInfo=tmrScroll,tmrScroll,-1,Enabled
Public Property Get Enabled() As Boolean
    Enabled = tmrScroll.Enabled
End Property

' Get the control started.
Public Property Let Enabled(ByVal New_Enabled As Boolean)
    tmrScroll.Enabled() = New_Enabled
    PropertyChanged "Enabled"

        ' See if the control is enabled.
    If tmrScroll.Enabled Then
```

```
        ' Start at the rightmost part of the control.
        CurX = ScaleWidth

        ' Set MinX depending on the value of ScrollUntilGone.
        If m_ScrollUntilGone Then
            MinX = -TextWidth(m_Text)
        Else
            MinX = 0
        End If
    End If
End Property


Public Property Get Distance() As Integer
    Distance = m_Distance
End Property


Public Property Let Distance(ByVal New_Distance As Integer)
    m_Distance = New_Distance
    PropertyChanged "Distance"
End Property


Public Property Get Text() As String
    Text = m_Text
End Property


Public Property Let Text(ByVal New_Text As String)
    m_Text = New_Text
    PropertyChanged "Text"

    If tmrScroll.Enabled Then
        ' Set MinX depending on the value of ScrollUntilGone.
        If m_ScrollUntilGone Then
            MinX = -TextWidth(m_Text)
        Else
            MinX = 0
        End If
    End If
End Property

'WARNING! DO NOT REMOVE OR MODIFY THE FOLLOWING COMMENTED LINES!
'MemberInfo=0,0,0,True
Public Property Get ScrollUntilGone() As Boolean
    ScrollUntilGone = m_ScrollUntilGone
End Property


Public Property Let ScrollUntilGone( _
    ByVal New_ScrollUntilGone As Boolean)

    m_ScrollUntilGone = New_ScrollUntilGone
    PropertyChanged "ScrollUntilGone"
```

```
    ' Set MinX depending on the value of ScrollUntilGone.
    If m_ScrollUntilGone Then
        MinX = -TextWidth(m_Text)
    Else
        MinX = 0
    End If
End Property
```

Within the code, you probably noticed several comments that begin with:

```
'WARNING! DO NOT REMOVE OR MODIFY THE FOLLOWING COMMENTED LINES!
```

These comments were added by the ActiveX Control Interface Wizard. This wizard was used to build some of the simpler property procedures used by the control. The wizard uses these comments to understand what the procedures do. If you remove them, the wizard will be unable to completely understand these routines in the future. The code will still work, but you will have to maintain these routines yourself without the wizard's help.

The TextScroller control contains lots of other code. It includes properties that modify the name, size, and other properties of the font used by the control. It also includes standard routines like UserControl_InitProperties and UserControl_ReadProperties that are required by any ActiveX control. These routines are straightforward so they are not reproduced here. You can see the complete source code on the CD-ROM. For more information on creating ActiveX controls in Visual Basic, see *Custom Controls Library* by Rod Stephens (John Wiley & Sons, 1998).

CHAPTER 6

Starting and Stopping

There are many ways you can start a program. You can double-click on it in Windows Explorer, double-click on a shortcut to it, drag a file onto the program's icon, or invoke it from a DOS command window.

This chapter explains the differences between these methods and tells how a program should react. It also explains how one program can start another.

47. Check Command-Line Parameters

Directory: CmdLine

When a program starts, it may receive command-line parameters. Example program CmdLine displays the command-line parameters it receives when it starts. It displays each space-separated parameter in a different line next to its parameter number.

The following section explains how program CmdLine works. The sections after that describe different ways to start a program with command-line arguments.

Program CmdLine.

How It Works

Visual Basic's Command$ statement returns a list of the program's command-line parameters separated by spaces. For instance, the following code displays the command-line parameters in a TextBox.

```
txtCmdLine.Text = Command$
```

Once a program reads its command-line parameters, it can take appropriate action. For instance, the parameters might include the names of input and output files or flags that tell the program how to act. The following code shows how program CmdLine reads and displays its command-line arguments.

```
' Display the command-line arguments.
Private Sub Form_Load()
Dim cmds As String
Dim pos As Integer
Dim txt As String
Dim i As Integer

    cmds = Trim$(Command$)
    i = 1
    Do
        ' Find the next space-separated parameter.
        pos = InStr(cmds, " ")
        If pos = 0 Then Exit Do
        txt = txt & Format$(i) & ":" & _
            Left$(cmds, pos - 1) & vbCrLf
        cmds = Trim$(Mid$(cmds, pos + 1))
        i = i + 1
    Loop

    ' Add the last parameter.
    If Len(cmds) > 0 Then _
        txt = txt & Format$(i) & ":" & _
            cmds & vbCrLf
```

```
        txtCmdLine.Text = txt
End Sub
```

There are many ways to start a program:

- Running it in the Visual Basic Integrated Development Environment (IDE)
- Executing it in a DOS window
- Starting it from another program
- Double-clicking it in the Windows Explorer
- Dragging files onto it in the Windows Explorer
- Double-clicking on a shortcut to the program
- Dragging files onto its shortcut

The following sections explain how these different methods affect command-line parameters.

Starting in the IDE

Normally when a program starts in the IDE, it receives no parameters. You can give the program parameters for testing purposes. In Visual Basic 4, select the Tools menu's Options command. Click the Advanced tab, and enter the command-line parameters in the Command Line Arguments box.

In Visual Basic 5 or 6, select the Project menu's Properties command at the bottom of the menu. Click the Make tab, and enter the parameters in the Command Line Arguments box.

When you start the program in the IDE, it receives the parameters you entered. When you compile the program, these parameters are ignored. The compiled program will not receive parameters unless it is started using one of the other methods to give it parameters.

Starting in a DOS Window

To pass a program command-line parameters in a DOS window, add the parameters after the program's name. For instance, the following code executes the program CmdLine.exe, passing it the two parameters Input.txt and Output.txt.

```
C:\> CmdLine.exe Input.txt Output.txt
```

Starting from Another Program

There are a few ways one Visual Basic program can start another. The simplest is the Shell statement. The program simply passes the Shell statement a string containing the name of the program, followed by any command-line parameters it should receive. The following code starts program CmdLine with two parameters, much as the previous DOS command does.

```
Shell "CmdLine.exe Input.txt Output.txt"
```

Using Windows Explorer

When you double-click on a program in Windows Explorer, the program executes without command-line arguments.

If you drag one or more files onto a program in Windows Explorer, the program receives as command-line parameters the fully qualified path names of the files separated by spaces. The program can use InStr to separate the file names and use them appropriately. For instance, many programs that display or edit files open each of the files named by the parameters.

Using Shortcuts

Normally if you double-click on a program's shortcut, the program starts with no command-line parameters. You can edit the shortcut, however, so that it gives the program parameters.

Right-click on the shortcut and select the Properties command. Click on the Shortcut tab, and enter the parameters after the program's name in the Target field. Enter the program name and parameters just as you would type them in a DOS window. Now, when you double-click on the shortcut, the program starts with these parameters.

If you drag files onto a program's shortcut, the program receives the file names as parameters instead of the parameters specified in the shortcut.

48.   Check Environment Variables

Directory: Environ

Windows provides a rich execution environment for running programs. This environment includes environment variables that contain values associated with the Windows session. These values are typically defined in Autoexec.bat or other startup batch files.

Example program Environ displays the values of its environment variables. Enter a variable name, and click the Show button to see a particular value. Click the ShowAll button to see a list of all the variables.

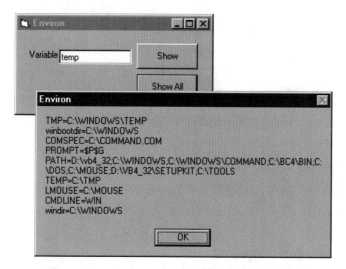

Program Environ.

How It Works

A Visual Basic program can read environment variables using the Environ function. If the program passes Environ the name of a variable, the function returns that variable's value. If the variable is not defined, the function returns a blank string.

If the program passes Environ an index, the function returns the name and value of the environment variable with that index. Again, if the variable is not defined, the function returns a blank string.

The following code shows how program Environ works. The ShowAll_Click event handler uses the fact that the Environ function returns a blank string if a variable is undefined. This routine passes Environ the values 1, 2, 3, and so on until the function returns a blank string.

```
Option Explicit

' Show the value of the named variable.
Private Sub cmdShow_Click()
    MsgBox Environ$(txtVarName.Text)
End Sub

' Show a list of all environment variables.
Private Sub cmdShowAll_Click()
Dim i As Integer
Dim txt As String
Dim new_value As String

    ' List values until we find a blank one.
    i = 1
    Do
        new_value = Environ$(i)
```

```
        If Len(new_value) = 0 Then Exit Do
        txt = txt & new_value & vbCrLf
        i = i + 1
    Loop

    ' Display the results.
    MsgBox txt
End Sub
```

Using the Environ function, a program can read environment variables and take appropriate action. For instance, you can define variables in Autoexec.bat to define system-wide values for use by all of your programs.

49. Start Another Program

Directory: Start

Visual Basic's Shell command allows a program to start another program. Shell takes two parameters. The first is the name of the program to start, followed by any command-line parameters it should receive. The second is a flag that tells Visual Basic how to start the new program. Table 6.1 lists values this parameter can take.

Example program Start starts other programs. Use the option buttons to select the program's Start mode. Enter the program's path, followed by any command-line parameters you want it to receive, and click the Start button.

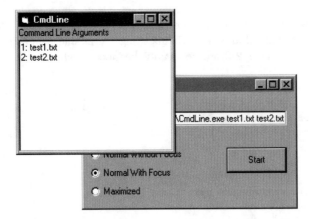

Program Start.

Table 6.1   Shell Function Start Mode Parameters

PARAMETER	MEANING
1	Start normal with focus
3	Start maximized
4	Start normal without focus
6	Start minimized

How It Works

Program Start is relatively straightforward. The following code shows how it works.

```
Option Explicit

Private StartMode As Integer

' Record the new start mode.
Private Sub optStartMode_Click(Index As Integer)
    Select Case Index
        Case 0 ' Minimized.
            StartMode = 6
        Case 1 ' Normal without focus.
            StartMode = 4
        Case 2 ' Normal with focus.
            StartMode = 1
        Case 3 ' Maximized.
            StartMode = 3
    End Select
End Sub

' Start the indicated program.
Private Sub cmdStart_Click()
    On Error Resume Next
    Shell txtProgram.Text, StartMode

    If Err.Number <> 0 Then _
        MsgBox Err.Description
End Sub
```

When a program starts another using Shell, the call to the Shell statement returns immediately. The first program does not wait for the second to finish running. Both applications run at the same time.

☆ ☆
④ ⑤ ⑥

50. Change Environment Variables

Directory: StartEnv

The previous section explains how a program can start another program using the Shell statement. The section before that shows how a program can read environment variables. You can combine these two techniques to pass environment variable values to a newly started program.

Example program StartEnv demonstrates this technique. Enter the path to a program, the name of an environment variable (which need not already exist), and a value for that variable. Then click the Start button. The program sets the environment variable's value and uses Shell to start the other program. The new program can use the Environ function to find the value of this and other variables.

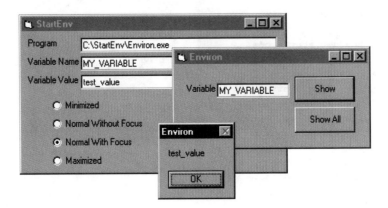

Program StartEnv.

How It Works

Visual Basic's Environ function lets a program read environment variables, but Visual Basic does not have a function that modifies those values. A program can use the SetEnvironmentVariable API function to set an environment variable's value.

When a program starts another program using the Shell statement, the new program inherits the environment variables of the first program. This includes any new values set using SetEnvironmentVariable so that the new program can read those values using the Environ function.

Program StartEnv uses the following code to set an environment variable and then start a new program.

```
Option Explicit

Private StartMode As Integer
```

```
#If Win32 Then
    ' SetEnvironmentVariable exists only in 32-bit systems.
    Private Declare Function SetEnvironmentVariable Lib "kernel32" _
        Alias "SetEnvironmentVariableA" (ByVal lpName As String, _
        ByVal lpValue As String) As Long
#End If

' Start the indicated program.
Private Sub cmdStart_Click()
Dim var_name As String
Dim var_value As String

    ' Set the environment variable.
    var_name = txtVarName.Text
    var_value = txtVarValue.Text
    SetEnvironmentVariable var_name, var_value

    ' Start the program.
    On Error Resume Next
    Shell txtProgram.Text, StartMode

    If Err.Number <> 0 Then _
        MsgBox Err.Description
End Sub
```

A program can set environment variables using the SetEnvironmentVariable API function, but it cannot later read those values using the Environ function. It can read the new value using the GetEnvironmentVariable API function if it must, but it would be more efficient for the program to simply keep track of any values it has changed.

☆ ☆
④ ⑤ ⑥

51. See if the IDE Is Running

Directory: InIDE

Sometimes it is useful for a program to know whether it is running in Visual Basic's Integrated Development Environment (IDE) or as a compiled executable. For instance, a program might provide an extra menu full of testing and debugging commands while it is running in the IDE, but it would hide that menu from end users while it is running as a compiled executable.

Example program InIDE displays text indicating whether it is running in the IDE or as a compiled executable.

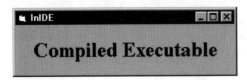

Program InIDE.

How It Works

Visual Basic does not have a statement that determines whether the program has been compiled, but a program can tell whether it is running in the IDE by using a simple trick.

Debug.Print statements are removed from a program when it is compiled into an executable image. The trick is to place code in a Debug.Print statement that generates an error. The program can use an error handler to catch the error. If the error occurs, the program must be running in the IDE. If the program has been compiled, the Debug.Print statement has been removed so the error will not occur.

```
' Return True if the program is running in the IDE.
Public Function InIDE() As Boolean
    On Error Resume Next
    Debug.Print 1 / 0
    InIDE = (Err.Number <> 0)
End Function
```

52. Allow Only One Instance

☆ ☆
④ ⑤ ⑥

Directory: OneApp

Visual Basic's App.PrevInstance statement returns True if there is already an instance of the program running. A program can use this to allow only one instance of itself to be running at any given time. This can be handy for programs where more than one instance is never necessary.

For instance, suppose a program checks a directory for new files every five minutes. Whenever it finds a new file, the program prints it. Having two such programs running at the same time would waste both computing power and paper on the printer. Only one instance of the program should ever run at the same time.

Example program OneApp ensures that only one instance of it ever runs at one time.

Program OneApp.

How It Works

When it detects another instance of itself, program OneApp tells the user. It then uses the AppActivate statement to try to activate the previous instance, and it exits. Unfortunately, this code does not work on all systems. It works for Windows NT 4.0, but it does not correctly activate the previous instance in Windows 95.

```
' See if there is already an instance running.
' If so, set focus to that instance and unload.
Public Sub CheckPreviousInstance()
    If App.PrevInstance Then
        ' Tell the user.
        MsgBox "This program is already running."

        ' Activate the previous instance.
        AppActivate App.Title

        ' Send a key (here SHIFT-key) to set the
        ' form from the previous instance to the
        ' top of the screen.
        SendKeys "+", True

        ' Terminate the new instance.
        Unload Me
    End If
End Sub
```

Note that a program's instances are tracked based on the executable file. If you copy the executable into another file, the user can run one instance of each executable.

53. Get the Windows Version

Directory: WinVer

Occasionally, it is useful for a program to know what version of Windows is running. Example program WinVer displays information about the Windows version and build number.

Program WinVer.

How It Works

The GetVersionInfo subroutine shown in the following code uses the GetVersionEx API function to retrieve Windows version information. GetVersionEx fills in values in an OSVERSIONINFO data structure. Subroutine GetVersionInfo uses those values to return the Windows version and build number.

```
Option Explicit

Private Type OSVERSIONINFO
    dwOSVersionInfoSize As Long
    dwMajorVersion As Long
    dwMinorVersion As Long
    dwBuildNumber As Long
    dwPlatformId As Long
    szCSDVersion As String * 128
End Type

#If Win32 Then
    Private Declare Function GetVersionEx Lib "kernel32" _
        Alias "GetVersionExA" ( _
        ByRef lpVersionInformation As OSVERSIONINFO) As Long
#Else
    Private Declare Function GetVersionEx Lib "Kernel" ( _
        ByRef lpVersionInformation As OSVERSIONINFO) As Integer
#End If

Private Const VER_PLATFORM_WIN32_NT = 2
Private Const VER_PLATFORM_WIN32_WINDOWS = 1
Private Const VER_PLATFORM_WIN32s = 0

' Return the operating system version and build.
Public Sub GetVersionInfo(version As String, build As String)
Dim info As OSVERSIONINFO
Dim txt As String

    info.dwOSVersionInfoSize = Len(info)
    GetVersionEx info

    If info.dwPlatformId = VER_PLATFORM_WIN32_WINDOWS Then
        version = "Windows95 "
    Else
        version = "WindowsNT "
```

```
        End If
        version = version & Format$(info.dwMajorVersion) & _
            "." & Format$(info.dwMinorVersion)

        build = Format$(info.dwBuildNumber)
    End Sub
```

54. Unload All Forms   ④ ⑤ ⑥

Directory: Unload

There are two main ways to end a program. First, the program can unload all of its forms. When all the forms are unloaded and the currently running code finishes, the program stops.

Second, the program can use Visual Basic's End statement. This makes the program stop immediately. Unfortunately, this means the forms are not unloaded properly. Their Form_Unload event handlers are not invoked so the forms cannot perform any necessary cleanup tasks. For instance, they cannot close open files and databases.

Visual Basic also does not always stop the program cleanly. It sometimes makes the program crash as it is exiting.

To prevent this kind of crash, a program should always finish by unloading all of its forms. For a complicated program that displays many forms and dialogs, finding and unloading all the loaded forms can be difficult.

Example program Unload demonstrates one method for unloading all of an application's forms quickly and easily. Click on the new form buttons to create several forms. When you close any form, the program closes all the forms and exits.

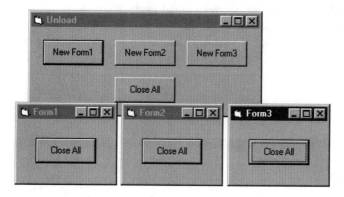

Program Unload.

How It Works

The UnloadAll subroutine shown in the following code makes unloading every form easy. UnloadAll first checks its static Boolean variable Unloading. If Unloading is True, the subroutine is already running. The new instance of the subroutine is unnecessary so it exits.

UnloadAll then sets Unloading to True so that later instances of the routine will exit. This is particularly useful if several forms invoke UnloadAll in their Form_Unload event handlers.

Next the subroutine unloads all of the forms in the Forms collection. It unloads the forms, starting with the last form in the collection and moving backward through the collection to the first. This is simpler than unloading the forms in their normal order: If the subroutine removed the first form, the collection would renumber the others to fill in the gap. The routine would then need to remove the new first form. Things are simpler if the routine works from the last form toward the first.

```
' Unload all loaded forms.
Public Sub UnloadAll()
Static Unloading As Boolean
Dim i As Integer

    ' Do nothing if we are already unloading.
    If Unloading Then Exit Sub
    Unloading = True

    For i = Forms.Count - 1 To 0 Step -1
        Unload Forms(i)
    Next i

    Unloading = False
End Sub
```

The UnloadAll subroutine cannot always unload every form. A form may refuse to unload by setting the Cancel parameter to False in its Form_QueryUnload event handler. For instance, if a form contains unsaved data, it may ask the user whether it should save the data, discard the data, or cancel the exit operation. In this case, the program should cancel its exit.

☆ ☆
④ ⑤ ⑥

55. **Run a DOS Batch File**

Directory: DosBatch

Just as a program can use the Shell statement to run an executable program, it can also use Shell to execute a DOS batch file. Recent versions of DOS, such as the version that comes with Windows NT, can even pass parameters to the batch file. The program simply adds the parameters after the batch file's name.

Example program DosBatch demonstrates this technique. Enter the name of a batch file and any parameters you want to pass to it. Then click the Run Batch File button to run the file.

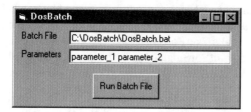

Program DosBatch.

How It Works

The following code shows how program DosBatch runs batch files.

```
' Run the batch file.
Private Sub cmdRun_Click()
    Shell txtBatchFile.Text & " " & _
        txtParameters.Text, vbNormalFocus
End Sub
```

56. Wait for Another Program

☆ ☆ ☆
④ ⑤ ⑥

Directory: RunWait

The Shell statement runs a program asynchronously. That means the two programs execute independently at their own speeds. Sometimes it is important that the first program wait until the second program is finished before it continues.

Example program RunWait starts another program and then waits until it completes. Enter the complete path to an executable program and click the Start button. Program RunWait presents a message box that says "About to start the program." When you close this dialog, RunWait starts the other program and waits for it to finish. When you close the other program, RunWait presents a message box that says "Done running the program."

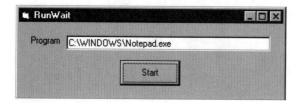

Program RunWait.

How It Works

The ShellAndWait subroutine shown in the following code uses the Shell statement to start a new program. It saves the process ID of that program returned by Shell. The routine hides the main program and uses the OpenProcess API function to get the process handle for the new program. It then calls WaitForSingleObject to wait until that process completes. The subroutine passes WaitForSingleObject the parameter INFINITE to indicate that it wants to wait as long as necessary for the process to complete.

WaitForSingleObject returns when the second program ends. Subroutine ShellAndWait uses the CloseHandle API function to free resources it used and then makes the main program visible again.

```
Option Explicit

' The process functions exist only in 32-bit systems.
Private Declare Function OpenProcess Lib "kernel32" ( _
    ByVal dwDesiredAccess As Long, ByVal bInheritHandle As Long, _
    ByVal dwProcessId As Long) As Long
Private Declare Function WaitForSingleObject Lib "kernel32" ( _
    ByVal hHandle As Long, ByVal dwMilliseconds As Long) As Long
Private Declare Function CloseHandle Lib "kernel32" ( _
    ByVal hObject As Long) As Long

Private Const SYNCHRONIZE = &H100000
Private Const INFINITE = -1&

' Start the other program and wait for it.
Private Sub cmdStart_Click()
    Beep
    ShellAndWait txtProgram.Text
    Beep
End Sub

' Start the indicated program and wait for it to
' finish, hiding while we wait.
Private Sub ShellAndWait(ByVal program_name As String)
Dim process_id As Long
Dim process_handle As Long

    ' Start the program using Shell.
    On Error GoTo ShellError
    process_id = Shell(program_name, vbNormalFocus)
    On Error GoTo 0

    ' Hide.
    Me.Visible = False
    DoEvents

    ' Wait for the program to finish.
```

```
        ' Get the process handle.
        process_handle = OpenProcess(SYNCHRONIZE, 0, process_id)
        If process_handle <> 0 Then
            WaitForSingleObject process_handle, INFINITE
            CloseHandle process_handle
        End If

        ' Reappear.
        Me.Visible = True
        Exit Sub

ShellError:
    MsgBox "Error starting program " & _
        txtProgram.Text & vbCrLf & _
        Err.Description
    End Sub
```

This program has some strange side effects in the Visual Basic Integrated Development Environment (IDE). While the WaitForSingleObject function is running, Visual Basic cannot update its windows. If you obscure the IDE's windows, they may not repaint properly.

57. Invoke Default Actions

Directory: StartDef

When you double-click on a file in Windows Explorer, the system examines the file's extension. It tries to find an application that understands that extension. If it finds such an application, the system invokes it, passing it the file's name. For instance, if you have Microsoft Word installed on your system and you double-click on a file with a .doc extension, your system will probably open the document using Word.

Example program StartDef performs a similar task. When you enter the name of a file and click the Start button, the program attempts to open the file with the appropriate default application.

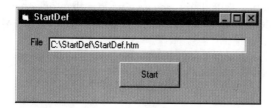

Program StartDef.

How It Works

Visual Basic's Shell statement allows a program to start an application, but it does not find and execute the default application for a file. If the file is not executable, Shell fails.

The ShellExecute API function provides this additional feature. If it is passed the name of a nonexecutable file, ShellExecute opens the file using the appropriate default application. For instance, if the program passes ShellExecute a file with an .htm extension, the system opens the file using its default Web browser.

The following code shows how program StartDef uses ShellExecute to process files.

```
Option Explicit

#If Win32 Then
    Private Declare Function ShellExecute Lib "shell32.dll" _
        Alias "ShellExecuteA" (ByVal hwnd As Long, _
        ByVal lpOperation As String, ByVal lpFile As String, _
        ByVal lpParameters As String, ByVal lpDirectory As String, _
        ByVal nShowCmd As Long) As Long
#Else
    Private Declare Function ShellExecute Lib "Shell.dll" ( _
        ByVal hwnd As Integer, ByVal lpOperation As String, _
        ByVal lpFile As String, ByVal lpParameters As String, _
        ByVal lpDirectory As String, ByVal nShowCmd As Integer) _
        As Integer
#End If

Private Const SW_SHOW = 5

' Start the indicated program.
Private Sub cmdStart_Click()
    If ShellExecute(hwnd, "open", txtProgram.Text, _
        vbNullString, vbNullString, SW_SHOW) <= 32 _
    Then _
        MsgBox "Error starting the default application."
End Sub
```

The ShellExecute function returns the instance handle for the new application if it is opened successfully. If the function fails, it returns a value less than or equal to 32 to indicate the reason why it failed. Consult the online documentation to see what the exact error codes mean.

CHAPTER 7

Network Programming

O ver the past few years, networking, the Internet, and the World Wide Web have grown explosively. Networking applications are more common than ever, and even simple applications that have little real need for networking are incorporating Web features.

Microsoft made network programming easier for Visual Basic programmers by introducing the WebBrowser and InternetTransfer controls in Visual Basic 5. This chapter explains how a Visual Basic program can take advantage of these controls and a few useful API functions to provide networking features. This is far from the end of the story for network programming. For a more complete introduction to the topic, consult a book on network programming.

58. Map a Network Share ④ ⑤ ⑥

Directory: MapShare

One of the most basic networking functions a program can perform is to map a network share. Example program MapShare does this. Enter the remote share name and password, and the local drive letter. Then click the Map Share button.

Program MapShare.

How It Works

The WNetAddConnection function contained in the library mpr.dll mounts remote shared directories for the local system. WNetAddConnection takes three parameters: the name of the remote share to mount, the password for the remote share if one is required, and the local drive letter where the remote share should be mounted.

The following code shows how program MapShare uses WNetAddConnection.

```
Option Explicit

' mpr.dll is a 32-bit DLL.
#If Win32 Then
    Private Declare Function WNetAddConnection Lib "mpr.dll" _
        Alias "WNetAddConnectionA" (ByVal lpszNetPath As String, _
        ByVal lpszPassword As String, ByVal lpszLocalName As String) _
        As Long
#End If

' Map the share.
Private Sub cmdMapShare_Click()
Dim local_letter As String
Dim share_name As String
Dim password As String

    lblResult.Caption = "Working..."
    Screen.MousePointer = vbHourglass
    DoEvents

    ' Get the local letter. Add a colon (:)
    ' if necessary.
```

```
        local_letter = txtLocalLetter.Text
        If InStr(local_letter, ":") = 0 _
            Then local_letter = local_letter & ":"

        ' Get the remote share name and password.
        share_name = txtShareName.Text
        password = txtPassword.Text

        ' Mount the share.
        If MapShare(local_letter, share_name, password) Then
            lblResult.Caption = "Error mapping share."
        Else
            lblResult.Caption = "Share mapped."
        End If

        Screen.MousePointer = vbDefault
    End Sub

' Map the networked share. Return True if we fail.
Private Function MapShare(ByVal local_letter As String, _
    ByVal share_name As String, ByVal password As String) As Boolean

        MapShare = _
            (WNetAddConnection(share_name, _
                password, local_letter) > 0)
    End Function
```

WNetAddConnection mounts a share for the entire system, not just for the program that uses it. Once a program mounts a share, other programs such as Windows Explorer can treat the share as if it were a locally mounted disk.

59. Display a Web Document

 ⑤ ⑥

Directory: ShowWeb

The WebBrowser control introduced in Visual Basic 5 allows a program to display a Web document easily. Example program ShowWeb uses this control to display Web documents. Enter a Web address in the URL box, and click the Show button to see the document.

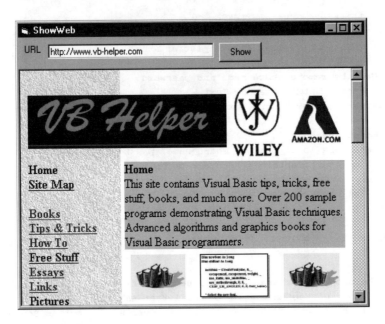

Program ShowWeb.

How It Works

To use the WebBrowser control, install it on a form. Then use the control's properties and methods to display Web documents. The following code shows how program ShowWeb controls its WebBrowser control.

```
Option Explicit

' Make the WebBrowser as large as possible.
Private Sub Form_Resize()
Dim hgt As Single

    hgt = ScaleHeight - wbrURL.Top
    If hgt < 120 Then hgt = 120
    wbrURL.Move 0, wbrURL.Top, ScaleWidth, hgt
End Sub


' Navigate to the indicated URL.
Private Sub cmdShow_Click()
    wbrURL.Navigate txtURL.Text
End Sub


' Make the browser visible.
Private Sub wbrURL_DownloadComplete()
    wbrURL.Visible = True
End Sub
```

The WebBrowser control has many other useful features including the ability to go forward, backward, or home, to refresh its display, and to display or hide different tool bars. To learn more about the WebBrowser control, consult the online help.

60. Display HTML Code

⑤ ⑥

Directory: URLText

The InternetTransfer control introduced in Visual Basic 5 allows a program to manipulate files on the Internet. Example program URLText uses this control to display the HTML code of a Web document. Enter a Web address in the URL box, and click the ShowText button to see the HTML code.

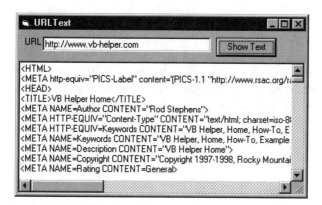

Program URLText.

How It Works

The following code shows how program URLText uses its InternetTransfer control. The key is the control's OpenURL method. This method returns the HTML text of a Web document.

```
Option Explicit

Private Sub cmdShowText_Click()
Dim response As Variant

    MousePointer = vbHourglass
    txtResult.Text = ""
    DoEvents

    ' Open the URL.
    response = inetURL.OpenURL(txtURL.Text)

    ' Display the response.
```

```
        txtResult.Text = response

        MousePointer = vbDefault
End Sub

' Make the TextBox as large as possible.
Private Sub Form_Resize()
Dim hgt As Single

    hgt = ScaleHeight - txtResult.Top
    If hgt < 120 Then hgt = 120
    txtResult.Move 0, txtResult.Top, ScaleWidth, hgt
End Sub

' Cancel any pending commands.
Private Sub Form_Unload(Cancel As Integer)
    inetURL.Cancel
End Sub
```

The InternetTransfer control's properties and methods provide many other features. They allow a program to use the HyperText Transfer Protocol (HTTP) and File Transfer Protocol (FTP). A program can use the control to perform tasks such as uploading and downloading files from FTP sites. To learn more about the InternetTransfer control, see the online help.

61. Parse HTML Code

Directory: URLParse

The previous section explains how to use the InternetTransfer control to download a Web document's HTML code. Once the program has downloaded that code, it can parse it to look for specific pieces of information.

Example program URLParse uses an InternetTransfer control to download information about books from Amazon.com's Web site. Enter the International Standard Book Number (ISBN) for a book in the ISBN field, and click the Get Information button. The program builds an appropriate Web address to display Amazon.com's information for that book. It uses the InternetTransfer control to read the response text and parses the result to find the book's title, author, and price.

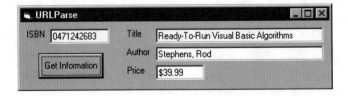

Program URLParse.

How It Works

Many Web sites use special codes to indicate a search. By entering appropriate codes in the URL, a Web browser tells the site what information to retrieve. Amazon.com displays information for a book when it sees a URL of the form http://www.amazon .com/exec/obidos/ISBN=X where X is the book's 10-digit ISBN.

You can often learn the format of the URL you need by navigating to the site using your browser. Find the information you want to view, and then look at the URL displayed by your browser.

The following code shows how program URLParse retrieves book information. The program creates the appropriate URL and uses the InternetTransfer control to retrieve a response. Subroutine ParseResponse looks through the result to find the book's title, author, and price.

Note that the formats of the responses generated by a Web site are subject to the whim of the site's administrator. Subroutine ParseResponse uses key text values to search for the data it needs. If the response format changes, a few modifications to these values should allow the program to find the data in its new location.

```
Option Explicit

' Get information about the entered ISBN.
Private Sub cmdGetInformation_Click()
Dim query_url As String
Dim response As Variant

    MousePointer = vbHourglass
    txtTitle.Text = ""
    txtAuthor.Text = ""
    txtPrice.Text = ""
    DoEvents

    ' Prepare a URL to get the information.
    query_url = _
        "http://www.amazon.com/exec/obidos/ISBN=" & _
        txtISBN.Text

    ' Open the URL.
    response = inetInformation.OpenURL(query_url)

    ' Parse the response.
    ParseResponse CStr(response)

    MousePointer = vbDefault
End Sub

' Parse the response string to extract book information.
Private Sub ParseResponse(ByVal response As String)
```

```vb
Const TITLE_START = "<font size=+1><b>"
Const TITLE_END = "</b>"
Const AUTHOR_START = "Author="
Const AUTHOR_END = "/"
Const PRICE_START1 = "Our Price:"
Const PRICE_START2 = ">"
Const PRICE_END = "<"


Dim pos1 As Integer
Dim pos2 As Integer

    ' Make sure we found something.
    If InStr(response, AUTHOR_START) = 0 Then
        ' The book was not found.
        txtTitle.Text = "*** Book Not Found ***"
        Exit Sub
    End If


    ' Find the book's title.
    pos1 = InStr(response, TITLE_START)
    pos1 = pos1 + Len(TITLE_START)
    pos2 = InStr(pos1, response, TITLE_END)
    txtTitle.Text = Clean(Mid$(response, pos1, pos2 - pos1))


    ' Find the book's author.
    pos1 = InStr(pos2, response, AUTHOR_START)
    pos1 = pos1 + Len(AUTHOR_START)
    pos2 = InStr(pos1, response, AUTHOR_END)
    txtAuthor.Text = Clean(Mid$(response, pos1, pos2 - pos1))


    ' Find the book's price.
    pos1 = InStr(pos2, response, PRICE_START1)
    pos1 = pos1 + Len(PRICE_START1)
    pos1 = InStr(pos1, response, PRICE_START2)
    pos1 = pos1 + Len(PRICE_START2)
    pos2 = InStr(pos1, response, PRICE_END)
    txtPrice.Text = Clean(Mid$(response, pos1, pos2 - pos1))
End Sub

' Replace %xx with a character where xx is the hex
' code for a character.
Private Function Clean(ByVal txt As String) As String
Dim pos As Integer
Dim num_text As String
Dim num As Integer

    pos = 1
    Do
        ' Find the next %.
        pos = InStr(pos, txt, "%")
        If pos = 0 Then Exit Do
```

```
    ' Find the number's hex string value.
    num_text = "&H" & Mid$(txt, pos + 1, 2)

    ' Convert the string value into a number.
    num = CInt(num_text)

    ' Replace the code with the character.
    txt = Left$(txt, pos - 1) & _
        Chr$(num) & Mid$(txt, pos + 3)
    Loop

    Clean = txt
End Function

' Cancel any pending commands.
Private Sub Form_Unload(Cancel As Integer)
    inetInformation.Cancel
End Sub
```

Using similar techniques, a program could download practically any kind of information from the Web. For instance, a program could download stock quotes from the Web and parse the results to find the stock values within the HTML code.

Taming TextBoxes

Visual Basic's TextBox control provides many useful features including copy, cut, and paste, scroll bars, and multiline text entry. The RichTextBox control provides additional features including the ability to display multiple fonts and character styles in a single piece of text. This chapter explains ways you can get even more out of the TextBox and RichTextBox controls.

62. Show New Text

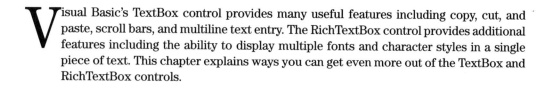

Directory: ScrText

When a program adds new text to a TextBox, that text is not necessarily visible. For instance, the following code adds new text to the end of a TextBox. If the current text is long, the new text may be scrolled off the bottom of the control so that it is not visible to the user.

```
txtAlerts.Text = txtAlerts.Text & vbCrLf & "Missing log file."
```

Example program ScrText ensures that new text is visible. Click the Add Text button to make the program add five lines of text to the TextBox. If the Scroll With Text box is checked, the program makes the new text visible. If the box is not checked, the new text may not be visible.

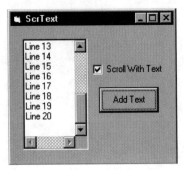

Program ScrText.

How It Works

When a TextBox's insertion position changes, the control automatically adjusts itself if necessary so that the new insertion position is visible. You can use this fact to make new text visible by moving the insertion position to the new text's location. The following code moves the insertion position to the end of the text.

```
txtAlerts.Text = txtAlerts.Text & vbCrLf & "Missing log file."
txtAlerts.SelStart = Len(txtAlerts.Text)
```

Program ScrText uses similar code to make its new text visible.

63. Clear All TextBoxes

Directory: ClearTxt

A nice feature provided by programs with many TextBoxes is the ability to clear every TextBox at once. For instance, Web pages that contain many text fields often have a Reset button that blanks all the fields.

Example program ClearTxt lets the user clear all of its TextBoxes. Click the Clear Text button to clear the TextBoxes.

Program ClearTxt.

How It Works

A form's Controls collection holds references to all the controls on the form. A program can use this collection to examine and modify all the controls easily. The following code examines a form's controls and blanks those that are TextBoxes.

```
Dim ctl As Control

    For Each ctl In Controls
        If TypeOf ctl Is TextBox Then _
            ctl.Text = ""
    Next ctl
```

You can modify this code to operate on other controls. For instance, it could uncheck CheckBoxes, select OptionButtons with Index property 0, and so forth.

---

64. Automatically Select Text

 ④ ⑤ ⑥

Directory: AutoSel

In times past when few computers had a mouse, many data entry programs automatically selected text when the input focus moved into a field. This made it easy for the user to keep or replace the field's current contents. To keep the current contents, the user pressed the Tab key and moved to the next field. To replace the text, the user simply started typing. Because the text was selected, it would be replaced.

With modern point-and-click interfaces, this feature has become less common. It is still convenient, however, if the user is likely to want to either replace all of a TextBox's contents or leave the contents unchanged.

Example program AutoSel automatically selects text when focus moves to a field. Use the Tab key to move from field to field.

Program AutoSel.

How It Works

The SelectField subroutine shown in following code selects all of the text in a TextBox. The txtName_GotFocus event handler shows how a program can automatically select a TextBox's contents when that control gains the input focus.

```
' Select all the text in this TextBox.
Private Sub SelectField(ByVal text_box As TextBox)
    text_box.SelStart = 0
    text_box.SelLength = Len(text_box.Text)
End Sub

' Select this field's contents.
Private Sub txtName_GotFocus()
    SelectField txtName
End Sub
```

Each TextBox in program AutoSel has a GotFocus event handler that invokes Select-Field.

65. Convert Carriage Returns to Tabs   ④ ⑤ ⑥

Directory: CrToTab

Normally, if the user presses the Return key while a single-line TextBox has the input focus, a Visual Basic program beeps. You can change this behavior using Visual Basic code.

Example program CrToTab ignores Return keys in single-line TextBoxes. If the Replace With Tabs box is checked, the program converts Return keys into Tab keys so pressing Return moves the focus to the next field. If this box is not checked, the program ignores carriage returns quietly.

Program CrToTab.

How It Works

A program can use KeyPress event handlers to watch for Return keys. Rather than placing an event handler on every TextBox, it is easier to set the form's KeyPreview property to True. Then the program can process all key events at the form level before they are passed on to the TextBoxes.

The following code shows how a program can handle Return keys in single-line TextBoxes. The code first verifies that the key is a Return key and that the control receiving it is a single line TextBox. It then sets the KeyAscii parameter to 0 to make the program discard the character.

The event handler then uses SendKeys to send the control a Tab character. This makes the focus move to the next control just as if the user pressed Tab instead of Return.

```
Private Sub Form_KeyPress(KeyAscii As Integer)
Const ASC_CR = 13 ' ASCII code for carriage return.

    ' If this is not a carriage return, do nothing.
    If KeyAscii <> ASC_CR Then Exit Sub

    ' If the control with focus is not a TextBox, do nothing.
    If Not (TypeOf ActiveControl Is TextBox) _
        Then Exit Sub

    ' If the control's MultiLine property is true, do nothing.
    If ActiveControl.MultiLine Then Exit Sub

    ' Ignore the carriage return.
    KeyAscii = 0

    ' Send a tab key.
    SendKeys "{TAB}"
End Sub
```

Note that the Return key still inserts a new line in multiline TextBoxes. This can be annoying to users who grow accustomed to using the Return key to tab through the fields. Each time the user presses Return, focus moves to the next control except when the current control is a multiline TextBox. Then the program starts inserting blank lines in the control's text. In some applications, you may want to avoid this annoyance by removing the SendKeys statement and simply ignoring the Return key instead of replacing it with a Tab.

66. Make a RichTextBox Editor

☆ ☆ ☆
④ ⑤ ⑥

Directory: RichEdit

The RichTextBox control is an enhanced TextBox that provides many additional formatting features. Example program RichEdit uses a RichTextBox control to implement a simple text editor. It implements several standard menu items in addition to several text formatting commands.

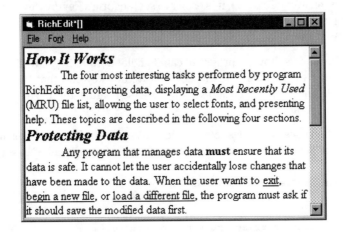

Program RichEdit.

How It Works

The three most interesting tasks performed by program RichEdit are protecting data, displaying a most recently used (MRU) file list, and allowing the user to select fonts. These topics are described in the following sections.

Protecting Data

Any program that manages data must ensure that its data is safe. It cannot let the user accidentally lose changes that have been made to the data. When the user wants to exit, begin a new file, or load a different file, the program must ask if it should save the modified data first.

Program RichEdit uses the DataModified Boolean variable to keep track of whether the current data has been modified since it was loaded or last saved.

Whenever the program's RichTextBox detects a change, its Change event handler invokes subroutine SetDataModified. This routine updates DataModified and sets the program's caption so it displays an asterisk if the data is modified. For instance, if the file's title is MyData.txt, the routine makes the program's caption read "RichEdit*[MyData.txt]."

```
Option Explicit

Private FileName As String   ' The full file name.
Private FileTitle As String  ' The file name without path.

Private DataModified As Boolean

Private Sub rchEditor_Change()
    SetDataChanged True
End Sub

' Set DataModified. Display an asterisk in the
' form's Caption next to the file name if
' appropriate.
Private Sub SetDataModified(changed As Boolean)
    ' Don't bother if it's already been done.
    If DataModified = changed Then Exit Sub

    DataModified = changed
    If changed Then
        Caption = "RichEdit*[" & FileTitle & "]"
    Else
        Caption = "RichEdit [" & FileTitle & "]"
    End If
End Sub
```

When the user wants to exit, load a different file, or start a new file, the program calls the DataSafe function. This function returns True if it is safe to remove the old data.

DataSafe begins by checking the value of DataModified. If DataModified is False, the current data has not been modified so it can safely be discarded. DataSafe returns True to indicate that it is safe to proceed with the operation that will remove the current data.

If the data has been modified, DataSafe warns the user and asks if it should save the changes. If the user clicks the No button, the user does not want to save the data so it is safe to discard. DataSafe returns True.

If the user clicks the Cancel button, the user has decided not to continue with the operation that would remove the current data. DataSafe returns False to tell the calling routine that it is not safe to remove the current data.

Finally, if the user clicks the Yes button, the user wants to save the data. DataSafe invokes the mnuFileSave_Click event handler just as if the user had selected the Save menu item from the File menu. This routine saves the modified data, prompting the user for a file name if necessary. If the save succeeds, the program sets DataModified to False. DataSafe sets its return value to Not DataModified. This tells the calling routine that the data is safe if the data was properly saved.

```
' Return True if the data is safe.
Private Function DataSafe() As Boolean
    ' No problem if the data is unmodified.
    If Not DataModified Then
        DataSafe = True
        Exit Function
    End If

    ' See if the user wants to save changes.
    Select Case MsgBox("The data has been modified. " & _
            Do you want to save the changes?", vbYesNoCancel)
        Case vbYes
            ' Save the data. Procedure SaveData
            ' will reset DataModified.
            mnuFileSave_Click
            DataSafe = Not DataModified

        Case vbNo
            ' Discard the changes to the data.
            DataSafe = True

        Case vbCancel
            ' Cancel.
            DataSafe = False
    End Select
End Function
```

The RichTextBox's Change event handler calls SetDataModified to mark the data as modified. The program also calls SetDataModified when the data is freshly loaded or created and it has not yet been modified. For instance, the following code executes when the user selects the File menu's New command. It first verifies that the current data is safe. It then blanks the text document and the file name and calls SetDataModified to indicate that the data has not been modified yet.

```
' Start a new file.
Private Sub mnuFileNew_Click()
    ' Make sure the existing data is safe.
    If Not DataSafe Then Exit Sub

    ' Start a new document.
    rchEditor.Text = ""
```

```
    ' Save the file name and title.
    FileTitle = ""
    FileName = ""

    ' Make sure the caption gets updated.
    DataModified = True
    SetDataModified False
End Sub
```

This technique is quite flexible and is useful in any program that allows the user to modify data.

MRU List

Most recently used (MRU) file lists have become standard on commercial applications. As Figure 8.1 shows, program RichEdit displays the last four files it accessed in its MRU list.

Program RichEdit uses three routines to manage its MRU list. LoadMRUList loads the list from the system registry. DisplayMRUList updates the menu items in the program's File menu to display the MRU choices. SaveFileName adds a name to the MRU list in the File menu and updates the registry.

When the program starts, it calls subroutine LoadMRUList to load the MRU file names from the Registry. The file names are stored in the Registry in the RichEdit section, MRUList subsection. The files' names are stored in keys named Name1, Name2, Name3, and Name4. The files' names without path information are stored in the keys Title1, Title2, Title3, and Title4. Subroutine LoadMRUList uses Visual Basic's GetSetting statement to read the file names and titles and store them in the MRUName and MRUTitle collections. It then calls DisplayMRUList to update the File menu.

```
    ' The MRU list.
    Private MRUName As Collection
    Private MRUTitle As Collection
```

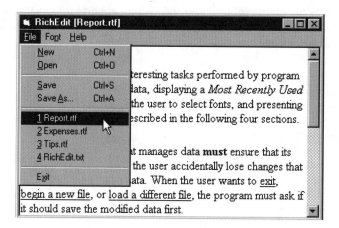

Figure 8.1   Example program RichEdit uses a four-item MRU list.

```
' Load the MRU list.
Private Sub LoadMRUList()
Dim i As Integer
Dim file_title As String
Dim file_name As String

    ' Load the saved entries.
    Set MRUName = New Collection
    Set MRUTitle = New Collection
    For i = 1 To 4
        file_name = GetSetting("RichEdit", _
            "MRUList", "Name" & Format$(i), "")
        If Len(file_name) > 0 Then
            file_title = GetSetting("RichEdit", _
                "MRUList", "Title" & Format$(i), "")
            MRUTitle.Add file_title
            MRUName.Add file_name
        End If
    Next i

    ' Display the MRU items.
    DisplayMRUList
End Sub
```

Program RichEdit's File menu contains five menu items that initially have their Visible properties set to False. These items come just before the menu's Exit command. The first four are all named mnuFileMRUItem and have Index properties 1, 2, 3, and 4. This is where the MRU file names will be displayed.

The fifth menu item is named mnuFileMRUSep. Its Caption property is set to a dash (-) so it displays as a separator in the menu. This is the separator that lies between the MRU file names and the Exit command in the menu.

Subroutine DisplayMRUList examines the strings in the MRUName and MRUTitle collections. For each nonblank entry, it sets the caption of one of the mnuFileMRUItem menu items and makes that item visible. It sets the Visible property for any unused MRU menu items to False so they are not displayed. If any MRU item is visible, the routine also makes the separator visible.

```
' Display the MRU list.
Private Sub DisplayMRUList()
Dim i As Integer

    ' Load the used entries.
    For i = 1 To 4
        If i > MRUName.Count Then Exit For
        mnuFileMRUItem(i).Caption = "&" & _
            Format$(i) & " " & MRUTitle(i)
        mnuFileMRUItem(i).Visible = True
    Next i
```

```
        ' Hide unneeded entries.
        For i = MRUName.Count + 1 To 4
            mnuFileMRUItem(i).Visible = False
        Next i

        ' Show the separator if necessary.
        mnuFileMRUSep.Visible = (MRUName.Count > 0)
    End Sub
```

When the user saves a file with a new name or opens a file, the program calls subroutine SaveFileName. This routine records the file's name and title in the FileName and FileTitle variables. It then searches the MRUName and MRUTitle collections to see if the file is already in the MRU file list. If it is, the routine removes it from the collections so that it will not appear twice when it is added again.

SaveFileName then inserts the new file title at the beginning of the MRU collections. This puts the file at the top of the MRU list. If the list contains more than four items, the program removes the last one. This item will not appear on the MRU list anyway because subroutine DisplayMRUList considers at most four files, but removing this item prevents the MRU collections from becoming cluttered.

Next, SaveFileName uses Visual Basic's SaveSetting command to save the new MRU list in the Registry. Finally, the routine invokes DisplayMRUList to update the items shown in the program's File menu.

```
    ' Save the file name and title. Update the MRU list.
    Private Sub SaveFileName(ByVal fname As String, ByVal ftitle As String)
    Dim i As Integer

        FileTitle = ftitle
        FileName = fname

        ' See if the file is already in the MRU list.
        For i = 1 To 4
            If i > MRUName.Count Then Exit For
            If LCase$(MRUName(i)) = LCase$(fname) Then
                ' It is here. Remove it.
                MRUName.Remove i
                MRUTitle.Remove i
                Exit For
            End If
        Next i

        ' Add the file at the top of the list.
        If MRUName.Count > 0 Then
            MRUName.Add fname, , 1
            MRUTitle.Add ftitle, , 1
        Else
            MRUName.Add fname
            MRUTitle.Add ftitle
        End If
```

```
    ' If there are more than 4 files in the
    ' collections, remove the last one.
    If MRUName.Count > 4 Then
        MRUName.Remove 5
        MRUTitle.Remove 5
    End If

    ' Save the modified MRU list.
    For i = 1 To 4
        If i > MRUName.Count Then
            fname = ""
            ftitle = ""
        Else
            fname = MRUName(i)
            ftitle = MRUTitle(i)
        End If
        SaveSetting "RichEdit", "MRUList", _
            "Name" & Format$(i), fname
        SaveSetting "RichEdit", "MRUList", _
            "Title" & Format$(i), ftitle
    Next i

    ' Redisplay the MRU items.
    DisplayMRUList
End Sub
```

A few commercial applications provide a configuration dialog that allows the user to specify the number of items that should be displayed in the MRU list. This feature is not widely implemented, but you could modify the code presented here to implement it if you like. While this feature does not seem to be turning into a standard, it does not hurt because the program can default to the more typical four-item MRU list until the user changes it.

Formatting Fonts

The RichTextBox control provides several properties that affect the appearance of the text it displays. The SelBold, SelItalic, SelStrikethru, and SelUnderline properties are Boolean values that determine whether the selected text has a **bold**, *italic*, ~~strike through~~, or <u>underlined</u> style. The RichEdit program provides simple menu entries to let the user change these values.

When the user opens the program's Font menu, its mnuFormat_Click event handler executes. This routine examines the properties of the currently selected text and places check marks beside the appropriate menu items. For instance, if the selected text is bold, the event handler checks the Bold menu item. To make checking these values easier, the routine uses function FontAttributeValue.

FontAttributeValue determines whether a property value is Null and returns a default value if it is. The RichTextBox control returns Null for a property value if it is ambiguous. For instance, if the user selects two words, only one of which is bold, the control's SelBold property is Null. In that case the program leaves the Bold menu item unchecked.

```
' Get the proper settings.
Private Sub mnuFormat_Click()
    mnuFormatBold.Checked = _
        FontAttributeValue(rchEditor.SelBold, False)
    mnuFormatItalic.Checked = _
        FontAttributeValue(rchEditor.SelItalic, False)
    mnuFormatUnderline.Checked = _
        FontAttributeValue(rchEditor.SelUnderline, False)
    mnuFormatStrikethrough.Checked = _
        FontAttributeValue(rchEditor.SelStrikethru, False)
End Sub


' Return a font attribute value. Return the default
' if the value is Null.
Private Function FontAttributeValue(ByVal attr_value As Variant, _
    ByVal default As Variant) As Variant

    If IsNull(attr_value) Then
        FontAttributeValue = default
    Else
        FontAttributeValue = attr_value
    End If
End Function
```

When the user selects one of these menu items, the program sets the selected text's property to the opposite of the value displayed by the corresponding menu. For instance, if the Italic command is marked in the menu, the selected text is currently italicized. If the user selects this menu item, the program switches the text to nonitalic.

```
Private Sub mnuFormatItalic_Click()
    rchEditor.SelItalic = Not mnuFormatItalic.Checked
End Sub
```

The RichTextBox control also allows the user to specify different fonts and font sizes for the selected text. The program's Font command in the Font menu presents the Common Dialog control's font selection dialog. It initializes the dialog's font properties using the selected text's values. If the user clicks the dialog's OK button, the program applies the new properties to the text.

```
' Let the user select new font characteristics.
Private Sub mnuFormatFont_Click()
    ' Set the font attributes.
    dlgFont.FontBold = _
        FontAttributeValue(rchEditor.SelBold, False)
    dlgFont.FontItalic = _
        FontAttributeValue(rchEditor.SelItalic, False)
    dlgFont.FontUnderline = _
        FontAttributeValue(rchEditor.SelUnderline, False)
    dlgFont.FontStrikethru = _
```

```
                    FontAttributeValue(rchEditor.SelStrikethru, False)
        dlgFont.FontName = _
            FontAttributeValue(rchEditor.SelFontName, "")
        dlgFont.FontSize = _
            FontAttributeValue(rchEditor.SelFontSize, 0)

        ' Let the user select the font attributes.
        On Error Resume Next
        dlgFont.flags = cdlCFScreenFonts
        dlgFont.ShowFont
        If Err.Number = cdlCancel Then
            ' The user canceled.
            Exit Sub
        ElseIf Err.Number <> 0 Then
            MsgBox "Error" & Str$(Err.Number) & " selecting font." & _
                vbCrLf & Err.Description
            Exit Sub
        End If
        On Error GoTo 0

        ' Set the font.
        rchEditor.SelBold = dlgFont.FontBold
        rchEditor.SelItalic = dlgFont.FontItalic
        rchEditor.SelUnderline = dlgFont.FontUnderline
        rchEditor.SelStrikethru = dlgFont.FontStrikethru
        rchEditor.SelFontName = dlgFont.FontName
        rchEditor.SelFontSize = dlgFont.FontSize
    End Sub
```

The RichTextBox control provides other properties that let a program perform such tasks as justifying text, creating bulleted lists, and using hanging indentation. You can easily modify program RichEdit to provide access to these features.

67. Set TextBox Tabs

Directory: TextTabs

Aligning text using a proportionally spaced font can be difficult. Tab stops can make aligning text much easier. While Visual Basic's TextBox control does not support tabs, the underlying Windows control used by a TextBox does.

Example program TextTabs uses tabs to align text. When it starts, it defines the tab locations and displays some text in three columns.

```
 TextTabs                    _ □ X
Bacon Burger              3.00
       Tomato             0.15
       Extra Cheese       0.20
Large Fries               0.99
Medium Softdrink          1.05
----------
Subtotal                  5.39
Tax                       0.38
Total                     5.77
```

Program TextTabs.

How It Works

To set tab stops in a TextBox, program TextTabs uses the SendMessage API function to send the control the EM_SETTABSTOPS message. The call to SendMessage also sends the control the number of the tab stops and an array containing their positions in dialog units. The exact size of a dialog unit depends on the particular system, but they are relatively small.

The following code shows how the program sets two tab stops for the txtReceipt control.

```
Option Explicit

Private Declare Function SendMessage Lib "user32" _
    Alias "SendMessageA" (ByVal hwnd As Long, ByVal wMsg As Long, _
    ByVal wParam As Long, lParam As Any) As Long
Private Const EM_SETTABSTOPS = &HCB
    :
Dim tabs(1 To 2) As Long

    tabs(1) = 20
    tabs(2) = 130

    ' Set the tabs.
    SendMessage txtReceipt.hwnd, EM_SETTABSTOPS, 2, tabs(1)
```

If the number of tab stops in the call to SendMessage is 0, the TextBox ignores the fourth parameter and sets tabs every 32 dialog units.

If the number of tab stops is 1, the fourth parameter should be a long integer specifying the spacing between tab stops. For instance, the following code sets tab stops every 60 dialog units.

```
SendMessage txtReceipt.hwnd, EM_SETTABSTOPS, 1, 60
```

Once the program has established tab stops, the TextBox control automatically positions text that contains tab characters. The following code displays three column headings aligned at the left margin and the first two tab stops.

```
txtCustomers.Text = "Cust #" & vbTab & "Name" & vbTab & "Address"
```

Note that the user cannot normally enter tabs into a TextBox. When the user presses the Tab character, Visual Basic takes control and moves the input focus to the next control instead of sending the character to the TextBox. The program must insert the tab characters itself.

68. Set TextBox Margins

Directory: Margins

Just as Visual Basic's TextBox control does not support the tab stops provided by the underlying Windows control, it also does not support margins. Using the SendMessage API function, you can set margins for a TextBox. Example program Margins demonstrates this technique.

Program Margins.

How It Works

To set margins in a TextBox, a program should send the control the EM_SETMARGINS message. SendMessage's third parameter should be the constant EC_LEFTMARGIN to set the left margin, EC_RIGHTMARGIN to set the right margin, or both values combined with the Or operator to set both margins. The last parameter should be a long integer holding the left margin plus the right margin times 65,536 (&H10000 in hex).

Unfortunately, when a program sets new margins, the right margin does not immediately take effect. It only takes effect the next time the TextBox reformats its text. The SetTextBoxMargins subroutine shown in the following code adds a blank character to the TextBox's contents to force the control to honor the new right margin. It then removes the extra character to restore the text to its original value.

```
Private Declare Function SendMessage Lib "user32" _
    Alias "SendMessageA" (ByVal hWnd As Long, ByVal wMsg As Long, _
    ByVal wParam As Long, ByVal lParam As Long) As Long


Private Const EM_SETMARGINS = &HD3
Private Const EC_LEFTMARGIN = &H1
Private Const EC_RIGHTMARGIN = &H2

' Set the TextBox's margins.
Private Sub SetTextBoxMargins(ByVal text_box As TextBox, _
    ByVal left_margin As Integer, ByVal right_margin As Integer)
Dim long_value As Long
Dim txt As String
Dim sel_start As Integer
Dim sel_length As Integer

    ' Set the margins.
    long_value = right_margin * &H10000 + _
        left_margin
    SendMessage text_box.hWnd, _
        EM_SETMARGINS, _
        EC_LEFTMARGIN Or EC_RIGHTMARGIN, _
        long_value

    ' Reset the text to make the right margin take effect.
    sel_start = text_box.SelStart
    sel_length = text_box.SelLength
    txt = text_box.Text
    text_box.Text = txt & " "
    text_box.Text = txt
    text_box.SelStart = sel_start
    text_box.SelLength = sel_length
End Sub
```

☆ ☆
④ ⑤ ⑥

69. **Double-Click to Strike Out Lines**

Directory: StrikeLn

This example is really more an exercise in finding and modifying a line of text in a Rich-TextBox than it is an important way to strike out a line of text.

Example program StrikeLn strikes or unstrikes text when you double-click on a line. When you double-click on a line, the insertion position moves to the line you clicked and the program strikes or unstrikes the line.

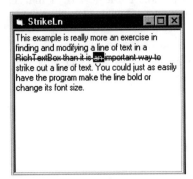

Program StrikeLn.

How It Works

The StrikeLine subroutine shown in the following code switches the strikeout state of the line that contains the RichTextBox's selection position. Working with a variable is much faster than working directly with the control's Text property, so the routine begins by copying the control's text into a string variable. It will work on the copy to save time.

StrikeLine searches the text for the last carriage return/line feed combination before the insertion point. It then checks whether the position of that carriage return is after all of the text. If it is, the user did not double-click on a line of text so the subroutine exits without modifying any text.

The subroutine then searches for the next carriage return/line feed combination. It sets the control's SelStart property to the beginning of the line and its SelLength property to include all of the text in the line. Then it toggles the text's SelStrikethru property.

```
' Strike or unstrike the line that contains SelStart.
Private Sub StrikeLine(rch As RichTextBox)
Dim txt As String
Dim txtlen As Integer
Dim crlen As Integer
Dim start_pos As Integer
Dim end_pos As Integer
Dim pos1 As Integer
Dim pos2 As Integer

    ' Find the previous carriage return.
    txt = rch.Text
    pos2 = 0
    Do While pos2 <= rchBody.SelStart
        pos1 = pos2
```

```
            pos2 = InStr(pos2 + 1, txt, vbCrLf)
            If pos2 = 0 Then Exit Do
    Loop
    If pos1 < 1 Then
        start_pos = 1
    Else
        start_pos = pos1 + Len(vbCrLf)
    End If

    ' See if the user clicked after all the text.
    If start_pos >= Len(txt) Then Exit Sub

    ' Find the next carriage return.
    end_pos = InStr(start_pos, txt, vbCrLf)
    If end_pos = 0 Then end_pos = Len(txt)

    rch.SelStart = start_pos - 1
    rch.SelLength = end_pos - start_pos
    rch.SelStrikethru = Not rch.SelStrikethru
End Sub
```

You could easily modify program StrikeLn to make the line bold, change its font size, or modify it in some other way.

70. Display the Clicked Word

Directory: WordClck

Occasionally a program needs to know what word a user has clicked in a TextBox. For instance, when the user clicks a certain word, the program might open another document. This would allow the program to implement a simple hypertext feature.

Example program WordClck displays the word clicked by the user. When the user clicks on a word, the program displays it in the label at the bottom of the form.

Program WordClck.

How It Works

The WordClicked function shown in the following code begins at a TextBox's insertion position given by its SelStart property. It searches forward and backward through the text looking for the ends of the word at that position. It stops when it encounters a character that is not a letter, number, or underscore. You could change the characters it looks for to change the definition of a word. For instance, you might make the routine stop only when it found an invisible character such as a space or carriage return.

WordClicked returns the text between the start and end of the word.

```
' Return the word at SelStart.
Public Function WordClicked(ByVal txtbox As TextBox) As String
Dim pos As Integer
Dim start_pos As Integer
Dim end_pos As Integer
Dim ch As String
Dim txt As String

    pos = txtbox.SelStart

    ' Find the start of the word.
    txt = txtbox.Text
    For start_pos = pos To 1 Step -1
        ch = Mid$(txt, start_pos, 1)
        ' Allow digits, letters, and underscores.
        If Not ( _
            (ch >= "0" And ch <= "9") Or _
            (ch >= "a" And ch <= "z") Or _
            (ch >= "A" And ch <= "Z") Or _
            ch = "_" _
        ) Then Exit For
    Next start_pos
    start_pos = start_pos + 1

    ' Find the end of the word.
    For end_pos = pos To Len(txt)
        ch = Mid$(txt, end_pos, 1)
        ' Allow digits, letters, and underscores.
        If Not ( _
            (ch >= "0" And ch <= "9") Or _
            (ch >= "a" And ch <= "z") Or _
            (ch >= "A" And ch <= "Z") Or _
            ch = "_" _
        ) Then Exit For
    Next end_pos
    end_pos = end_pos - 1

    If start_pos <= end_pos Then
        WordClicked = Mid$(txt, start_pos, end_pos - start_pos + 1)
```

```
        Else
            WordClicked = ""
        End If
    End Function
```

71. Find the Word under the Mouse   ④ ⑤ ⑥

Directory: WordUndr

The previous section showed how to find the word clicked by the user in a TextBox. A program can also determine which word is under the cursor when the user moves the mouse over a TextBox. Example program WordUndr displays the word under the mouse as the mouse moves. As you move the mouse over the text, the label at the bottom of the form displays the word under the mouse.

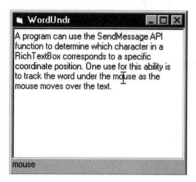

Program WordUndr.

How It Works

A program can use the SendMessage API function to determine which character in a RichTextBox corresponds to a specific coordinate position. Subroutine RichWord-Position, shown in the following code, takes as inputs X and Y coordinates. It initializes the X and Y components of a POINTAPI structure and passes the structure to the SendMessage function with the EM_CHARFROMPOS message. This message makes SendMessage return the character position in the text box that is at the indicated location.

RichWordPosition then searches forward and backward through the control's text looking for the ends of the word at that position. This search is similar to the search described in the previous section.

Subroutine RichWordPosition returns the positions of the first and last characters in the word at the specified X and Y coordinates through its start_pos and end_pos parameters.

```vb
Private Type POINTAPI
    X As Long
    Y As Long
End Type
Private Declare Function SendMessage Lib "user32" _
    Alias "SendMessageA" (ByVal hWnd As Long, ByVal wMsg As Long, _
    ByVal wParam As Long, lParam As Any) As Long
Private Const EM_CHARFROMPOS& = &HD7

' Find the position of the word under the mouse.
Public Sub RichWordPosition(ByVal rch As RichTextBox, _
    ByVal X As Single, ByVal Y As Single, _
    start_pos As Integer, end_pos As Integer)
Dim pt As POINTAPI
Dim pos As Integer
Dim ch As String
Dim txt As String

    ' Make start_pos < end_pos in case we fail.
    start_pos = 0
    end_pos = -1

    ' Convert the position to pixels.
    pt.X = ScaleX(X, ScaleMode, vbPixels)
    pt.Y = ScaleY(Y, ScaleMode, vbPixels)

    ' Get the character number.
    pos = SendMessage(rch.hWnd, EM_CHARFROMPOS, 0&, pt)
    If pos <= 0 Then Exit Sub

    ' Find the start of the word.
    txt = rch.Text
    For start_pos = pos To 1 Step -1
        ch = Mid$(rch.Text, start_pos, 1)
        ' Allow digits, letters, and underscores.
        If Not ( _
            (ch >= "0" And ch <= "9") Or _
            (ch >= "a" And ch <= "z") Or _
            (ch >= "A" And ch <= "Z") Or _
            ch = "_" _
        ) Then Exit For
    Next start_pos
    start_pos = start_pos + 1

    ' Find the end of the word.
    For end_pos = pos To Len(txt)
        ch = Mid$(txt, end_pos, 1)
        ' Allow digits, letters, and underscores.
        If Not ( _
            (ch >= "0" And ch <= "9") Or _
            (ch >= "a" And ch <= "z") Or _
```

```
            (ch >= "A" And ch <= "Z") Or _
            ch = "_" _
        ) Then Exit For
    Next end_pos
    end_pos = end_pos - 1
End Sub
```

Function RichWordUnder uses the RichWordPosition subroutine to find the position of the word under the mouse. It then returns the text value of that word.

```
' Return the word under the mouse.
Public Function RichWordUnder(rch As RichTextBox, _
    X As Single, Y As Single) As String
Dim start_pos As Integer
Dim end_pos As Integer

    RichWordPosition rch, X, Y, start_pos, end_pos

    If start_pos <= end_pos Then
        RichWordUnder = _
            Mid$(rch.Text, start_pos, end_pos - start_pos + 1)
    Else
        RichWordUnder = ""
    End If
End Function
```

72. Give Different Words Different Cursors ☆ ☆ ④ ⑤ ⑥

Directory: WordCurs

The previous section explains how to use SendMessage to display the word in a Rich-TextBox that is under the mouse. Using a similar technique, a program can provide other forms of feedback when the mouse moves over the text. Example program Word-Curs uses this method to display a pointing hand when the mouse is over a Web address.

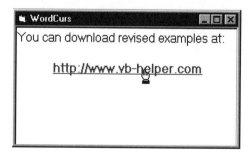

Program WordCurs.

How It Works

The RichSetMouse subroutine shown in the following code calculates the character position at the given coordinates. It then sets the RichTextBox control's MousePointer property to vbCustom if that character lies between positions URL_start and URL_stop. If the control's MouseIcon property is set to a custom icon, the control displays that icon as the mouse pointer.

If the character under the mouse does not lie between these positions, the subroutine sets the control's MousePointer property to vbDefault. That makes the control display the default I-beam cursor.

```vb
Private URL_start As Integer
Private URL_stop As Integer
        :
    ' Initialize URL_start and URL_stop, etc.
        :
' Set the mouse pointer appropriately.
Public Sub RichSetMouse(rch As RichTextBox, X As Single, Y As Single)
Static showing_hand As Boolean

Dim pt As POINTAPI
Dim pos As Integer

    ' Convert the position to pixels.
    pt.X = ScaleX(X, ScaleMode, vbPixels)
    pt.Y = ScaleY(Y, ScaleMode, vbPixels)

    ' Get the character number.
    pos = SendMessage(rch.hWnd, EM_CHARFROMPOS, 0&, pt)

    ' See if it is over the URL text.
    If (pos >= URL_start) And (pos <= URL_stop) Then
        ' We want the hand pointer.
        If Not showing_hand Then
            MousePointer = vbCustom
            showing_hand = True
        End If
    Else
        ' We want the default pointer.
        If showing_hand Then
            MousePointer = vbDefault
            showing_hand = False
        End If
    End If
End Sub
```

☆ ☆
④ ⑤ ⑥

73. Validate Fields

Directory: Validate

Many applications display TextBoxes where the user will enter values that must be validated. For instance, phone number and numeric fields must have proper formats.

When the user tries to move the focus out of a field, the program can validate its contents. If there is a mistake, the program can warn the user and force focus back into that field. This technique is common in Windows applications, but it is very intrusive. It breaks the user's train of thought and forces the user to deal with the problem immediately.

Furthermore, some fields cannot be adequately validated when the user moves to another field. The allowed values of one field may depend on another.

An alternative strategy is to mark a field as invalid when focus leaves it, but not to force the focus back into that field. The user can then continue working until all of the fields have been filled. When the user tries to accept the form's values, the program can validate the fields again and ask the user to correct any problems. Example program Validate uses this approach.

Program Validate.

How It Works

When focus enters a field, program Validate calls the SetValid subroutine to make the field appear normally. SetValid sets the control's ForeColor and BackColor properties to match those of the hidden control lblGood. This control's only purpose is to define the colors that normal controls should have.

When focus leaves a field, the program invokes the field's validation routine. If the validation fails, the program calls subroutine SetInvalid. This routine marks the control as invalid by setting its ForeColor and BackColor properties to match those of the hidden control lblBad.

The following code shows subroutines SetValid and SetInvalid, together with the validation code for a text field that allows only letters.

```
' Reset the field's colors.
Private Sub txtLetters_GotFocus()
    SetValid txtLetters
End Sub


' Make sure the data passes edits.
Private Sub txtLetters_LostFocus()
    If InvalidLetters(txtLetters.Text) Then _
        SetInvalid txtLetters
End Sub


' Set the control's colors for a valid field.
Private Sub SetValid(ctl As TextBox)
    ctl.ForeColor = lblGood.ForeColor
    ctl.BackColor = lblGood.BackColor
End Sub


' Set the control's colors for an invalid field.
Private Sub SetInvalid(ctl As TextBox)
    ctl.ForeColor = lblBad.ForeColor
    ctl.BackColor = lblBad.BackColor
End Sub


' Return true if the field contains anything other
' than letters.
Function InvalidLetters(txt As String) As Boolean
Dim ch As String
Dim i As Integer

    ' Assume it will fail.
    InvalidLetters = True

    For i = 1 To Len(txt)
        ch = UCase$(Mid$(txt, i, 1))
        If ch < "A" Or ch > "Z" Then Exit Function
    Next i

    ' The value is valid.
    InvalidLetters = False
End Function
```

When the user clicks the Validate program's Cancel button, the form simply unloads. This is the correct action for a data entry form. Because the user is canceling whatever action the form performs, it does not matter whether the field values are valid.

When the user clicks the program's OK button, the form revalidates all of its fields. If a field fails its validation now, the program presents a dialog box asking the user to fix the problem. When the user closes the dialog, the program returns focus to the invalid field.

If all of the fields pass their validations, the form unloads. In an application where the form is a dialog box and not the program's only form, the program would continue.

```
' Perform form-level validations.
Private Sub cmdOk_Click()
    ' Validate the fields.
    If InvalidLetters(txtLetters.Text) Then
        MsgBox "The Letters field must contain letters."
        GoToField txtLetters
        Exit Sub
    End If

    If InvalidDigits(txtDigits.Text) Then
        MsgBox "The Integer field must contain an integer."
        txtDigits.SetFocus
        Exit Sub
    End If

    If txtSameAsDigits.Text <> txtDigits.Text Then
        MsgBox "The Same As Integer field must match the Integer field."
        txtSameAsDigits.SetFocus
        Exit Sub
    End If

    If InvalidOdd(txtOddNumber.Text) Then
        MsgBox "The Odd Number field must contain an odd number."
        txtOddNumber.SetFocus
        Exit Sub
    End If

    If InvalidEven(txtEvenNumber.Text) Then
        MsgBox "The Even Number field must contain an even number."
        txtEvenNumber.SetFocus
        Exit Sub
    End If

    ' We passed all edits. Unload.
    Unload Me
End Sub
```

74. Make All Text Visible

Directory: SizeText

Sometimes it is important for the user to be able to see all of a TextBox control's text at all times. In that case, the program can resize the TextBox whenever its text is modified. Example program SizeText makes its TextBox just big enough to display all of its text. As you type, the program automatically resizes the control when necessary.

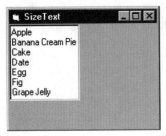

Program SizeText.

How It Works

The SizeTextBox subroutine shown in the following code resizes a TextBox so that it is just big enough to display all of its text. The routine uses the form's TextHeight and Text-Width methods to see how big the printed text is. These routines allow enough room for the text even if it contains multiple lines of different lengths.

If the TextBox is displaying a border, SizeTextBox adds some extra space for the border. It then compares this calculated height and width to the control's current dimensions. If the TextBox does not already have the correct size, the subroutine resizes it.

```
Private Sub SizeTextBox(ByVal text_box As TextBox)
Dim hgt As Single
Dim wid As Single

    ' Make the form's font match the TextBox's.
    Set Font = text_box.Font

    ' See how big the text is.
    wid = TextWidth(text_box.Text)
    hgt = TextHeight(text_box.Text)

    ' Add in room for borders.
    If text_box.BorderStyle = vbFixedSingle Then
        wid = wid + ScaleX(120, vbTwips, ScaleMode)
        hgt = hgt + ScaleY(120, vbTwips, ScaleMode)
    End If

    ' Resize the control.
    If (text_box.Height <> hgt) Or _
       (text_box.Width <> wid) _
    Then
        text_box.Move text_box.Left, text_box.Top, _
            wid, hgt
    End If
End Sub
```

Some programs might need the TextBox's height or width to remain unchanged. For instance, a program might make the TextBox as wide as possible while still fitting its form. In that case, you could modify the SizeTextBox subroutine to change only the TextBox's height.

75. Hide a TextBox's Caret

☆ ☆ ☆
⑤ ⑥

Directory: NoCaret

Example program NoCaret suppresses the insertion caret in its two upper TextBoxes. Even when they have the input focus, these controls do not display a caret.

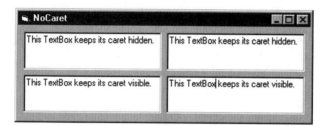

Program NoCaret.

How It Works

The HideCaret API function hides a TextBox's caret. Unfortunately, the TextBox restores its caret when it receives one of several messages. Hiding the caret and keeping it hidden is not trivial.

To keep the caret hidden, the program must install a new WindowProc to intercept Windows messages. When the new WindowProc receives a WM_RESERVED or WM_PAINT message, it calls the HideCaret API function to keep the caret hidden. It then calls the original WindowProc using the CallWindowProc function so the program can process the message normally.

The following code shows routines that a program can use to hide the caret. These routines should be placed in a .bas module. The SetNoCaret routine takes a TextBox as a parameter and installs the NoCaretWindowProc function as the control's WindowProc. NoCaretWindowProc looks for the WM_RESERVED and WM_PAINT messages and takes appropriate action.

Because installing a custom WindowProc routine requires the AddressOf operator introduced in Visual Basic 5, this technique will not work in earlier versions of Visual Basic.

```
Option Explicit

Private Declare Function CallWindowProc Lib "user32" _
    Alias "CallWindowProcA" (ByVal lpPrevWndFunc As Long, _
```

```
        ByVal hwnd As Long, ByVal msg As Long, ByVal wParam As Long, _
        ByVal lParam As Long) As Long
Private Declare Function SetWindowLong Lib "user32" _
        Alias "SetWindowLongA" (ByVal hwnd As Long, ByVal nIndex As Long, _
        ByVal dwNewLong As Long) As Long
Private Declare Function HideCaret Lib "user32" (ByVal hwnd As Long) _
        As Long


Private CaretWindowProc  As Long


' Set this control's WindowProc to NoCaretWindowProc
' so it keeps its caret hidden.
Public Sub SetNoCaret(ByVal text_box As TextBox)
Const GWL_WNDPROC = (-4)


    ' Set the new WindowProc.
    CaretWindowProc  = SetWindowLong( _
        text_box.hwnd, GWL_WNDPROC, _
        AddressOf NoCaretWindowProc)
End Sub


' When we receive a WM_PAINT or WM_RESERVED
' message, hide the caret.
Public Function NoCaretWindowProc(ByVal hwnd As Long, _
        ByVal msg As Long, ByVal wParam As Long, ByVal lParam As Long) _
        As Long
Const WM_RESERVED = &H100E
Const WM_PAINT = &HF


    If (msg = WM_PAINT) Or (msg = WM_RESERVED) _
        Then HideCaret hwnd


    ' Process the message normally.
    NoCaretWindowProc = CallWindowProc( _
        OldWindowProc, hwnd, _
        msg, wParam, lParam)
End Function
```

When program NoCaret starts, its Form_Load event handler calls the SetNoCaret subroutine passing it the hwnd properties of the TextBoxes that should have their carets disabled.

Keep in mind that replacing the WindowProc can be dangerous. If you change the code and make a mistake, the Visual Basic development environment will crash and you will lose any changes you have made since the last time you saved your work. For this reason, save often.

76. Replace a TextBox's Context Menu ☆ ☆ ④ ⑤ ⑥

Directory: CtxNew

Visual Basic automatically provides TextBox controls with a context menu. If you right-click on a TextBox, the context menu appears, as shown in Figure 8.2. This menu lets the user copy, cut, and paste to the clipboard.

The context menu is convenient, but it can interfere with a program's ability to validate text input. For instance, suppose a program uses the following event handler to ensure that the user enters only digits into a TextBox. This code prevents the user from typing other characters directly into the TextBox. It also prevents the user from pressing Ctrl-V to paste text from the clipboard into the TextBox. Unfortunately, the user can still use the context menu to paste letters into the TextBox. The event handler is not triggered when the menu pastes text, so the program cannot protect itself properly.

```
' Allow only digits 0-9. In particular, do not allow Ctrl-V.
Private Sub txtStandard_KeyPress(KeyAscii As Integer)
    If KeyAscii < Asc("0") Or KeyAscii > Asc("9") _
        Then KeyAscii = 0
End Sub
```

Disabling the context menu is complicated and is described in the next section. It is relatively easy to replace it, however, with a menu of your own.

Example program CtxNew replaces the standard context menu with a menu of its own. This menu contains the single command Copy. When it is invoked, this command copies the TextBox's selected text into the clipboard. Because the Paste command is not present, the user cannot circumvent the program's validation code.

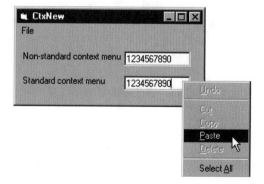

Figure 8.2 If you right-click on a TextBox, a context menu appears.

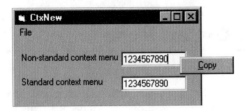

Program CtxNew.

How It Works

To replace the context menu, create a menu bar for the form as you would for any other application. Create a submenu named mnuPopup. Give that menu the choices you want the user to be able to invoke from the context menu and give those commands event handlers. Then use the following code to display the new menu instead of the standard menu when the user right-clicks on the TextBox.

```
' If this is a right button, display the new menu.
Private Sub txtNonstandard_MouseDown(Button As Integer, _
    Shift As Integer, X As Single, Y As Single)

    If Button = vbRightButton Then
        ' Release the standard menu's mouse grab.
        ReleaseCapture

        ' Display the new popup.
        PopupMenu mnuPopup
    End If
End Sub
```

Unfortunately, if you omit the PopupMenu command, this code does not remove the standard context menu. If you do not display the new menu, the old one still appears.

77. Disable a TextBox's Context Menu ⑤ ⑥

Directory: CtxNone

The previous section explains how to replace Visual Basic's default TextBox context menu with one of your own. Removing the context menu completely is harder, but it is still possible.

Example program CtxNone disables the context menus in its two upper TextBoxes. When you right-click on these controls, no menu appears.

Program CtxNone.

How It Works

Completely disabling a TextBox's context menu is much harder than replacing it with a customized menu. In fact, to use this technique, the program must install a custom WindowProc. Because that requires the AddressOf operator introduced in Visual Basic 5, this technique will not work in earlier versions of Visual Basic. In earlier versions, you should use the method described in the previous section to replace the context menu instead of removing it completely.

To prevent the standard context menu from appearing, the program must install a new WindowProc to intercept Windows messages. The new WindowProc ignores all WM_CONTEXTMENU messages. It processes all other messages normally using the control's original WindowProc function.

The following code shows routines that a program can use to ignore TextBox context menus. The RemoveContextMenu routine takes a TextBox as a parameter and installs the NoContextMenuWindowProc function as the control's WindowProc. NoContextMenuWindowProc ignores WM_CONTEXTMENU messages.

```
Option Explicit

Declare Function CallWindowProc Lib "user32" _
    Alias "CallWindowProcA" (ByVal lpPrevWndFunc As Long, _
    ByVal hWnd As Long, ByVal msg As Long, ByVal wParam As Long, _
    ByVal lParam As Long) As Long
Declare Function SetWindowLong Lib "user32" _
    Alias "SetWindowLongA" (ByVal hWnd As Long, ByVal nIndex As Long, _
    ByVal dwNewLong As Long) As Long


Private ContextMenuWindowProc As Long

' Give the TextBox a new WindowProc so it does
' not display a context menu when right-clicked.
Public Sub RemoveContextMenu(ByVal text_box As TextBox)
Const GWL_WNDPROC = (-4)

    ContextMenuWindowProc = SetWindowLong( _
        text_box.hWnd, GWL_WNDPROC, _
        AddressOf NoContextMenuWindowProc)
```

```
End Sub

' Pass along all messages except the one that
' makes the context menu appear.
Public Function NoContextMenuWindowProc(ByVal hWnd As Long, _
    ByVal msg As Long, ByVal wParam As Long, ByVal lParam As Long) _
    As Long
Const WM_CONTEXTMENU = &H7B

    If msg <> WM_CONTEXTMENU Then _
        NoContextMenuWindowProc = _
            CallWindowProc( _
            ContextMenuWindowProc, hWnd, msg, _
            wParam, lParam)
End Function
```

When program CtxNone starts, its Form_Load event handler calls subroutine Remove-ContextMenu, passing it the hwnd properties of the TextBoxes that should have their context menus disabled.

Keep in mind that replacing the WindowProc can be dangerous. If you change the code and make a mistake, the Visual Basic development environment will crash and you will lose any changes you have made since the last time you saved your work. For this reason, save often.

78. Right Justify Single-Line Text ④ ⑤ ⑥

Directory: RJustify

In Visual Basic 4 and 5, single-line TextBoxes are always left justified even if the control's Alignment property is set to 1 - Right Justify. With a little work, however, it is still possible to right justify a single-line TextBox. Example program RJustify displays right justified text in a single line.

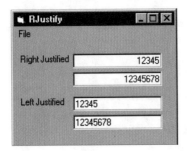

Program RJustify.

How It Works

Although single-line TextBoxes cannot display right justified text, multiline TextBoxes can. To display right justified text, a program can use a multiline TextBox that is only tall enough to show one line of text. If the user presses the carriage return key inside the TextBox, however, the program starts a new line. Because the TextBox is only one line tall, some of the text will be hidden.

To prevent this, the TextBox's KeyPress event handler should catch and ignore Return keys. It must also ignore ^V so the user cannot paste a Return key into the TextBox. Finally, it must use one of the methods described in the previous sections to replace or disable the TextBox's context menu so the user cannot paste a Return key into it in that way. Program RJustify replaces the standard context menu with one that does not include a Paste command.

Because the code used by program RJustify is the same as code presented in previous sections, it is not repeated here. To see the code, read those sections or load the program from the CD-ROM.

Using ListBoxes and ComboBoxes

L istBoxes and ComboBoxes are very similar. Both allow the user to select an item from a list of choices. By restricting the values the user can select to specific allowed values, these controls help the user make valid selections. This chapter describes some of the ways a program can take full advantage of the capabilities of these two types of controls.

79. Find Selected Items

Directory: ShowSels

The ListBox control's ListIndex property gives the index of the item that is selected in the ListBox. Often a program can check this property to see what item the user has selected.

If the control's MultiSelect property is 1 (Simple) or 2 (Extended), however, the user can select more than one item at a time. In that case, a single ListIndex property cannot give the indexes of all the selected items.

Example program ShowSels demonstrates a method for determining which items have been selected. The program displays a list of animals in a ListBox with MultiSelect set to 2 (Extended). Hold down the Control key and click on the animals to select them. Whenever you change the selected animals, the program lists the selected items in the TextBox on the right.

Program ShowSels.

How It Works

To see which items are selected when MultiSelect is not 0 (None), a program can use the control's Selected property. This value returns True if the indicated item is selected. For instance, the following code determines whether the first item in the list is selected.

```
If lstItems.Selected(0) Then ...
```

The following code shows how program ShowSels displays its list of selected items.

```
Option Explicit

' Start with nothing selected.
Private Sub Form_Load()
    lstItems.ListIndex = -1
End Sub

' The user clicked an item. Update the display.
Private Sub lstItems_Click()
Dim i As Integer
Dim txt As String

    For i = 0 To lstItems.ListCount - 1
        ' See if item i is selected.
        If lstItems.Selected(i) Then _
            txt = txt & lstItems.List(i) & vbCrLf
    Next i

    txtSelected.Text = txt
End Sub
```

80. Find an ItemData Value

Directory: ItemData

The ListBox and ComboBox controls both provide an ItemData property that lets you associate numeric data values with the items in the list. For example, lstItems.ItemData(0) returns the value associated with the first item in the list lstItems.

There is no control property or method that locates an item with a particular ItemData value, but a program can use a simple search to find an ItemData value.

Example program ItemData shows how to locate items with particular ItemData values. This program displays a ComboBox and a ListBox containing a series of department names with their telephone extensions. Each entry's ItemData value is set to its extension. For instance, the Finance department's entry reads "Finance 8121." This entry's ItemData value is 8121. Enter an extension in the TextBox, and click the Find button to make the program locate the corresponding item in both controls.

Program ItemData.

How It Works

A program can locate a particular ItemData value by searching all of the ItemData values until it finds the one it needs. The following code shows how program ItemData works.

```
Option Explicit

' Find the items with the given ItemData value.
Private Sub cmdFind_Click()
    SelectItemData lstItems, txtExtension
    SelectItemData cboItems, txtExtension
End Sub


' Search a control's ItemData property for the
' target value. If found select the item.
```

```
Public Sub SelectItemData(ctl As Control, target As Integer)
Dim i As Long

    ' Only do this for ListBoxes and ComboBoxes.
    If TypeName(ctl) <> "ListBox" And _
        TypeName(ctl) <> "ComboBox" _
            Then Exit Sub

    ' Examine all the items.
    For i = 0 To ctl.ListCount - 1
        If ctl.ItemData(i) = target Then
            ctl.ListIndex = i
            Exit Sub
        End If
    Next

    ' The target was not found. Select nothing.
    ctl.ListIndex = -1
End Sub
```

81. Change Dropdown Height   ④ ⑤ ⑥

Directory: CboHgt

Normally when the user clicks on a ComboBox, the control presents a dropdown list with a certain standard height. This height is not necessarily appropriate for all programs. For instance, a ComboBox might contain one more item than will fit in the default height. In that case, it will be a little awkward for the user to have to scroll to find the last option. If the dropdown area were a little taller, the user could see all the choices at once.

Fortunately, a program can use the MoveWindow API function to resize a ComboBox's dropdown area. Example program CboHgt does just that. The ComboBox on the left has the standard dropdown height. The one on the right has been modified so that its dropdown area reaches almost to the bottom of the form.

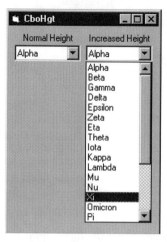

Program CboHgt.

How It Works

The following code shows how program CboHgt resizes its right ComboBox. The MoveWindow API function measures distances in pixels, so the SizeCombo subroutine performs its calculations in pixels.

```
Option Explicit

#If Win32 Then
    Private Declare Function MoveWindow Lib "user32" ( _
        ByVal hWnd As Long, ByVal X As Long, ByVal Y As Long, _
        ByVal nWidth As Long, ByVal nHeight As Long, _
        ByVal bRepaint As Long) As Long
#Else
    Private Declare Sub MoveWindow Lib "User" ( _
        ByVal hWnd As Integer, ByVal X As Integer, _
        ByVal Y As Integer, ByVal nWidth As Integer, _
        ByVal nHeight As Integer, ByVal bRepaint As Integer)
#End If

' Resize a ComboBox's dropdown display area.
Public Sub SizeCombo(frm As Form, cbo As ComboBox)
Dim cbo_left As Integer
Dim cbo_top As Integer
Dim cbo_width As Integer
Dim cbo_height As Integer
Dim old_scale_mode As Integer

    ' Change the Scale Mode on the form to Pixels.
    old_scale_mode = frm.ScaleMode
    frm.ScaleMode = vbPixels
```

```
' Save the ComboBox's Left, Top, and Width
' in pixels.
cbo_left = cbo.Left
cbo_top = cbo.Top
cbo_width = cbo.Width

' Calculate the new height of the combo box.
cbo_height = frm.ScaleHeight - cbo.Top - 5
frm.ScaleMode = old_scale_mode

' Resize the combo box window.
MoveWindow cbo.hwnd, cbo_left, cbo_top, _
    cbo_width, cbo_height, 1
End Sub
```

The worst case occurs when a ComboBox contains only a few more items than will fit on its dropdown list. In that case, it is usually better to enlarge the dropdown list so that it can display all of the items. If the list contains many more items than will fit at one time, the user will not mind scrolling through the list as much.

82. Change Dropdown Width

☆ ☆
④ ⑤ ⑥

Directory: CboWid

The previous section explains how to use the MoveWindow API function to make a ComboBox's dropdown area taller than normal. Using the SendMessage API function, a program can make the dropdown area wider than normal.

Example program CboWid uses this approach to let the user select an acronym. The left ComboBox has a standard width. When you open its dropdown area, the choices are truncated. The right ComboBox has a dropdown area large enough to display all of the text for its list of items.

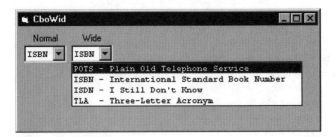

Program CboWid.

How It Works

The following code shows how program CboWid resizes its right ComboBox. The Size-Combo subroutine examines each of the items in the ComboBox. It uses the form's TextWidth function to see how wide these items are. It then resizes the dropdown area to make it wide enough to display the widest of the items.

```
Option Explicit

#If Win32 Then
    Private Declare Function SendMessage Lib "user32" _
        Alias "SendMessageA" (ByVal hWnd As Long, ByVal wMsg As Long, _
        ByVal wParam As Long, lParam As Long) As Long
#End If

Private Const CB_SETDROPPEDWIDTH = &H160

Private Sub Form_Load()
    #If Win32 = False Then
        MsgBox "This example only works in 32-bit Visual Basic."
        End
    #End If

    ' Resize the ComboBox's dropdown area.
    SizeCombo Me, cboWide
End Sub


' Resize a ComboBox's dropdown display area so it
' is wide enough to hold its widest item.
Public Sub SizeCombo(frm As Form, cbo As ComboBox)
Dim old_font As Object
Dim old_scale_mode As Integer
Dim cbo_left As Integer
Dim cbo_top As Integer
Dim cbo_width As Integer
Dim cbo_height As Integer
Dim i As Integer
Dim max_width As Long
Dim new_width As Long

    ' Change the Scale Mode on the form to Pixels
    ' and the font to the ComboBox's font.
    old_scale_mode = frm.ScaleMode
    frm.ScaleMode = vbPixels
    Set old_font = frm.Font
    Set frm.Font = cbo.Font

    ' Save the ComboBox's Left, Top, and Width
    ' in pixels.
    cbo_left = cbo.Left
```

```
    cbo_top = cbo.Top
    cbo_width = cbo.Width

    ' Find the widest ComboxBox item.
    max_width = 10
    For i = 0 To cbo.ListCount - 1
        new_width = frm.TextWidth(cbo.List(i))
        If max_width < new_width Then _
            max_width = new_width
    Next i

    ' Allow room for the scroll bar.
    max_width = max_width + 25

    ' Restore the original ScaleMode.
    frm.ScaleMode = old_scale_mode
    Set frm.Font = old_font

    ' Set the width for the dropdown list.
    SendMessage cbo.hWnd, _
        CB_SETDROPPEDWIDTH, max_width, 0
End Sub
```

This technique can be particularly useful on forms that are very crowded. When the ComboBox is closed, only the leftmost part of the selected list item is visible. That part of the item entries can show a brief description or abbreviation of the selected item. For instance, in program CboWid, the items' abbreviations are visible when the ComboBoxes are closed.

When the user clicks on the ComboBox, it expands to show the list entries in full. The leftmost part of the entries can give a short abbreviation while the full entries give additional description that takes up space only when the dropdown area is visible.

83.   Set Tabs in a ListBox

Directory: ListTabs

When a program uses a proportionally spaced font, some characters are wider than others. That means columns of text will generally not line up neatly unless the program takes special action. For instance, a form can use its CurrentX property to line up columns of text, as shown in the following code.

```
Private Sub Form_Paint()
Const COLUMN_1 = 1440
Const COLUMN_2 = 2880

Dim TextValue(1 To 10, 1 To 2) As String
```

```
Dim i As Integer

    ' Initialize the strings.
        :

    ' Display the strings.
    CurrentY = 1440
    For i = 1 To 10
        CurrentX = COLUMN_1
        Print TextValue(i, 1);
        CurrentX = COLUMN_2
        Print TextValue(i, 2)
    Next i
End Sub
```

A program can use the SendMessage API function with the LB_SETTABSTOPS message to line up entries in a ListBox that uses a proportionally spaced font. Example program ListTabs demonstrates this technique.

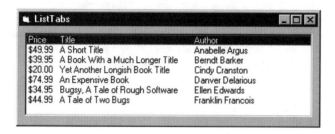

Program ListTabs.

How It Works

The following code shows how program ListTabs works.

```
Option Explicit

#If Win32 Then
    Private Declare Function SendMessage Lib "user32" _
        Alias "SendMessageA" (ByVal hWnd As Long, ByVal wMsg As Long, _
        ByVal wParam As Long, lParam As Any) As Long
#End If

Private Const LB_SETTABSTOPS = &H192

Private Sub Form_Load()
Dim tabs(1 To 2) As Long

    #If Win32 = False Then
        MsgBox "This program works only in 32-bit Visual Basic."
```

```
          End
#End If


' Define the tabs (in pixels).
tabs(1) = 30
tabs(2) = 150


' Set the tabs.
SetListTabs lstAligned, 2, tabs


' Enter some values.
lstAligned.AddItem "Price" & vbTab & "Title" & vbTab & "Author"
lstAligned.AddItem "$49.99" & vbTab & _
    "A Short Title" & vbTab & "Anabelle Argus"
lstAligned.AddItem "$39.95" & vbTab & _
    "A Book With a Much Longer Title" & vbTab & "Berndt Barker"
lstAligned.AddItem "$20.00" & vbTab & _
    "Yet Another Longish Book Title" & vbTab & "Cindy Cranston"
lstAligned.AddItem "$74.99" & vbTab & _
    "An Expensive Book" & vbTab & "Danver Delarious"
lstAligned.AddItem "$34.95" & vbTab & _
    "Bugsy, A Tale of Rough Software" & vbTab & "Ellen Edwards"
lstAligned.AddItem "$44.99" & vbTab & _
    "A Tale of Two Bugs" & vbTab & "Franklin Francois"
End Sub


' Set the ListBox's tabs.
Private Sub SetListTabs(ByVal lst As ListBox, ByVal num As Long, _
    tabs() As Long)

    SendMessage lstAligned.hWnd, LB_SETTABSTOPS, 2, tabs(1)
End Sub
```

84. Move Items between Lists

Directory: MoveList

Many programs allow the user to move items from one list to another. For instance, Visual Basic 5's ActiveX Control Interface Wizard uses two lists to allow the user to pick standard control properties. The user clicks buttons to move items back and forth between a list of selected properties and a list of unselected properties.

Example program MoveList shows how to let a user move items between two lists. Select one or more items in the left list and click the > button to move them into the right list. Click the >> button to move all of the items into the right list. Use the < and << buttons to move items from the right list to the left list.

Program MoveList.

How It Works

There are two main tasks a program must perform to provide this kind of interface. First, when the user clicks on a list, the program must enable the correct buttons. For instance, when no items are selected in the left list, the > button should be disabled because no items have been selected to move into the right list. Second, the program must move the correct items when the user clicks a button.

The following code shows how program MoveList accomplishes these tasks. When the user clicks on the left or right list and when the form initially loads, the program calls subroutine EnabledButtons. This routine examines the lists' Selected values to see if any items are selected in the lists. It enables or disables the > and < buttons accordingly.

EnabledButtons also determines whether the lists are empty and enables or disables the >> and << buttons accordingly. For instance, if the right list is empty, the program cannot move any items into the left list so it disables the << button.

When the user clicks on the < button, the cmdMoveLeft_Click event handler executes. This routine examines the Selected values for the items in the right list to see which are selected. When it finds one that is selected, it adds that item to the left list and removes it from the right list. This routine examines the items in decreasing order so it considers those with the largest indexes first. That prevents confusion caused by the control renumbering items as they are removed from the list.

The subroutine that moves selected items from the left list into the right list and the routines that move all items from one list to another are similar.

```
' Enable the appropriate buttons.
Private Sub lstLeft_Click()
    EnableButtons
End Sub

' Enable the appropriate buttons.
Private Sub lstRight_Click()
    EnableButtons
End Sub
```

```vb
Private Sub Form_Load()
    ' Put some values in the left list.
    lstLeft.AddItem "Ape"
    lstLeft.AddItem "Bear"
    lstLeft.AddItem "Cat"
    lstLeft.AddItem "Dog"
    lstLeft.AddItem "Eagle"
    lstLeft.AddItem "Frog"
    lstLeft.AddItem "Giraffe"
    lstLeft.AddItem "Hen"
    lstLeft.AddItem "Ibex"
    lstLeft.AddItem "Jackel"

    ' Enable the appropriate buttons.
    EnableButtons
End Sub

' Enable the appropriate buttons.
Private Sub EnableButtons()
Dim i As Integer

    ' See if an item is selected in the left list.
    For i = lstLeft.ListCount - 1 To 0 Step -1
        If lstLeft.Selected(i) Then Exit For
    Next i
    cmdMoveRight.Enabled = (i >= 0)

    ' See if an item is selected in the right list.
    For i = lstRight.ListCount - 1 To 0 Step -1
        If lstRight.Selected(i) Then Exit For
    Next i
    cmdMoveLeft.Enabled = (i >= 0)

    ' See if the right list has any items.
    cmdMoveLeftAll.Enabled = (lstRight.ListCount > 0)

    ' See if the left list has any items.
    cmdMoveRightAll.Enabled = (lstLeft.ListCount > 0)
End Sub

' Move the items selected in the right list
' into the left list.
Private Sub cmdMoveLeft_Click()
Dim i As Integer

    ' Remove the selected items.
    For i = lstRight.ListCount - 1 To 0 Step -1
        ' Move this item.
        If lstRight.Selected(i) Then
            lstLeft.AddItem lstRight.List(i)
            lstRight.RemoveItem i
```

```
            End If
        Next i


        ' Enable the correct buttons.
        EnableButtons
    End Sub

    ' Move the items selected in the left list
    ' into the right list.
    Private Sub cmdMoveRight_Click()
    Dim i As Integer

        ' Remove the selected items.
        For i = lstLeft.ListCount - 1 To 0 Step -1
            ' Move this item.
            If lstLeft.Selected(i) Then
                lstRight.AddItem lstLeft.List(i)
                lstLeft.RemoveItem i
            End If
        Next i


        ' Enable the correct buttons.
        EnableButtons
    End Sub

    ' Move all items into the left list.
    Private Sub cmdMoveLeftAll_Click()
    Dim i As Integer

        ' Move the items.
        For i = lstRight.ListCount - 1 To 0 Step -1
            ' Move this item.
            lstLeft.AddItem lstRight.List(i)
            lstRight.RemoveItem i
        Next i


        ' Enable the correct buttons.
        EnableButtons
    End Sub

    ' Move all items into the right list.
    Private Sub cmdMoveRightAll_Click()
    Dim i As Integer

        ' Move the items.
        For i = lstLeft.ListCount - 1 To 0 Step -1
            ' Move this item.
            lstRight.AddItem lstLeft.List(i)
            lstLeft.RemoveItem i
        Next i
```

```
    ' Enable the correct buttons.
        EnableButtons
    End Sub
```

This kind of interface is useful when the user must select one or more items from a very long list, particularly if the user is likely to select only a few items. In that case, the user can see all of the selected items in the right list, but the unselected items in the left list do not take up much room.

If the user is selecting from a very short list, you should consider using a series of OptionButtons instead of this two-list interface.

85. Save and Restore a ComboBox

Directory: SaveCbo

An application can use simple file operations to load a ComboBox's data from a file when the program starts and save any changes when it stops. Example program SaveCbo demonstrates this technique. Enter a value in the ComboBox, and click the Add button to make it part of the list of choices. Click the Remove button to remove the selected item from the list. When you close and restart the program, the changes you have made will be reloaded automatically.

Program SaveCbo.

How It Works

Program SaveCbo stores information about its ComboBox in the file animals.dat. This file begins with the number of items in the ComboBox and the index of the currently selected item. It then contains the list values. The following shows a small sample file.

```
6,5
"Aardvark"
"Badger"
"Cow"
"Frog"
"Giraffe"
"Ibex"
```

The program does all its interesting processing in its Form_Load and Form_Unload event handlers. The Form_Load subroutine opens the file animals.dat for input. It reads the number of items in the ComboBox and the index of the selected item. It then reads each of the ComboBox item values and adds them to the ComboBox. Finally, it selects the item that was selected when the file was created.

Subroutine Form_Unload opens the file animals.dat for output. It saves the number of items in the ComboBox and the index of the selected item. It then saves each of the ComboBox item values and closes the file.

```
' Load the data from last time.
Private Sub Form_Load()
Dim fnum As Integer
Dim num_items As Integer
Dim list_index As Integer
Dim txt As String
Dim i As Integer

    cboAnimals.Clear

    On Error GoTo NoFile
    fnum = FreeFile
    Open App.Path & "\animals.dat" For Input As fnum
    On Error GoTo CloseFile

    ' Read the number of items and the index of
    ' the selected item.
    Input #fnum, num_items, list_index

    ' Read the list items.
    For i = 0 To num_items - 1
        Input #fnum, txt
        cboAnimals.AddItem txt
    Next i
    cboAnimals.ListIndex = list_index

CloseFile:
    Close fnum
NoFile:

End Sub

' Save the data for next time.
Private Sub Form_Unload(Cancel As Integer)
Dim fnum As Integer
Dim i As Integer

    fnum = FreeFile
    Open App.Path & "\animals.dat" For Output As fnum
```

```
' Write the number of items and the index of
' the selected item.
Write #fnum, cboAnimals.ListCount, _
    cboAnimals.ListIndex

' Write the list items.
For i = 0 To cboAnimals.ListCount - 1
    Write #fnum, cboAnimals.List(i)
Next i

    Close fnum
End Sub
```

There are several other ways a program can save and load data. For instance, it could save the data in a database or in the system registry. It could also save the data for more than one control in the same file.

Also note that saving changes in the Form_Unload event handler is not completely foolproof. If the user makes changes to the ComboBox and then the program crashes without exiting normally, Form_Unload never executes so the user's changes are lost. If it is important that the changes always be saved, and if saving the values does not take too long, the program should save them as soon as the changes are made instead of waiting until the form unloads.

86. **Match ListBox Prefixes**

Directory: FindItem

When a ListBox control has the input focus, you can press a letter to make the list jump to the first item that begins with that letter. If you press the letter again, the list moves to the next item that starts with the same letter. You can continue pressing the letter to move through the items starting with that letter.

This method of selection is convenient when the list contains only a few items that begin with the same letter, but if many items have the same first letter, selecting a particular item this way can be tedious. You may need to press the letter many times before you find the item you want.

Example program FindItem demonstrates a technique for making item selection easier. Enter the first few letters of an item in the program's TextBox. The program selects the first item in the list that matches all the letters you enter.

Program FindItem.

How It Works

Program FindItem sends its ListBox control the LB_SELECTSTRING message to make it find and select the first item that begins with the prefix you enter in the TextBox. The following code shows how program FindItem works. The parameter -1 passed to SendMessage tells the ListBox to start searching the list after the item with index -1. That makes it search starting at the first item in the list.

```
Option Explicit

Private Declare Function SendMessage Lib "user32" _
    Alias "SendMessageA" (ByVal hWnd As Long, ByVal wMsg As Long, _
    ByVal wParam As Long, ByVal lParam As String) As Long
Private Const LB_SELECTSTRING = &H18C

' Select the first item that matches this value.
Private Sub txtValue_Change()
    SendMessage lstWords.hWnd, LB_SELECTSTRING, _
        -1, txtValue.Text
End Sub
```

★ ★ ★

87. Detect ComboBox Dropdown

Directory: CboDown

Occasionally, it is useful for a program to know when a ComboBox control is about to display its dropdown list. For instance, the choices available in the ComboBox's dropdown list might depend on items selected by the user. When the ComboBox is about to drop down, the program can update the items in its list.

In Visual Basic 5 and 6, a program can subclass to intercept Windows messages. When it sees the WM_COMMAND message, it can examine the message's parameters to see if the program is receiving a ComboBox dropdown event. If so, it can take whatever action is necessary.

Example program CboDown uses this method. Select some items in the ListBox on the left. Then click on the ComboBox's dropdown arrow to make it present its dropdown list. When you click on the ComboBox, the program copies the items you have selected in the ListBox into the ComboBox's dropdown list.

Program CboDown.

How It Works

The following code shows declarations and routines used by program CboDown and stored in the .bas module APIStuff.bas.

Subroutine CatchDropDown prepares the program to catch dropdown events. It saves the hWnd of the form and ComboBox, and it stores references to the ListBox and ComboBox controls. It then installs the NewWindowProc function as the form's new WindowProc routine. Whenever the form receives a Windows message, the system calls this function.

Function NewWindowProc checks the Window message to see if it is a WM_COMMAND message. If it is, the function then determines whether the message's command is CBN_DROPDOWN and whether the ComboBox that is about to display its dropdown list is the ComboBox to which it has a reference. If the message satisfies these conditions, the program is about to drop the ComboBox down so NewWindowProc copies the selected ListBox choices into the ComboBox's dropdown list.

```
Option Explicit

' The old WindowProc address.
Private OldWindowProc As Long

' The hWnd for the ComboBox.
Private ComboHwnd As Long
```

```
' The ComboBox control.
Private TheComboBox As ComboBox

' The ListBox control from which we are taking
' the ComboBox's values.
Private TheListBox As ListBox

' API declarations.
Private Declare Function CallWindowProc Lib "user32" _
    Alias "CallWindowProcA" (ByVal lpPrevWndFunc As Long, _
    ByVal hWnd As Long, ByVal msg As Long, ByVal wParam As Long, _
    ByVal lParam As Long) As Long
Private Declare Function SetWindowLong Lib "user32" _
    Alias "SetWindowLongA" (ByVal hWnd As Long, ByVal nIndex As Long, _
    ByVal dwNewLong As Long) As Long

Private Const GWL_WNDPROC = (-4)
Private Const WM_COMMAND = &H111
Private Const CBN_DROPDOWN = 7

' Install the new WindowProc.
Public Sub CatchDropDown(ByVal hWnd As Long, _
    ByVal cbo As ComboBox, ByVal lst As ListBox)

    ' Save the two controls and the ComboBox's hWnd.
    ComboHwnd = cbo.hWnd
    Set TheComboBox = cbo
    Set TheListBox = lst

    ' Subclass to catch ComboBox drop events.
    OldWindowProc = SetWindowLong( _
        hWnd, GWL_WNDPROC, _
        AddressOf NewWindowProc)
End Sub

' Look for the ComboBox dropdown.
Public Function NewWindowProc(ByVal hWnd As Long, _
    ByVal msg As Long, ByVal wParam As Long, ByVal lParam As Long) _
    As Long
Dim i As Integer

    ' See if this is a WM_COMMAND message.
    If msg = WM_COMMAND Then
        ' See if this message was generated by ComboBox
        ' and see if it is a CBN_DROPDOWN command.
        If ComboHwnd = (lParam And &HFFFF) And _
            (wParam \ &H10000) = CBN_DROPDOWN _
        Then
                ' The ComboBox is being dropped down.
                ' Start with no items in the ComboBox.
            TheComboBox.Clear
```

```
              ' Add the items selected in the ListBox
              ' to the ComboBox.
              For i = 0 To TheListBox.ListCount - 1
                  If TheListBox.Selected(i) Then
                      ' This item is selected.
                      TheComboBox.AddItem TheListBox.List(i)
                  End If
              Next i
          End If
      End If


      ' Call the original WindowProc.
      NewWindowProc = CallWindowProc( _
          OldWindowProc, hWnd, msg, wParam, _
          lParam)
  End Function
```

The code that follows shows how the CboDown program's main form uses the functions in module APIStuff.bas. Compared to the previous code, this code is simple. The important statement is the call to the CatchDropDown subroutine.

```
  Private Sub Form_Load()
      ' Create some list values.
      lstValues.AddItem "Ape"
      lstValues.AddItem "Bear"
      lstValues.AddItem "Cat"
      lstValues.AddItem "Dog"
      lstValues.AddItem "Eagle"
      lstValues.AddItem "Fox"
      lstValues.AddItem "Giraffe"

      ' Subclass to catch the dropdown events.
      CatchDropDown hWnd, cboValues, lstValues
  End Sub
```

As is the case with all subclassing programs, it is extremely important that this program terminate normally. If you stop it using the Run menu's End command or if the program crashes, the Visual Basic development environment will crash as well. You will lose any changes you have made since the last time you saved. To avoid wasting a lot of time, save your work often.

Using ListView and TreeView

The TreeView control displays hierarchical data much as Windows Explorer displays the directories and files on a disk or CD-ROM. The ListView control displays a list of items using icons, small icons, a list, or a multicolumn report. Both of these controls provide advanced display features, but they are difficult to use.

The sections in this chapter explain how to use these controls. Note that these controls were introduced in Visual Basic 5, so the examples presented in this chapter work only in Visual Basic 5 and 6.

88. Use a ListView Control

Directory: ListView

Using a ListView control is not easy. To make the control work, you must associate the ListView control with two ImageList controls containing pictures to use for the data items' large and small icons. You can then use the ColumnHeaders collection to build columns and the ListItems collection to add entries to the ListView.

Example program ListView follows these steps. Use the View menu's commands to display the data in icon, small icon, list, or report format. Click on an item to make the program display information about that item at the bottom of the form. Click on a column in the report view to make the control sort the items using that column. Click the same column again to reverse the sort order.

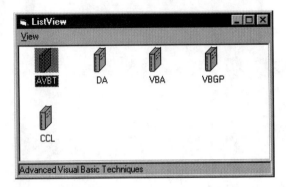

Program ListView.

How It Works

The following code shows how program ListView manages its data. The Form_Load event handler calls the AddEntry subroutine several times to add text values to three data arrays. AddEntry enlarges the arrays, saves the new values, and updates variables that keep track of the maximum width needed to display the text in each array.

Form_Load then uses the ListView control's ColumnHeaders collection to create column headers for three columns. It passes the collection's Add routine the width needed to display the longest string in each column.

Next, the program sets the ListView control's Icon and SmallIcon properties to the ImageList controls that contain the large and small icons it should use to represent the data. The ImageList controls' pictures were set at design time. Right-click on the controls and select the Properties command to examine or modify the pictures.

Form_Load then loops through the values stored in the data arrays. For each, it creates a new list item using the ListItem collection's Add method. It sets the new item's Icon and SmallIcon properties to indicate the indexes of the images in the ImageList controls that should be used to represent the item. Finally, it gives the new item two subitems to represent the second and third columns of data in the control's report display.

Compared to the Form_Load event handler, the rest of the program is straightforward. The Form_Resize event handler makes the ListView control as large as possible.

When you click on a column header in the report display, the control's lsvBooks_ColumnClick event handler executes. It sets the control's SortIndex property to make the control sort using the column that was clicked. If that column is already selected, the routine switches the value of the SortOrder property so the control reverses its sort order.

When you click on an item, the control's lsvBooks_ItemClick event handler simply displays the corresponding book's title in the label at the bottom of the form.

Finally, when you invoke one of the View menu's commands, the mnuViewChoice_Click event handler executes. It just sets the ListView control's View property to indicate the type of display it should provide. The ListView automatically generates the icon, small icon, list, or report view.

```
Option Explicit

' Variables to store the data.
Private NumBooks As Integer
Private abbrevs() As String
Private titles() As String
Private isbns() As String
Private abbrev_width As Single
Private title_width As Single
Private isbn_width As Single

' Initialize the data.
Private Sub Form_Load()
Dim list_item As ListItem
Dim i As Integer

    ' Set minimum column widths.
    abbrev_width = TextWidth("Abbrev")
    title_width = TextWidth("Title")
    isbn_width = TextWidth("ISBN")

    ' Create the text entries.
    AddEntry "AVBT", "Advanced Visual Basic Techniques", _
        "0-471-18881-6"
    AddEntry "DA", "Ready-to-Run Delphi 3.0 Algorithms", _
        "0-471-25400-2"
    AddEntry "VBA", "Ready-to-Run Visual Basic Algorithms", _
        "0-471-24268-3"
    AddEntry "VBGP", "Visual Basic Graphics Programming", _
        "0-471-15533-0"
    AddEntry "CCL", "Custom Controls Library", _
        "0-471-24267-5"

    ' Create the column headers.
    lsvBooks.ColumnHeaders.Add , , "Abbrev", abbrev_width
    lsvBooks.ColumnHeaders.Add , , "Title", title_width
    lsvBooks.ColumnHeaders.Add , , "ISBN", isbn_width

    ' Select the report view.
    mnuViewChoice_Click lvwReport

    ' Associate the ImageList controls with the
    ' ListView's Icons and SmallIcons properties.
    lsvBooks.Icons = imgLarge
    lsvBooks.SmallIcons = imgSmall

    ' Create the items.
    For i = 1 To NumBooks
        Set list_item = lsvBooks.ListItems.Add(, , abbrevs(i))
        list_item.Icon = 1
        list_item.SmallIcon = 1
```

```
            list_item.SubItems(1) = titles(i)
            list_item.SubItems(2) = isbns(i)
        Next i
End Sub


' Add a new entry to the text arrays.
Private Sub AddEntry(ByVal new_abbrev As String, _
        ByVal new_title As String, ByVal new_isbn As String)

        ' Make room for the new entries.
        NumBooks = NumBooks + 1
        ReDim Preserve abbrevs(1 To NumBooks)
        ReDim Preserve titles(1 To NumBooks)
        ReDim Preserve isbns(1 To NumBooks)

        ' Save the new entries.
        abbrevs(NumBooks) = new_abbrev
        titles(NumBooks) = new_title
        isbns(NumBooks) = new_isbn

        ' See if these are the longest so far.
        If abbrev_width < TextWidth(new_abbrev) Then _
            abbrev_width = TextWidth(new_abbrev)
        If title_width < TextWidth(new_title) Then _
            title_width = TextWidth(new_title)
        If isbn_width < TextWidth(new_isbn) Then _
            isbn_width = TextWidth(new_isbn)
End Sub


' Make the ListView control as big as possible.
Private Sub Form_Resize()
Dim hgt As Single

    hgt = ScaleHeight - lblInfo.Height
    If hgt < 120 Then hgt = 120
    lblInfo.Move 0, hgt, ScaleWidth
    lsvBooks.Move 0, 0, ScaleWidth, hgt
End Sub


' Sort using this column.
Private Sub lsvBooks_ColumnClick( _
        ByVal ColumnHeader As ComctlLib.ColumnHeader)
Dim sort_key As Integer

        ' If the column is already the sort index,
        ' switch its sort order.
        sort_key = ColumnHeader.Index - 1
        If sort_key = lsvBooks.SortKey Then
            ' Switch the sort order.
            lsvBooks.SortOrder = 1 - lsvBooks.SortOrder
        Else
```

```
    ' Sort using this column ascending.
        lsvBooks.SortKey = sort_key
        lsvBooks.SortOrder = lvwAscending
    End If


    lsvBooks.Sorted = True
End Sub

' Display information about the selected item.
Private Sub lsvBooks_ItemClick(ByVal Item As ComctlLib.ListItem)
    lblInfo.Caption = titles(Item.Index)
End Sub

Private Sub mnuViewChoice_Click(Index As Integer)
Dim i As Integer

    ' Display the selected view style.
    lsvBooks.View = Index

    ' Check this menu item.
    For i = 0 To 3
        If i = Index Then
            mnuViewChoice(i).Checked = True
        Else
            mnuViewChoice(i).Checked = False
        End If
    Next i
End Sub
```

89. Use a TreeView Control

☆ ☆
⑤ ⑥

Directory: AddNodes

Like the ListView control, the TreeView control provides a complex data display. Also, like the ListView control, the TreeView control is not easy to use.

The TreeView control represents hierarchical data using a tree-like arrangement of objects. The control's Nodes collection holds objects representing all the data items in the hierarchy. These objects are related to each other in a parent-child fashion. The Add function provided by the Nodes collection adds a new node to the tree. It allows the program to specify which object should be the new object's parent node in the tree.

For instance, the following code creates a new object and assigns it to the object variable the_group. The variable the_factory is the object that should be the new object's parent. The new object has key value "Engineering group" and a text value of "Engineering." The final two arguments to the Add routine give the indexes in an ImageList control of icons that represent the new node normally and when it is selected.

```
Set the_group = OrgTree.Nodes.Add(the_factory, tvwChild, _
    "Engineering group", "Engineering", 1, 2)
```

Example program AddNodes displays corporate personnel data. The company contains factories, each containing groups that contain people. Click on the minus sign next to an entry to collapse it and hide its detail data. Click on the plus sign next to an entry to expand it and show its detail.

Program AddNodes also lets you add new nodes at run time. Use the commands in the Nodes menu to add new factories, groups, and people. The program lets you add a node only if it can figure out where it belongs in the hierarchy. For example, if you click on a factory node, the program will disable the Add Person menu item because it cannot figure out which group should hold a new person. If you click on a group, the program will allow you to add new people to that group.

Note that the program uses the names of the factories, groups, and people as keys into the Nodes collection. Because collections cannot contain duplicate key values, you cannot use the same name for more than one factory, group, or person.

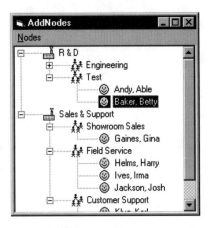

Program AddNodes.

How It Works

The following code shows how program AddNodes works. When the form loads, its Form_Load event handler starts by placing several icons in the imlNodes ImageList control. These icons will represent the nodes in the tree. Form_Load then sets the TreeView control's ImageList property to imlNodes to associate the TreeView control with the ImageList control.

The program then repeats a sequence of steps several times to create the tree nodes. First, it uses the Nodes collection's Add method to build a new factory node that has no parent. It then uses Add to create a group node that has the factory as its parent. Next, the program creates several person nodes within the group. It then invokes the Ensure-Visible method for the last person it created. That forces the control to expand the person's group and factory so the person is visible to the user.

Form_Load then creates more groups for that factory. When it has given that factory enough groups and people, it creates another factory and repeats the process.

The program's mnuAddFactory_Click event handler prompts the user for the new factory's name. It uses the Add method to create the new factory node with no parent.

The mnuAddGroup_Click event handler prompts the user for a new group's name. It examines the currently selected node to see which factory should contain the new group. If the selected node is a person or group, it moves up the tree until it finds the corresponding factory. It then uses the Add method to create the new group within this factory.

The mnuAddPerson_Click event handler follows a similar procedure. It identifies the group where the new person should be inserted and creates the new person object.

When the user opens the Nodes menu, the mnuNodes_Click event handler executes. This routine examines the currently selected node in the TreeView control. Depending on the kind of node selected, it enables and disables the Add Factory, Add Group, and Add Person menu items.

The NodeType function returns a numeric value indicating a node's type. This function relies on the fact that the program uses an f, g, or p as the first character in the key value for the nodes. For instance, a person node named "Bob" would have key value "p Bob." NodeType simply examines the first character in the node's key to see whether it is a factory, group, or person.

```
Option Explicit

' Data item types.
Private Enum ObjectType
    otNone = 0
    otFactory = 1
    otGroup = 2
    otPerson = 3
    otFactory2 = 4
    otGroup2 = 5
    otPerson2 = 6
End Enum

' Return the node's object type.
Private Function NodeType(test_node As Node) As ObjectType
    If test_node Is Nothing Then
        NodeType = otNone
    Else
        Select Case Left$(test_node.Key, 1)
            Case "f"
                NodeType = otFactory
            Case "g"
                NodeType = otGroup
            Case "p"
                NodeType = otPerson
        End Select
```

```
        End If
End Function


' Prepare the ImageList and TreeView controls.
Private Sub Form_Load()
Dim i As Integer
Dim factory As Node
Dim group As Node
Dim person As Node

    ' Load pictures into the ImageList.
    For i = 1 To 6
        imlNodes.ListImages.Add , , TreeImage(i).Picture
    Next i

    ' Attach the TreeView to the ImageList.
    trvCompany.ImageList = imlNodes

    ' Create some nodes.
    Set factory = trvCompany.Nodes.Add(, , _
        "f R & D", "R & D", otFactory, otFactory2)
    Set group = trvCompany.Nodes.Add(factory, tvwChild, _
        "g Engineering", "Engineering", otGroup, otGroup2)
    Set person = trvCompany.Nodes.Add(group, tvwChild, _
        "p Cameron, Charlie", "Cameron, Charlie", otPerson, otPerson2)
    Set person = trvCompany.Nodes.Add(group, tvwChild, _
        "p Davos, Debbie", "Davos, Debbie", otPerson, otPerson2)
    person.EnsureVisible

    Set group = trvCompany.Nodes.Add(factory, tvwChild, _
        "g Test", "Test", otGroup, otGroup2)
    Set person = trvCompany.Nodes.Add(group, tvwChild, _
        "p Able, Andy", "Andy, Able", otPerson, otPerson2)
    Set person = trvCompany.Nodes.Add(group, tvwChild, _
        "p Baker, Betty", "Baker, Betty", otPerson, otPerson2)
    person.EnsureVisible

    Set factory = trvCompany.Nodes.Add(, , _
        "f Sales & Support", "Sales & Support", otFactory, otFactory2)
    Set group = trvCompany.Nodes.Add(factory, tvwChild, _
        "g Showroom Sales", "Showroom Sales", otGroup, otGroup2)
    Set person = trvCompany.Nodes.Add(group, tvwChild, _
        "p Gaines, Gina", "Gaines, Gina", otPerson, otPerson2)
    person.EnsureVisible

    Set group = trvCompany.Nodes.Add(factory, tvwChild, _
        "g Field Service", "Field Service", otGroup, otGroup2)
    Set person = trvCompany.Nodes.Add(group, tvwChild, _
        "p Helms, Harry", "Helms, Harry", otPerson, otPerson2)
    Set person = trvCompany.Nodes.Add(group, tvwChild, _
        "p Ives, Irma", "Ives, Irma", otPerson, otPerson2)
```

```
    Set person = trvCompany.Nodes.Add(group, tvwChild, _
        "p Jackson, Josh", "Jackson, Josh", otPerson, otPerson2)
    person.EnsureVisible

    Set group = trvCompany.Nodes.Add(factory, tvwChild, _
        "g Customer Support", "Customer Support", otGroup, otGroup2)
    Set person = trvCompany.Nodes.Add(group, tvwChild, _
        "p Klug, Karl", "Klug, Karl", otPerson, otPerson2)
    Set person = trvCompany.Nodes.Add(group, tvwChild, _
        "p Landau, Linda", "Landau, Linda", otPerson, otPerson2)
    person.EnsureVisible
End Sub

' Make the TreeView as large as possible.
Private Sub Form_Resize()
    trvCompany.Move 0, 0, ScaleWidth, ScaleHeight
End Sub

' Add a new factory.
Private Sub mnuAddFactory_Click()
Dim name As String
Dim factory As Node

    name = InputBox("Factory Name", "New Factory", "")
    If name = "" Then Exit Sub

    Set factory = trvCompany.Nodes.Add(, , _
        "f " & name, name, otFactory, otFactory2)
    factory.EnsureVisible
End Sub

' Add a new group.
Private Sub mnuAddGroup_Click()
Dim name As String
Dim factory As Node
Dim group As Node

    name = InputBox("Group Name", "New Group", "")
    If name = "" Then Exit Sub

    ' Find the factory that should hold the new group.
    Set factory = trvCompany.SelectedItem
    If NodeType(factory) = otPerson Then _
        Set factory = factory.Parent
    If NodeType(factory) = otGroup Then _
        Set factory = factory.Parent

    Set group = trvCompany.Nodes.Add(factory, tvwChild, _
        "g " & name, name, otGroup, otGroup2)
    group.EnsureVisible
End Sub
```

```vb
' Add a new person.
Private Sub mnuAddPerson_Click()
Dim name As String
Dim group As Node
Dim person As Node

    name = InputBox("Person Name", "New Person", "")
    If name = "" Then Exit Sub

    ' Find the group that should hold the new person.
    Set group = trvCompany.SelectedItem
    If NodeType(group) = otPerson Then _
        Set group = group.Parent

    Set person = trvCompany.Nodes.Add(group, tvwChild, _
        "p " & name, name, otPerson, otPerson2)
    person.EnsureVisible
End Sub

' The user is opening the Nodes menu. See which
' menu items should be enabled.
Private Sub mnuNodes_Click()
Dim selected_node As Node
Dim selected_type As ObjectType

    Set selected_node = trvCompany.SelectedItem
    If selected_node Is Nothing Then
        selected_type = otNone
    Else
        selected_type = NodeType(selected_node)
    End If

    ' You can always add a factory.

    ' You can add a group if a factory, person, or
    ' group is selected.
    mnuAddGroup.Enabled = (selected_type <> otNone)

    ' You can add a person if a group or person
    ' is selected.
    mnuAddPerson.Enabled = (selected_type = otPerson) _
        Or (selected_type = otGroup)
End Sub
```

90. Let the User Drag TreeView Nodes

Directory: DragNode

The AddNodes program described in the previous section allows the user to add nodes to a TreeView control at run time. With a little more work, the program can also let the user drag and drop nodes from one part of the tree to another.

Example program DragNode lets the user rearrange nodes in this manner. Click on a node, and drag it into a new position. The program will let you drop nodes only where they are appropriate. For instance, you can drop a person only into a group, not into a factory or another person.

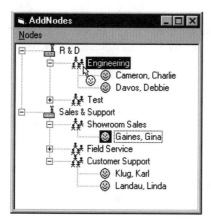

Program DragNode.

How It Works

The following code shows how the DragNode program handles drag-and-drop. The code that handles other TreeView operations, such as adding new nodes, is identical to the code used by program AddNodes so it is not repeated here. You can read about it in the previous section.

The first step in the drag-and-drop operation is determining when the user presses on a node. In the TreeView's MouseDown event handler, program DragNode uses the control's HitTest function to determine which node is under the mouse. It saves a reference to that node for later use.

The TreeView control's MouseMove event handler starts the drag-and-drop operation. If the user is dragging with the left mouse button down, the routine saves the type of the node being dragged. It then selects the node in the TreeView control. That makes the node appear selected when no other node is highlighted. The event handler then sets the TreeView control's DragIcon to an icon that matches the type of the node being dragged. It invokes the control's Drag method to begin the drag.

As the user drags the node over the TreeView control, it receives DragOver events. Its event handler uses the control's HitTest function to find the target node that the mouse is now over. If the target node is already highlighted from a previous DragOver event, the subroutine exits to avoid unnecessary recalculations.

If this is a new target node, the DragOver event handler determines the node's type. If the source node being dragged can legally be dropped on this kind of target node, the program uses the TreeView's DropHighlight property to highlight the target node.

The final step in the drag-and-drop is the drop. When the user drops the source node onto the TreeView control, the control receives a DragDrop event. The event handler checks the control's DropHighlight property to find the node on which the target should be dropped. If this property is Nothing, the source node was dropped on a node where it is not allowed. For instance, the user may have dropped a person on a factory node. In that case, the subroutine does nothing.

If the TreeView control's DropHighlight property holds a reference to a node, the event handler sets the source node's Parent property to the node stored in DropHighlight. That makes the source node a child of the target node and the TreeView automatically updates its display.

```vb
' Node drag and drop variables.
Private SourceNode As Object
Private SourceType As ObjectType
Private TargetNode As Object


' Save the node pressed so we can drag it later.
Private Sub trvCompany_MouseDown(Button As Integer, Shift As Integer, _
    x As Single, y As Single)

    Set SourceNode = trvCompany.HitTest(x, y)
End Sub

' Start a drag if one is not in progress.
Private Sub trvCompany_MouseMove(Button As Integer, Shift As Integer, _
    x As Single, y As Single)

    If Button = vbLeftButton Then
        ' Start a new drag. Note that we do not get
        ' other MouseMove events while the drag is
        ' in progress.

        ' See what node we are dragging.
        SourceType = NodeType(SourceNode)

        ' Select this node. When no node is highlighted,
        ' this node will be displayed as selected. That
        ' shows where it will land if dropped.
        Set trvCompany.SelectedItem = SourceNode
```

```vb
        ' Set the drag icon for this source.
        trvCompany.DragIcon = IconImage(SourceType)
        trvCompany.Drag vbBeginDrag
    End If
End Sub


' The mouse is being dragged over the control.
' Highlight the appropriate node.
Private Sub trvCompany_DragOver(Source As Control, _
    x As Single, y As Single, State As Integer)
Dim target As Node
Dim highlight As Boolean

    ' See what node we're above.
    Set target = trvCompany.HitTest(x, y)

    ' If it's the same as last time, do nothing.
    If target Is TargetNode Then Exit Sub
    Set TargetNode = target

    highlight = False
    If Not (TargetNode Is Nothing) Then
        ' See what kind of node we're above.
        If NodeType(TargetNode) + 1 = SourceType Then _
            highlight = True
    End If

    If highlight Then
        Set trvCompany.DropHighlight = TargetNode
    Else
        Set trvCompany.DropHighlight = Nothing
    End If
End Sub

' The user is dropping. See if the drop is valid.
Private Sub trvCompany_DragDrop(Source As Control, _
    x As Single, y As Single)

    If Not (trvCompany.DropHighlight Is Nothing) Then
        ' It's a valid drop. Set source node's
        ' parent to be the target node.
        Set SourceNode.Parent = trvCompany.DropHighlight
        Set trvCompany.DropHighlight = Nothing
    End If

    Set SourceNode = Nothing
    SourceType = otNone
End Sub
```

91. Save and Restore a TreeView

Directory: SaveTree

The SaveCbo program described in Chapter 9, "Using ListBoxes and ComboBoxes," shows how to save and load ComboBox values from a file. When the program exits, it saves the values in a file. When the program starts, it reloads the values from the file. A program can use a similar technique to save and load a TreeView control's values when the program exits and starts.

Example program SaveTree uses this technique. In most respects the program is similar to program DragNode, described in the previous section. Use the menus to create new nodes, and drag nodes into new positions. Click on nodes to expand or collapse them. When the program exits, it saves the TreeView's node data. When the program starts again, it reloads the TreeView data, selecting the previously selected node and restoring each node's collapsed or expanded state.

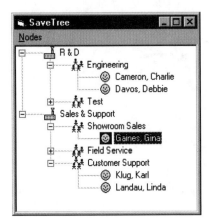

Program SaveTree.

How It Works

The code used by program SaveTree for adding and dragging nodes is similar to the code used by programs AddNodes and DragNode, described in the previous sections. Because this code is so similar, it is not repeated here. See the previous sections for more information about that code. The code that follows shows how this program saves and restores its tree data.

Program SaveTree uses the concept of a *serialization* to save and restore the complex information needed to describe a TreeView's data. A serialization is a linear representation of some kind of data. In this case, the program creates a string containing information that represents the TreeView data. The program includes a routine that creates a serialization from a TreeView control and another routine that initializes a TreeView control using the information in a serialization.

The following two sections explain how program SaveTree serializes and unserializes its TreeView control.

Serialization

Program SaveTree's Form_Unload event handler calls function SerializeTreeView to create a serialization for the TreeView control. It then writes the serialization string into the serialization file. All of the interesting work is performed by the serialization routines. The Form_Unload event handler itself is quite simple.

Function SerializeTreeView returns a serialization for a TreeView control. It returns a string of the form "TreeView(...)" where the parentheses contain a serialization for the top level nodes in the TreeView control that have no parents.

Each of the node serializations is represented by a string of the form "Root(...)" where these parentheses contain the serialization of the subtrees beneath those nodes. Combining these two types of strings gives a serialization of the form "TreeView(Root(...)Root(...)...)."

Function SerializeTreeView itself is fairly simple. It begins its return string with the value "TreeView(." It then examines each of the nodes in the TreeView control. For each node with no parent, the routine adds the string "Root(" and calls the SerializeNode function to find the serialization for the node. It finishes the string by adding closing parentheses.

Function SerializeNode returns the serialization for a node and its children. It takes as parameters the node to serialize and the number of times it should indent the serialization. The indentation is not necessary for the computer, but it makes the result easier to read.

SerializeNode starts with the string "BasicInfo(" followed by a series of values giving the node's ExpandedImage, Image, Key, Selected, SelectedImage, Tag, and Text values. It closes the node's basic information serialization with a parenthesis and then includes the serializations of the node's children. It packages each of these in a string of the form "Child(...)." The function calls itself recursively to calculate the child serializations. Note that the children may have children of their own, so the serialization may include many nested levels of serializations.

The following code shows the routines program SaveTree uses to serialize its TreeView data.

```
' Save the TreeView data into a file.
Private Sub Form_Unload(Cancel As Integer)
Dim txt As String
Dim fnum As Integer

    fnum = FreeFile
    Open App.Path & "\treeview.ser" For Output As fnum
    txt = SerializeTreeView(trvCompany)
```

```vb
        Write #fnum, txt
        Close fnum
End Sub


' Return a string representing the TreeView's data.
' Serializations neither begin nor end with vbCrLf.
Public Function SerializeTreeView(ByVal tree As TreeView) As String
Dim txt As String
Dim nl As String
Dim root_node As Node

    txt = "TreeView("
    nl = vbCrLf & "    "

    ' Serialize the root nodes.
    For Each root_node In tree.Nodes
        If root_node.Parent Is Nothing Then _
            txt = txt & nl & "Root(" & vbCrLf & _
                SerializeNode(root_node, 2) & _
                nl & ")"
    Next root_node

    txt = txt & vbCrLf & ")"

    SerializeTreeView = txt
End Function


' Return a string representing the Node's data.
' Serializations neither begin nor end with vbCrLf.
Public Function SerializeNode(ByVal par As Node, _
    ByVal indent As Integer) As String
Dim txt As String
Dim child As Node
Dim nl As String

    ' Serialize this node's basic information.
    txt = Space$(indent * 2) & "BasicInfo("
    nl = vbCrLf & Space$((indent + 1) * 2)

    txt = txt & nl & "Expanded(" & par.Expanded & ")"
    txt = txt & nl & "ExpandedImage(" & par.ExpandedImage & ")"
    txt = txt & nl & "Image(" & par.Image & ")"
    txt = txt & nl & "Key(" & par.Key & ")"
    txt = txt & nl & "Selected(" & par.Selected & ")"
    txt = txt & nl & "SelectedImage(" & par.SelectedImage & ")"
    txt = txt & nl & "Tag(" & par.Tag & ")"
    txt = txt & nl & "Text(" & par.Text & ")"

    nl = vbCrLf & Space$(indent * 2)
    txt = txt & nl & ")"
```

```
    ' Serialize the node's children.
    Set child = par.child
    Do While Not (child Is Nothing)
        txt = txt & nl & "Child(" & vbCrLf & _
            SerializeNode(child, indent + 1) & _
            nl & ")"
        Set child = child.Next
    Loop

    SerializeNode = txt
End Function
```

The result of these routines is a serialization that represents the entire tree. The following text shows the serialization file for a simple tree with one factory node that contains one group node. You can look on the CD-ROM for a much longer serialization file.

```
"TreeView(
  Root(
    BasicInfo(
      Expanded(True)
      ExpandedImage()
      Image(1)
      Key(f R & D)
      Selected(False)
      SelectedImage(4)
      Tag()
      Text(R & D)
    )
    Child(
      BasicInfo(
        Expanded(True)
        ExpandedImage()
        Image(2)
        Key(g Engineering)
        Selected(False)
        SelectedImage(5)
        Tag()
        Text(Engineering)
      )
    )
  )
)"
```

Unserialization

Program SaveTree's Form_Load event handler defines the constant LOAD_FROM_FILE. Set this constant to True to make the program load the TreeView from the file. Set it to False to make the program create a TreeView using code. This is useful for creating the initial serialization file.

If LOAD_FROM_FILE is True, the program opens the serialization file. It reads the entire file into a single text string. It then calls subroutine UnSerializeTreeView to parse the serialization and initialize the TreeView control.

Function GetToken is used extensively by the unserialization routines. GetToken takes as a parameter a serialization string with the format "TokenName(...)..." It returns the name of the first token in the string and the token's value. In this case, the token name is Token-Name, and the value of the token is whatever lies between the parentheses. Before it returns, the function removes this token and its value from the serialization string.

GetToken searches the serialization for the first opening parenthesis. Everything before that is the token's name. The function then examines the characters that follow. It keeps track of the number of opening parentheses that have not been matched with closing parentheses. When that number reaches zero, the function has found the parenthesis that matches the first opening parenthesis. Remember that the serialization may contain many levels of nested node serializations, so this parenthesis matching is needed to tell where the token's value ends. GetToken returns everything between the two matched parentheses as the token's value, and it removes the token from the serialization.

Subroutine UnserializeTreeView uses GetToken to get the first token from a serialization. It verifies that the token's name is TreeView. If it is not, there is something wrong with the serialization.

UnserializeTreeView then reads tokens from the serialization until the serialization is empty. Each of the tokens at this level should be of the form "Root(...)," so the function verifies that the tokens' names are Root. The routine then calls function UnSerialize-Node, passing it the root serializations to initialize the nodes in the TreeView control.

Function UnSerializeNode uses the GetToken function to read the BasicInfo token from a node's serialization. It then uses GetToken to read the node's property values out of the BasicInfo. It uses those values to create and initialize the node.

UnSerializeNode then uses GetToken to get any remaining tokens from the node's serialization. These tokens contain the serializations for the node's children and should be of the form "Child(...)." UnSerializeNode invokes itself recursively to unserialize the children.

```vb
' Prepare the ImageList and TreeView controls.
Private Sub Form_Load()

' Set LOAD_FROM_FILE False to create an initial data file.
#Const LOAD_FROM_FILE = True ' False.

Dim i As Integer
Dim txt As String
Dim fnum As Integer

#If LOAD_FROM_FILE Then
    ' No variables are needed here.
#Else
    Dim factory As Node
    Dim group As Node
```

```
            Dim person As Node
#End If

        ' Load pictures into the ImageList.
        For i = 1 To 6
            imlNodes.ListImages.Add , , TreeImage(i).Picture
        Next i

        ' Attach the TreeView to the ImageList.
        trvCompany.ImageList = imlNodes

        #If LOAD_FROM_FILE Then
            ' Load the serialization.
            fnum = FreeFile
            On Error Resume Next
            Open App.Path & "\treeview.ser" For Input As fnum
            If Err.Number = 0 Then
                ' We opened the file successfully. Read it.
                On Error GoTo 0
                Input #fnum, txt
                Close fnum

                ' Unserialize the TreeView.
                UnSerializeTreeView trvCompany, txt
            End If
        #Else
            ' Create some nodes.
                :
            ' This code is the same as the code in programs
            ' AddNodes and DragNode so it is not repeated here.
                :
        #End If
End Sub

' Break a token off of the string. Return the token's
' name and value through variables. Return token_name
' = "" if there are no more tokens. Remove the token
' from the string txt.
Public Sub GetToken(txt As String, token_name As String, _
    token_value As String)
Dim pos As Integer
Dim pos2 As Integer
Dim txt_len As Integer
Dim ch As String
Dim open_parens As Integer

    ' Remove leading vbCrLfs, spaces, etc.
    txt_len = Len(txt)
    pos = 1
    For pos = 1 To txt_len
        ' Find the first visible character.
        ch = Mid$(txt, pos, 1)
```

```vb
        If ch > " " And ch <= "~" Then Exit For
    Next pos

    If pos > 1 Then
        txt = Right$(txt, txt_len - pos + 1)
        txt_len = Len(txt)
    End If

    ' Find the open parenthesis.
    pos = InStr(txt, "(")
    If pos <= 1 Then
        ' No open parenthesis or no name.
        ' Return no token.
        txt = ""
        token_name = ""
        token_value = ""
        Exit Sub
    End If
    token_name = Left$(txt, pos - 1)

    ' Find the corresponding close parenthesis.
    open_parens = 1
    For pos2 = pos + 1 To txt_len
        ch = Mid$(txt, pos2, 1)
        Select Case ch
            Case "("
                open_parens = open_parens + 1
            Case ")"
                open_parens = open_parens - 1
                If open_parens = 0 Then Exit For
        End Select
    Next pos2
    ' Note: If there is no corresponding close
    ' parenthesis, pos2 = txt_len + 1. This makes us
    ' use the rest of the string.

    token_value = Mid$(txt, pos + 1, pos2 - pos - 1)
    If pos2 >= txt_len Then
        txt = ""
    Else
        txt = Right$(txt, txt_len - pos2 - 1)
    End If
End Sub

' Initialize the TreeView's data using a serialization.
Public Sub UnSerializeTreeView(ByVal tree As TreeView, _
    ByVal serialization As String)
Dim treeview_name As String
Dim treeview_value As String
Dim root_name As String
Dim root_value As String
```

```
    ' Make sure this is a TreeView serialization.
    GetToken serialization, treeview_name, treeview_value
    If treeview_name <> "TreeView" Then
        MsgBox "Error initializing TreeView. " & _
            "This is not a TreeView serialization."
        Exit Sub
    End If

    ' Remove all the nodes.
    tree.Nodes.Clear

    GetToken treeview_value, root_name, root_value
    Do While root_name <> ""
        ' This better be a root serialization.
        If root_name <> "Root" Then
            MsgBox "Error reading TreeView serialization. " & _
                "Expected 'Root' but found '" & _
                root_name & ".'"
            Exit Sub
        End If

        ' Unserialize the root. If there's an error,
        ' stop processing the serialization.
        If UnSerializeNode(tree, Nothing, root_value) Then Exit Sub

        ' Get the next root serialization.
        GetToken treeview_value, root_name, root_value
    Loop
End Sub

' Initialize the Node's data using a serialization.
' Return True if there is an error.
Public Function UnSerializeNode(ByVal tree As TreeView, _
    ByVal par As Node, ByVal serialization As String) As Boolean
Dim new_node As Node
Dim basic_name As String
Dim basic_value As String
Dim token_name As String
Dim token_value As String
Dim val_Expanded As Boolean
Dim val_ExpandedImage As Variant
Dim val_Image As Variant
Dim val_Key As String
Dim val_Selected As Boolean
Dim val_SelectedImage As Variant
Dim val_Tag As String
Dim val_Text As String

    ' Assume we will fail.
    UnSerializeNode = True
```

```
' Read the node's basic information.
GetToken serialization, basic_name, basic_value
If basic_name <> "BasicInfo" Then
    MsgBox "Error reading Node serialization. " & _
        "Expected 'BasicInfo' but found '" & _
        basic_name & ".'"
    Exit Function
End If

' Read the information categories.
GetToken basic_value, token_name, token_value
Do While token_name <> ""
    Select Case token_name
        Case "Expanded"
            val_Expanded = CBool(token_value)
        Case "ExpandedImage"
            If token_value = "" Then
                val_ExpandedImage = Empty
            Else
                val_ExpandedImage = CInt(token_value)
            End If
        Case "Image"
            If token_value = "" Then
                val_Image = Empty
            Else
                val_Image = CInt(token_value)
            End If
        Case "Key"
            val_Key = token_value
        Case "Selected"
            val_Selected = CBool(token_value)
        Case "SelectedImage"
            If token_value = "" Then
                val_SelectedImage = Empty
            Else
                val_SelectedImage = CInt(token_value)
            End If
        Case "Tag"
            val_Tag = token_value
        Case "Text"
            val_Text = token_value
    End Select

    ' Get the next value.
    GetToken basic_value, token_name, token_value
Loop
```

```
    ' Create the node.
    If par Is Nothing Then
        Set new_node = tree.Nodes.Add( _
            , tvwChild, val_Key, val_Text, val_Image, _
            val_SelectedImage)
    Else
        Set new_node = tree.Nodes.Add( _
            par, tvwChild, val_Key, val_Text, val_Image, _
            val_SelectedImage)
    End If

    ' Set the node's other values.
    new_node.Expanded = val_Expanded
    new_node.ExpandedImage = val_ExpandedImage
    new_node.Selected = val_Selected
    new_node.Tag = val_Tag

    ' Unserialize the node's children.
    GetToken serialization, token_name, token_value
    Do While token_name <> ""
        If token_name <> "Child" Then
            MsgBox "Error reading Node serialization. " & _
                "Expected 'Child' but found '" & _
                basic_name & ".'"
            Exit Function
        End If

        ' Unserialize the child.
        If UnSerializeNode(tree, new_node, token_value) _
            Then Exit Function

        ' Get the next child.
        GetToken serialization, token_name, token_value
    Loop

    ' No error occurred.
    UnSerializeNode = False
End Function
```

Serialization is a powerful concept. It lets a program store and recover complex data structures such as the TreeView control's data. In this program, the serialization is stored in a file. It could also be transmitted across a network, written into the system registry, or stored in a database and later loaded into another program. Because the serialization is a simple text string, it can be encrypted before it is stored and decrypted after it is loaded. Serializations allow programs to manipulate complex data structures quickly and easily.

☆ ☆ ☆
⑤ ⑥

92. Combine TreeViews and ListViews

Directory: TreeList

The TreeView and ListView controls work well together. Windows Explorer uses a TreeView control on the left to display a directory hierarchy. On the right, it uses a ListView control to show details about the files in the directory selected in the TreeView control.

Example program TreeList uses a ListView control to display details for people selected in a TreeView control. When you click on a person's node in the TreeView control on the left, the program displays information about that person in the ListView control on the right.

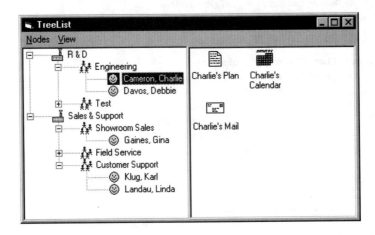

Program TreeList.

How It Works

Program TreeList is a combination of programs SaveTree and ListView, described earlier in this chapter. For more information on how the program manages its TreeView and ListView controls, read the descriptions of those programs.

The only really new code in program TreeList is in the TreeView's Click event handler. When the user clicks on a node in the tree, the trvCompany_Click subroutine executes. This routine clears the ListView control and verifies that the selected node represents a person. If the selected node represents a factory or group, the program does not display anything in the ListView control so the event handler exits.

If the selected node does represent a person, the routine adds data to the ListView control much as program ListView does. In this program, the event handler creates data items representing the person's plan, calendar, and mail. A real-world application would probably create different data items for each person. For instance, it might locate the person in a database and create ListView items based on the information it finds there.

```
' Display the data for this node in the ListView.
Private Sub trvCompany_Click()
Dim list_item As ListItem
Dim first_name As String
Dim txt As String
Dim pos As Integer
Dim col_width As Single

    ' Clear the ListView.
    lsvProjects.ListItems.Clear
    lsvProjects.ColumnHeaders.Clear

    ' Work only with people nodes.
    If NodeType(SourceNode) <> otPerson Then Exit Sub

    ' Display information for the person.
    If SourceNode Is Nothing Then Exit Sub

    ' Find the person's first name.
    pos = InStr(SourceNode.Text, ",")
    first_name = _
        Trim$(Mid$(SourceNode.Text, pos + 1)) & "'s "

    ' Fill in the ListView.
    txt = first_name & "Plan"
    If col_width < TextWidth(txt) Then col_width = TextWidth(txt)
    Set list_item = lsvProjects.ListItems.Add(, , txt)
    list_item.Icon = 1
    list_item.SmallIcon = 1

    txt = first_name & "Calendar"
    If col_width < TextWidth(txt) Then col_width = TextWidth(txt)
    Set list_item = lsvProjects.ListItems.Add(, , txt)
    list_item.Icon = 2
    list_item.SmallIcon = 2

    txt = first_name & "Mail"
    If col_width < TextWidth(txt) Then col_width = TextWidth(txt)
    Set list_item = lsvProjects.ListItems.Add(, , txt)
    list_item.Icon = 3
    list_item.SmallIcon = 3

    ' Create the column header, leaving room for the bitmaps.
    lsvProjects.ColumnHeaders.Add , , "Item", _
        col_width + ScaleX(16, vbPixels, vbTwips)
End Sub
```

The ListView and TreeView controls form a powerful combination. Using them together, you can add sophisticated data displays to your programs relatively quickly.

Using Other Controls

The first 10 chapters in this book describe some of the ways a program can use Timer, TextBox, ListBox, ComboBox, ListView, and TreeView controls. This chapter explains some of the less obvious issues that arise when you use other controls that come with Visual Basic. Most of these examples are quite simple. They merely highlight key features of certain useful controls.

93. Play an AVI Video File

Directory: PlayAVI

Visual Basic's Multimedia MCI control allows a Visual Basic program to play several different kinds of multimedia files including AVI video files. Program PlayAVI shows how a program can play an AVI video file. Enter the name of an AVI file and click the Play button to make the program play the file.

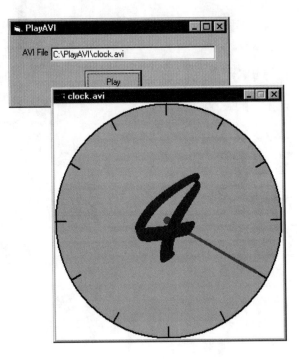

Program PlayAVI.

How It Works

The following code shows how program PlayAVI controls its MCI control programmatically. The program's Form_Load event handler initializes some of the control's properties. The Notify property indicates whether the MCI control generates notification events when it finishes playing a multimedia file. Program PlayAVI does not need this callback so it sets Notify to False.

The program sets the MCI control's Shareable property to False to indicate that more than one program cannot share this MCI device. Finally, Form_Load sets the Device-Type property to AVIVideo so the control knows it will be playing an AVI video file.

When you click the Play button, the cmdPlay_Click event handler actually plays the video file. This routine sets the control's FileName property to indicate the location of the AVI file. It then invokes the control's Open, Play, and Close commands.

The MCI control's Wait property determines whether it waits for the next command to finish before returning control to the program. Program PlayAVI sets Wait to True before each of the commands it executes so the control performs them in their proper sequence.

```
Option Explicit

Private Sub Form_Load()
    ' Select a default AVI file.
    txtFilename.Text = App.Path & "\clock.avi"

    ' Prepare the MCI control for AVI video.
```

```
      mciPlayer.Notify = False
      mciPlayer.Wait = True
      mciPlayer.Shareable = False
      mciPlayer.DeviceType = "AVIVideo"
End Sub


' Open the device and play the video.
Private Sub cmdPlay_Click()
    ' Set the file name.
    mciPlayer.filename = txtFilename.Text

    ' Open the MCI device.
    mciPlayer.Wait = True
    mciPlayer.Command = "Open"

    ' Play the video.
    mciPlayer.Wait = True
    mciPlayer.Command = "Play"

    ' Close the device.
    mciPlayer.Command = "Close"
End Sub
```

94. Play a Wave Audio File

Directory: PlayWAV

In addition to AVI video files, Visual Basic's MCI control can also play wave audio (.wav) files. Program PlayWAV shows how a program can play an audio file. Enter the name of a wave audio file and click the Play button to make the program play the file.

Program PlayWAV.

How It Works

The following code shows how program PlayWAV controls its MCI control programmatically. It is very similar to the code used by program PlayAVI. The only difference is that this program's Form_Load statement sets the MCI control's DeviceType to WaveAudio instead of AVIVideo.

```
Option Explicit

Private Sub Form_Load()
    ' Select a default AVI file.
    txtFilename.Text = App.Path & "\ringin.wav"

    ' Prepare the MCI control for WaveAudio.
    mciPlayer.Notify = False
    mciPlayer.Shareable = False
    mciPlayer.DeviceType = "WaveAudio"
End Sub

' Open the device and play the sound.
Private Sub cmdPlay_Click()
    ' Set the file name.
    mciPlayer.filename = txtFilename.Text

    ' Open the MCI device.
    mciPlayer.Wait = True
    mciPlayer.Command = "Open"

    ' Play the sound.
    mciPlayer.Wait = True
    mciPlayer.Command = "Play"

    ' Close the device.
    mciPlayer.Command = "Close"
End Sub
```

Because program PlayWAV plays sound, your computer must have sound support for the program to work correctly.

95. Make a Button Ignore Return Keys ④ ⑤ ⑥

Directory: IgnoreCR

Normally, a CommandButton fires if it has focus and the user presses the Space, Return, or Enter key. Some applications use the Enter and Return keys to perform special actions. For instance, if a form contains a button with Default property set to True, that button fires when the user presses the Return or Enter key even when the input focus is on another control. Unfortunately, if another button has the input focus, that button fires instead of the default button. A different button fires depending on which control has the focus.

To prevent confusion, you can make buttons ignore the Return and Enter keys. Then the user cannot invoke the form's default action by pressing Return or Enter while the focus is on one of the buttons, although these keys still work normally when the focus is on other controls.

Example program IgnoreCR demonstrates this strategy. The Reverse button is the form's default button. If you click this button or press the Return or Enter keys while focus is on this button or the TextBox, the Reverse button fires. If you press the Return or Enter key while the focus is on the Upper Case or Lower Case button, the key press is ignored.

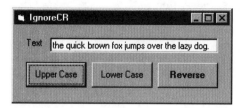

Program IgnoreCR.

How It Works

The following code shows how program IgnoreCR ignores Return and Enter keys. The Reverse button has its Default property set to True, but otherwise it works as usual.

The Upper Case and Lower Case buttons do not use Click event handlers. Instead, they execute their code in their KeyUp and MouseUp event handlers. The KeyUp event handlers execute their code when they detect Space keys. The MouseUp event handlers determine whether the mouse is currently above the button and execute their code only if it is. This prevents the code from executing if the user presses the button and then drags the mouse off the button before releasing it.

```
Option Explicit


' If this is a space character, invoke the
' appropriate command.
Private Sub cmdLowerCase_KeyUp(KeyCode As Integer, Shift As Integer)
    If KeyCode = vbKeySpace Then MakeLowerCase
End Sub


' If this is a space character, invoke the
' appropriate command.
Private Sub cmdUpperCase_KeyUp(KeyCode As Integer, Shift As Integer)
    If KeyCode = vbKeySpace Then MakeUpperCase
End Sub


' If the mouse is over the button, invoke the
' appropriate command.
Private Sub cmdLowerCase_MouseUp(Button As Integer, Shift As Integer, X
As Single, Y As Single)
    If X >= 0 And X <= cmdLowerCase.Width And _
        Y >= 0 And Y <= cmdLowerCase.Height _
            Then MakeLowerCase
End Sub
```

```
' If the mouse is over the button, invoke the
' appropriate command.
Private Sub cmdUpperCase_MouseUp(Button As Integer, Shift As Integer, X
As Single, Y As Single)
    If X >= 0 And X <= cmdUpperCase.Width And _
        Y >= 0 And Y <= cmdUpperCase.Height _
            Then MakeUpperCase
End Sub


' Reverse the string.
Private Sub cmdReverse_Click()
    MakeReversed
End Sub


' Convert the text into lowercase.
Private Sub MakeLowerCase()
    txtValue.Text = LCase$(txtValue.Text)
End Sub


' Convert the text into uppercase.
Private Sub MakeUpperCase()
    txtValue.Text = UCase$(txtValue.Text)
End Sub


' Reverse the text.
Private Sub MakeReversed()
Dim new_text As String
Dim old_text As String

    old_text - txtValue.Text
    Do While Len(old_text) > 0
        new_text = Left$(old_text, 1) & new_text
        old_text = Mid$(old_text, 2)
    Loop
    txtValue.Text = new_text
End Sub
```

96. Use a ProgressBar

Directory: ProgBar

A program can use a ProgressBar control to keep the user informed while a long process runs. The ProgressBar control displays a box that it fills with colored rectangles to indicate the program's progress. While the control itself is relatively simple, using it is a little harder.

Example program ProgBar performs a long task. Click the Start button to begin the long process. The program displays its progress in a new form. Click the Stop button on the progress form to stop the process before it finishes. Then click the button again to close the form.

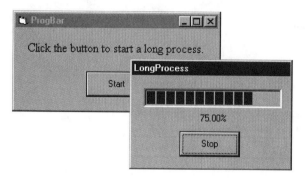

Program ProgBar.

How It Works

The following code shows how program ProgBar runs a long process. When you press the Start button, the main form simply displays the LongProcessForm. That form contains all of the program's interesting code, so only the ProgBar code is shown here.

When the process form loads, it uses the Show statement to make itself visible. It sets the form variable Running to True to indicate that the long process should run. It then calls subroutine RunLongProcess to run the long process. When RunLongProcess finishes, the Form_Load event handler changes its button's caption to Close. The button may have been disabled by code described later, so it also reenables the button.

The form's button checks the Running variable to see if the long process is still running. If it is, the button sets Running to False to stop it. It sets its caption to Stopping and disables itself. This lets the user know that the process will stop soon. If the long process is already stopped when the button is clicked, the button unloads the form.

Subroutine RunLongProcess simulates a long task. It performs 20 steps, each taking roughly a quarter second. Each time it performs one step, the program updates the ProgressBar and executes DoEvents. Calling DoEvents is important because it makes the ProgressBar update itself so the user can see the new display.

RunLongProcess then checks the value of the Running variable. If Running has been set to False, the user wants to cancel the process, so the routine exits the For loop controlling the 20 steps.

```
Option Explicit

' Indicates whether the long process is running.
Private Running As Boolean

' When the form loads, start the long process.
Private Sub Form_Load()
```

```
    ' Display the form.
    Show
    DoEvents

    ' Run the process.
    Running = True
    RunLongProcess

    ' The process is finished. Let the user close
    ' the form.
    Running = False
    cmdStop.Caption = "Close"
    cmdStop.Enabled = True
End Sub

' If the process is still running, stop it.
' Otherwise unload the form.
Private Sub cmdStop_Click()
    If Running Then
        ' Tell the process to stop.
        Running = False

        ' Disable the stop button.
        cmdStop.Caption = "Stopping"
        cmdStop.Enabled = False
        DoEvents
    Else
        ' Unload the form.
        Unload Me
    End If
End Sub

' Run a long process updating the status bar.
Private Sub RunLongProcess()
Dim progress As Integer
Dim stop_time As Single
Dim progress_value As Single

    ' Perform 20 steps of work.
    For progress = 1 To 20
        ' Waste about 1/4 second at each step.
        stop_time = Timer + 0.25
        Do While Timer < stop_time
            DoEvents
        Loop

        ' Update the status display.
        progress_value = progress / 20
        lblProgress.Caption = Format$(progress_value, "Percent")
        pbarLongProcess.Value = progress_value * 100
```

```
            ' Perform DoEvents to update the progress
            ' bar. This also lets the program handle
            ' the Stop button click.
            DoEvents

            ' If the user wants to stop, stop.
            If Not Running Then Exit For
        Next progress
    End Sub
```

Other programs that use a ProgressBar control follow a similar pattern. Every time it finishes a step in a long calculation, the program updates the ProgressBar. For a process that the user can interrupt, this is also a natural place to stop execution early.

97. Use a StatusBar

☆ ☆
④ ⑤ ⑥

Directory: StatBar

As the previous section explains, a ProgressBar keeps the user informed while a long process runs. A StatusBar can also provide feedback on what the program is doing.

Example program StatBar displays information in a StatusBar control. Click on one of the option buttons to make the program display the corresponding picture and text in its status bar.

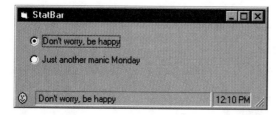

Program StatBar.

How It Works

The StatusBar control contains a collection of Panel objects. Each Panel object represents one of the StatusBar's panels. At design time, you can right-click on the StatusBar control and select the Properties command to see the control's property pages. The Panel tab lets you set the panels' properties. You can also use the StatusBar's Panels collection to manipulate the panels at run time.

The following code shows how program StatBar manages its panels. The StatusBar's three panels were created at design time using the property page dialog. The program's Form_Load event handler saves references to the panels and initializes their properties.

Form_Load sets the first panel's Picture property to the picture contained in an image control on the form. It gives the panel no bevel, sets its minimum allowed width to 10 twips, and indicates that it should resize itself to fit its contents.

The routine sets the second panel's AutoSize property to sbrSpring. That makes it take up any space that is left over by the other panels.

Form_Load sets the third panel's minimum width to 10 twips and sets AutoSize to sbr-Contents so the panel resizes to fit its contents. Finally, Form_Load sets the panel's Style property to sbrTime to make it automatically display the system time. The program does not need to do anything else to display the time.

The only other piece of code in the program is the event handler for the program's two option buttons. The optHappiness_Click subroutine sets the first panel's Picture property and the second panel's Text property so they show values that correspond to the option button selected.

```
Option Explicit

' Status bar panels.
Private PicturePanel As Panel
Private TextPanel As Panel

' Prepare the panels.
Private Sub Form_Load()
Dim time_panel As Panel

    ' Put a picture in the first panel.
    Set PicturePanel = sbrStatus.Panels(1)
    Set PicturePanel.Picture = imgHappiness(0).Picture
    PicturePanel.Bevel = sbrNoBevel
    PicturePanel.MinWidth = 10
    PicturePanel.AutoSize = sbrContents

    ' Blank the second panel.
    Set TextPanel = sbrStatus.Panels(2)
    TextPanel.AutoSize = sbrSpring
    TextPanel.Text = ""

    ' Initialize the time panel.
    Set time_panel = sbrStatus.Panels(3)
    time_panel.MinWidth = 10
    time_panel.AutoSize = sbrContents
    time_panel.Style = sbrTime
End Sub

' Display the correct picture and text.
Private Sub optHappiness_Click(Index As Integer)
    Set PicturePanel.Picture = imgHappiness(Index).Picture
    TextPanel.Text = optHappiness(Index).Caption
End Sub
```

98. Let the User Select a Font

Directory: PickFont

A program can use the Windows Common Dialog Control to allow the user to select a font. Example program PickFont lets you pick a font for a big Label control. Click the Pick Font button to make the font selection dialog appear. Select a font and click the OK button. The program then displays the font you selected.

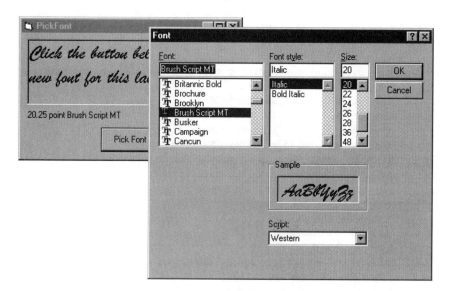

Program PickFont.

How It Works

The following code shows how program PickFont lets the user select a new font. The most interesting code is in the Pick Font button's Click event handler. It begins by setting properties for the Common Dialog Control dlgFont. The routine sets the CancelError property to True so that the dialog raises an error if the user cancels the dialog instead of clicking OK. It sets the Flags property to CF_SCREENFONTS to make the dialog list fonts that are available on the computer's screen. See the online help for other Flag values. The routine next sets the properties that describe the Label control's current font.

The button's event handler then displays the dialog by invoking its ShowFont method. It uses an On Error Resume Next statement to catch errors. Because the control's Cancel-Error property is True, the control will raise an error if the user cancels.

After the ShowFont method returns, the subroutine checks the Err object's Number property to see if an error occurred. If Err.Number is CDERR_CANCEL, the user canceled the dialog. If Err.Number is some other nonzero value, an unexpected error occurred. Finally, if Err.Number is zero, no error occurred. In that case, the program uses the values selected by the user to set the Label control's font.

```
' Display the name of the initial font.
Private Sub Form_Load()
    SetFontNameLabel
End Sub

' Let the user select a new font.
Private Sub cmdPickFont_Click()
Const CF_SCREENFONTS = &H1
Const CDERR_CANCEL = 32755

    ' Prepare the common dialog control.
    dlgFont.CancelError = True
    dlgFont.Flags = CF_SCREENFONTS
    dlgFont.FontName = lblText.FontName
    dlgFont.FontBold = lblText.FontBold
    dlgFont.FontItalic = lblText.FontItalic
    dlgFont.FontStrikethru = lblText.FontStrikethru
    dlgFont.FontUnderline = lblText.FontUnderline
    dlgFont.FontSize = lblText.FontSize

    ' Display the dialog.
    On Error Resume Next
    dlgFont.ShowFont

    ' See if the user canceled.
    If Err.Number = CDERR_CANCEL Then
        ' The user canceled. Do nothing.
    ElseIf Err.Number > 0 Then
        ' There was an unexpected error.
        MsgBox "Error " & Err.Number & _
            " selecting font." & vbCrLf & _
            Err.Description
    Else
        ' Apply the font.
        lblText.FontName = dlgFont.FontName
        lblText.FontBold = dlgFont.FontBold
        lblText.FontItalic = dlgFont.FontItalic
        lblText.FontStrikethru = dlgFont.FontStrikethru
        lblText.FontUnderline = dlgFont.FontUnderline
        lblText.FontSize = dlgFont.FontSize

        ' Display the font's name.
        SetFontNameLabel
    End If
End Sub
```

```
' Display the font's name and size.
Private Sub SetFontNameLabel()
    lblFontName.Caption = _
        Format$(lblText.Font.Size) & " point " & _
        lblText.Font.Name
End Sub
```

99. Let the User Select a File

☆ ☆
④ ⑤ ⑥

Directory: PickFile

A program can also use the Windows Common Dialog Control to let the user select a file. Example program PickFile lets you select a file. Click the Pick File button to make the file selection dialog appear. Select a file, and click the OK button. The program reads the file and displays its contents in a TextBox.

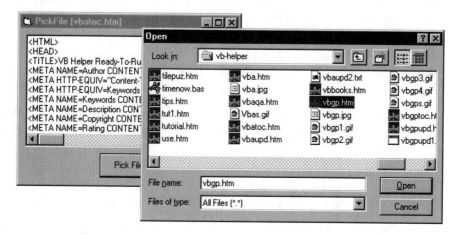

Program PickFile.

How It Works

The following code shows how program PickFile lets the user select a file. The program's Form_Load event handler performs one-time initialization of the Common Dialog Control. It uses the App.Path statement to set the dialog's InitDir property to be the program's current path. That makes the dialog begin searching for files in the program's current directory.

Form_Load also sets the control's Filter property. This is a list of the filter descriptions and filter values that the dialog should display, separated by vertical bar characters. Program PickFile uses the three filters listed in Table 11.1. To provide those values, the program gives the control the following Filter property value:

```
Text Files (*.txt)|*.txt|Data Files (*.dat)|*.dat|All Files (*.*)|*.*
```

Table 11.1   Filters Used by Program PickFile

DESCRIPTION	VALUE
Text Files (*.txt)	*.txt
Data Files (*.dat)	*.dat
All Files (*.*)	*.*

Note that the descriptions must include the values of the filters if you want the user to see them. For instance, if the description for data files did not include the text (*.dat), the user would not necessarily know that the program is looking for data files with a .dat extension.

The program's most interesting code lies in its cmdPickFile_Click event handler. It begins by setting properties for the Common Dialog Control. The routine sets the CancelError property to True to make the dialog raise an error if the user cancels the dialog instead of clicking OK. It sets the Flags property to OFN_FILEMUSTEXIST + OFN_HIDEREADONLY. The first value makes the dialog accept only files that actually exist. Without this flag, the control would allow the user to type in the name of a nonexistent file. The second flag hides the read-only check box that is normally displayed on the dialog. See the online help for other Flag values.

The button's event handler then invokes the control's ShowOpen method to display a file open dialog. The ShowSave method is similar except it opens a dialog that is appropriate for saving a file instead of loading one.

The program uses an On Error Resume Next statement to catch errors. Because the control's CancelError property is True, the control will raise an error if the user cancels the dialog.

After the ShowOpen method returns, the subroutine checks the Err object's Number property to see if an error occurred. If Err.Number is CDERR_CANCEL, the user canceled the dialog. If Err.Number is some other nonzero value, an unexpected error occurred.

If Err.Number is zero, no error occurred. In that case, the dialog's FileName property contains the name and path of the file the user selected. The FileTitle property contains the name of the file without its path. The program opens and reads the file named by the FileName property. It updates the form's caption to include the value in the FileTitle property so you can see what file is loaded.

The program strips the file's title from the right end of the file's name to find the directory that holds the file. It sets the dialog's InitDir property to this directory. The next time you click the Pick File button, the file selection dialog begins its search in this directory.

```
Option Explicit

' Set initial values for the dialog.
Private Sub Form_Load()
    dlgFile.InitDir = App.Path & "\"
    dlgFile.Filter = _
        "Text Files (*.txt)|*.txt|Data Files (*.dat)|*.dat|" & _
```

```
                "All Files (*.*)|*.*"
    End Sub


    ' Let the user select a file.
    Private Sub cmdPickFile_Click()
    Const CDERR_CANCEL = 32755
    Const OFN_FILEMUSTEXIST = &H1000
    Const OFN_HIDEREADONLY = &H4

    Dim fnum As Integer

        ' Prepare the common dialog control.
        dlgFile.CancelError = True
        dlgFile.Flags = OFN_FILEMUSTEXIST + OFN_HIDEREADONLY

        ' Display the dialog.
        On Error Resume Next
        dlgFile.ShowOpen

        ' See if the user canceled.
        If Err.Number = CDERR_CANCEL Then
            ' The user canceled. Do nothing.
        ElseIf Err.Number > 0 Then
            ' There was an unexpected error.
            MsgBox "Error " & Err.Number & _
                " selecting file." & vbCrLf & _
                Err.Description
        Else
            ' Open and read the file.
            fnum = FreeFile
            Open dlgFile.FileName For Input As fnum
            txtFileContents = Input$(LOF(fnum), fnum)
            Close fnum

            ' Display the file title.
            Caption = "PickFile [" & _
                dlgFile.FileTitle & "]"

            ' Strip the file title off the file name and use
            ' the result as the initial directory next time.
            dlgFile.InitDir = Left$(dlgFile.FileName, _
                Len(dlgFile.FileName) - Len(dlgFile.FileTitle))
        End If
    End Sub
```

Updating the dialog's InitDir property makes it easier for users to work in a single directory. The program begins looking for files where the user selected the previous file so the user does not need to navigate to the directory again.

Some programs use more than one initial directory for different kinds of files or for different file operations. For instance, the program might use separate Common Dialog

Controls for opening and saving files. The two dialogs would manage their initial directories separately. This would minimize the navigation required if the user frequently loads files in one directory and saves them in another.

☆ ☆
④ ⑤ ⑥

100. Use Tabs

Directory: TabStrip

One way to conserve space on a crowded screen is to place different sets of information in tabs. The user clicks on a tab to see the corresponding information. Example program TabStrip uses three tabs to display information. Click on the tabs to see personal, home address, and work address information.

Program TabStrip.

How It Works

Microsoft's TabStrip control provides a series of tabs. When the user clicks on a tab, the control moves that tab to the top, and it raises a Click event. However, the control does not display any controls for that tab. The program must provide code for hiding and displaying the tabs' contents.

The easiest way to manage the tab contents is to place a control array of container controls over the TabStrip control. The containers are usually PictureBox or Frame controls. Each container holds the controls that should be displayed for one tab. When the user clicks on a TabStrip tab, the program hides the previously displayed tab container and makes the newly selected container visible.

The following code shows how program TabStrip does this. When the program starts, the Form_Load event handler makes some initial adjustments to the picTab container controls. First, it calculates the dimensions the containers should have to fill the inside of the TabStrip control. It then hides the containers, removes their borders, and places them all on top of the TabStrip. It uses the Add method provided by the TabStrip control's Tabs collection to create one tab for each container. It uses the captions in the corresponding lblTabTitle Label controls to name the tabs.

These steps make designing the form easier. You could position the controls and set their BorderStyle and Visible properties at design time, but that would make it harder to tell the containers apart at design time. Note also that the lblTabTitle controls used to name the tabs have Visible properties set to False. They are used only to name the tabs and to identify the containers at design time, so they should be hidden from the user. Because the controls are positioned at run time, you can leave them spread out so that you can see them all at design time.

When the user clicks on a tab, the tabInformation_Click event handler executes. This routine first determines whether the tab clicked is already visible. If it is, the subroutine exits. If the clicked tab is not already selected, the subroutine hides the previously selected tab container and makes the new one visible.

```
Option Explicit

' The index of the selected tab.
Private SelectedTab As Integer

' Arrange the tab controls.
Private Sub Form_Load()
Dim l As Single
Dim t As Single
Dim w As Single
Dim h As Single
Dim i As Integer

    ' Calculate the tab PictureBox positions.
    l = tabInformation.Left + 30
    t = tabInformation.Top + 330
    w = tabInformation.Width - 80
    h = tabInformation.Height - 380

    ' Hide the tabs, remove their borders, and
    ' position them.
    For i = 0 To picTab.ubound
        picTab(i).Visible = False
        picTab(i).BorderStyle = vbBSNone
        picTab(i).Move l, t, w, h
    Next i

    ' Create one tab per PictureBox. Use the
    ' PictureBox's Tag property for the title.
    tabInformation.Tabs.Clear
    For i = 0 To picTab.ubound
        tabInformation.Tabs.Add , , lblTabTitle(i).Caption
    Next i
```

```
    ' Create some test data.
    MakeData

    ' Display the first tab.
    picTab(SelectedTab).Visible = True
End Sub

' Display the correct tab PictureBox.
Private Sub tabInformation_Click()
Dim selected_tab As Integer

    ' If this tab is already selected, do nothing.
    selected_tab = tabInformation.SelectedItem.Index - 1
    If selected_tab = SelectedTab Then Exit Sub

    ' Hide the previously selected tab.
    picTab(SelectedTab).Visible = False

    ' Display the newly selected tab.
    SelectedTab = selected_tab
    picTab(SelectedTab).Visible = True
End Sub
```

☆

101. Use Buttons with Pictures ⑤ ⑥

Directory: PicBtn

Starting with Visual Basic 5, CommandButtons in Visual Basic programs can display pictures. The PicBtn example program displays a picture in a CommandButton.

Program PicBtn.

How It Works

Using a picture in a CommandButton is not hard. Simply assign the button's Picture property to the picture it should display. Then set the button's Style property to 1 - Graphical. This step is forgotten by many who have not displayed pictures on buttons before. If you do not set the button's Style to Graphical, the button ignores its Picture property.

☆ ☆
⑤ ⑥

102. Make a Highlighting Control

Directory: HilitCtl

Using a control's MouseMove event handler, you can make a control highlight itself when the mouse is over it. Unfortunately, making the control unhighlight itself when the mouse leaves is a little harder because the control does not receive a MouseLeaving event.

You can solve this problem using a Timer. The Timer periodically checks the mouse position to see if it is still over the control. You can do this in a normal Visual Basic program. If you have many such controls, however, you need to keep track of a lot of tedious code. In Visual Basic 5 and 6, you can hide some of the complexity by creating an ActiveX control that highlights itself when the mouse is over it.

The HighlightLabel ActiveX control uses this approach. Program TestCtl demonstrates the control. While the mouse is over one of the program's HighlightLabel controls, the control makes itself bold and red.

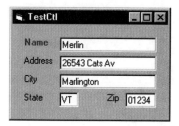

Program TestCtl.

How It Works

The HighlightLabel control used by program TestCtl has two main tasks: to highlight when the mouse is over it and to unhighlight when the mouse moves elsewhere. The HighlightLabel control contains a normal Label control named lblHighlight. That control's MouseMove event handler triggers when the mouse moves over the label. This routine checks to see if the control is already highlighted and, if it is, it does nothing. If the control is not already highlighted, the routine sets the label control's ForeColor and Font.Bold properties to highlight it.

Unhighlighting the control when the mouse leaves it is a little harder because the control does not receive an event telling it that the mouse has left. To solve this problem, the HighlightLabel control uses a Timer control. When the MouseMove event handler highlights the control, it also enables the Timer. Every tenth of a second, the Timer fires its Timer event handler. This routine uses the GetCursorPos API function to see where the mouse currently lies. It then uses ScreenToClient to translate the screen coordinates returned by GetCursorPos into the same coordinates used by the ActiveX control. The routine compares those coordinates to the control's position to see if the mouse is still over the label. If it is not, the routine unhighlights the control and disables the Timer.

The last interesting piece of code used by the HighlightLabel control is its Enabled property let routine. The control's Enabled property indicates whether it should highlight itself when the mouse is over it. When the value of Enabled changes, the Enabled property let procedure determines whether the mouse is currently over the control and updates the control accordingly.

The following code shows the most interesting parts of the HighlightLabel control's code. Many of the details of creating an ActiveX control have been omitted. For more information about custom control creation, see a book about ActiveX controls such as *Custom Controls Library* by Rod Stephens (John Wiley & Sons, 1998).

```vb
Option Explicit

Private highlighted As Boolean

Private Type POINTAPI
    X As Long
    Y As Long
End Type

Private Declare Function ScreenToClient Lib "user32" ( _
    ByVal hwnd As Long, lpPoint As POINTAPI) As Long
Private Declare Function GetCursorPos Lib "user32" ( _
    lpPoint As POINTAPI) As Long
        :
    <Code omitted>
        :
' The mouse is over the control. Highlight it.
Private Sub lblHighlight_MouseMove(Button As Integer, _
    Shift As Integer, X As Single, Y As Single)

    ' If highlighting is turned off or it's
    ' already highlighted, do nothing.
    If highlighted Or (Not m_Enabled) Then Exit Sub

    highlighted = True
    lblHighlight.ForeColor = m_HighlightColor
    lblHighlight.Font.Bold = True
    tmrHighlight.Enabled = True
End Sub

Private Sub tmrHighlight_Timer()
Dim pt As POINTAPI

    ' See where the cursor is.
    GetCursorPos pt

    ' Translate into window coordinates.
    ScreenToClient hwnd, pt
```

```
        ' See if we're still within the control.
        If pt.X < lblHighlight.Left Or pt.Y < lblHighlight.Top Or _
            pt.X > lblHighlight.Left + lblHighlight.Width Or _
            pt.Y > lblHighlight.Top + lblHighlight.Height _
        Then
            highlighted = False
            lblHighlight.ForeColor = vbBlack
            lblHighlight.Font.Bold = False
            tmrHighlight.Enabled = False
        End If
    End Sub


Public Property Let Enabled(ByVal New_Enabled As Boolean)
Dim pt As POINTAPI

    m_Enabled = New_Enabled
    PropertyChanged "Enabled"

    ' See if we need to change the highlighting.
    If m_Enabled Then
        ' If we are enabled, see if we should be disabled.
        ' See where the cursor is.
        GetCursorPos pt

        ' Translate into window coordinates.
        ScreenToClient hwnd, pt

        ' See if we're above the control.
        If Not ( _
            pt.X < lblHighlight.Left Or pt.Y < lblHighlight.Top Or _
            pt.X > lblHighlight.Left + lblHighlight.Width Or _
            pt.Y > lblHighlight.Top + lblHighlight.Height) _
        Then
            ' Pretend the mouse moved over us.
            lblHighlight_MouseMove 0, 0, 0, 0
        End If
    Else
        ' If we are disabled and currently
        ' highlighted, unhighlight.
        If highlighted Then
            highlighted = False
            lblHighlight.ForeColor = m_ForeColor
            lblHighlight.Font.Bold = False
            tmrHighlight.Enabled = False
        End If
    End If
End Property
```

CHAPTER 12

Managing Controls

Previous chapters explained ways of using specific kinds of controls. This chapter describes ways to manage controls in general. It covers such topics as using control arrays, creating controls at run time, enabling and disabling controls in a group, and using accelerators.

103. Learn Control Array Bounds

Directory: ArBounds

Many Visual Basic programmers are unaware that control arrays have LBound and UBound properties that give their lower and upper bounds. For instance, txtArray.UBound is the upper bound of the array of controls named txtArray. Example program ArBounds uses these properties to enter values in an array of TextBoxes.

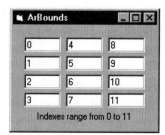

Program ArBounds.

How It Works

The array of TextBox controls used by ArBounds was created at design time. To build a similar array, create a TextBox and give it the txtNewArray. Select it, and press Ctrl-C to copy it. Then press Ctrl-V to paste a copy of the control onto the form. When Visual Basic asks if you want to create a control array, answer Yes. Visual Basic will give the first control an Index property value of 0 and the second control an Index value of 1. The program can refer to the controls as txtNewArray(0) and txtNewArray(1). You can now copy and paste as many controls as you like.

The following code shows how program ArBounds fills in the TextBox's values when it runs. The program uses the control array's LBound and UBound properties to determine the range of index values it must consider.

```
' Fill in the TextBox's values and display the
' lower and upper bounds of the control array.
Private Sub Form_Load()
Dim i As Integer

    For i = txtArray.LBound To txtArray.UBound
        txtArray(i).Text = Format$(i)
    Next i

    lblIndexes.Caption = "Indexes range from " & _
        Format$(txtArray.LBound) & " to " & _
        Format$(txtArray.UBound)
End Sub
```

A program can use LBound and UBound to avoid the need to keep track of the number of controls in a control array. For instance, suppose an expense report program allows the user to enter expense items in a control array of 20 TextBoxes. If you hard-code the indexes 0 through 19 into the program, you must change the value 19 if you later decide to change the number of TextBoxes. On the other hand, if the program uses the LBound and UBound properties to determine the range of indexes, the code will continue to work even if you add or remove controls at design time.

Note that the LBound and UBound properties do not tell the program whether every index between the bounds is present. For instance, the controls in a control array could have indexes 3, 4, and 6. In that case, LBound is 3 and UBound is 6. This does not tell the program that there is no control having index 5. To discover this fact, the program must try to access the controls. It can use an On Error statement to protect itself in case one of the indexes is unused.

104. Create Controls at Run Time Using Load ④ ⑤ ⑥

Directory: LoadCtl

You can add controls to a form at design time using Visual Basic's integrated development environment. You can also add new controls to a form at run time using control arrays. To do this, you must create a control array containing at least one control at design time. The easiest way to create a control array with one item is to place a control on the form and set its Index property to 0.

At run time, the program can use the Load statement to create new instances of the control array. For example, the following statement creates a new control in the lblNames control array with the index 12.

```
Load lblNames(12)
```

When the program creates a new control, the control's Visible property is initially False. That gives the program a chance to change the control's position and other properties before it becomes visible.

A program can use the Unload statement to remove a control it created earlier using Load. It cannot remove controls created at design time.

Example program LoadCtl demonstrates control creation and destruction. Click the Add button to create a new TextBox. Click Delete to remove the most recently created TextBox. Because the program can delete only those controls it created previously using the Load statement, it will not let you unload the first control.

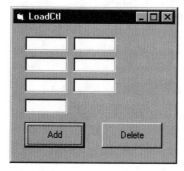

Program LoadCtl.

How It Works

The following code shows how program LoadCtl works. The Add button's event handler uses the UBound property to find the largest index currently in the txtControl control array. It uses the Load statement to create a control with the next larger Index value. The rest of the code in this routine positions the new control and makes it visible.

The Delete button's event handler uses UBound to find the index of the last control in the txtControl control array. If this index is 0, the corresponding control is the one that was created at design time. That control cannot be unloaded, so the event handler exits. If the largest index value is greater than 0, the routine uses the Unload statement to unload the control.

```vb
' Create a new control.
Private Sub cmdAdd_Click()
Dim new_index As Integer
Dim t As Single
Dim l As Single
Dim wid As Single
Dim hgt As Single

    ' Create the new control.
    new_index = txtControl.UBound + 1
    Load txtControl(new_index)

    ' Calculate the control's new position.
    hgt = txtControl(new_index - 1).Height
    wid = txtControl(new_index - 1).Width
    l = txtControl(new_index - 1).Left
    t = txtControl(new_index - 1).Top + hgt + 120
    If t + hgt + 120 >= cmdAdd.Top Then
        t = txtControl(0).Top
        l = l + wid + 120
    End If

    ' Position the new control and display it.
    txtControl(new_index).Move l, t
    txtControl(new_index).Visible = True
End Sub

' Delete the last control added.
Private Sub cmdDelete_Click()
Dim last_index As Integer

    ' Delete the last control.
    last_index = txtControl.UBound
    If last_index > 0 Then Unload txtControl(last_index)
End Sub
```

105. Create Controls at Run Time in Visual Basic 6   ⑥

Directory: LoadCtl2

In Visual Basic 4, 5, and 6, a program can add and remove controls in a control array at run time using the Load and Unload statements. In Visual Basic 6, a program can also create and remove controls completely from scratch using the Control collection's Add and Remove methods.

Example program LoadCtl2 shows how to use this technique. Click the Add button to create a new TextBox. Click Delete to remove the most recently created TextBox. The first TextBox in the program LoadCtl described in the previous section was created at design time so that program could not remove it. All of the TextBoxes created by program LoadCtl2 are created at run time so you can remove them all.

Program LoadCtl2.

How It Works

The following code shows how program LoadCtl2 works. The program uses an array to hold the TextBoxes it creates. The Add button's event handler uses the Controls collection's Add method to create a new control. Most of the code sizes and positions the new control.

The Delete button's event handler uses the Controls collection's Remove method to remove the most recently created TextBox. The routine uses the control's name as a key to identify it to the Remove method.

```
Option Explicit

Private Boxes() As TextBox
Private NumBoxes As Integer

' Create a new control.
Private Sub cmdAdd_Click()
```

```
Dim cmd_name As String
Dim t As Single
Dim l As Single
Dim wid As Single
Dim hgt As Single

    ' Create the new control.
    NumBoxes = NumBoxes + 1
    ReDim Preserve Boxes(1 To NumBoxes)
    cmd_name = "cmd" & Format$(NumBoxes)
    Set Boxes(NumBoxes) = _
        Controls.Add("VB.TextBox", cmd_name)

    ' Calculate the control's size and position.
    hgt = 285
    wid = 855
    If NumBoxes = 1 Then
        ' This is the first button.
        l = 240
        t = 240
    Else
        ' Position relative to the last button.
        l = Boxes(NumBoxes - 1).Left
        t = Boxes(NumBoxes - 1).Top + hgt + 120
    End If
    If t + hgt + 120 >= cmdAdd.Top Then
        t = 240
        l = l + wid + 120
    End If

    ' Position the new control and display it.
    Boxes(NumBoxes).Move l, t, wid, hgt
    Boxes(NumBoxes).Visible = True
End Sub


' Delete the last button.
Private Sub cmdDelete_Click()
Dim cmd_name As String

    ' Delete the last control.
    If NumBoxes > 0 Then
        cmd_name = "cmd" & Format$(NumBoxes)
        Controls.Remove cmd_name
        NumBoxes = NumBoxes - 1
    End If
End Sub
```

| 106. | **Enable the Controls in a Container** | ④ ⑤ ⑥ |

Directory: Enable

PictureBoxes and Frames are controls that can contain other controls. By examining the Container property for controls in a form's Controls collection, a program can identify the controls contained in a PictureBox or Frame.

Example program Enable uses this fact to enable and disable all of the controls within a frame. Click on the CheckBoxes at the bottom of the form to enable or disable the controls inside the corresponding Frame.

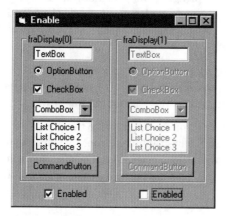

Program Enable.

How It Works

The key to program Enable is the SetContainerEnabled subroutine shown in the following code. This routine examines all of the controls on the form. It compares each control's Container property to the container passed into the routine. If the control lies within the container, the routine enables or disables the control.

```
' Enable or disable the controls within this container.
Private Sub SetContainerEnabled(ByVal container_ctl As Control, _
    ByVal is_enabled As Boolean)
Dim ctl As Control

    For Each ctl In Controls
        ' If this control lies inside the container,
        ' enable or disable it.
        If ctl.Container Is container_ctl Then
            ctl.Enabled = is_enabled
        End If
    Next ctl
End Sub
```

107. Use Accelerators

Directory: Accel

Keyboard accelerators allow you to use a program more easily without using a mouse. A control indicates that it has an accelerator with an underscored character. For instance, the underscored O on a button labeled <u>O</u>pen indicates that the button's accelerator is an O. You can press Alt-O to make the button trigger as if you had clicked on it with the mouse.

Example program Accel uses accelerators for its menu items, labels, and buttons. Press and release the Alt key to move focus to the program's main menu. You can then press the Escape key to move focus back to the form. You can also use the arrow keys or the menu accelerators to open the program's menus. Once a menu is open, selecting the accelerator for an item on the menu triggers that item.

While the menus are closed, you can trigger a command button by pressing Alt and the accelerator for the button. In program Accel, pressing Alt-O triggers the Open button. The Cancel button has no accelerator so you cannot trigger it in this way.

If you invoke the accelerator for a label control, focus passes to the next control in the tab sequence. In program Accel, TextBoxes have TabIndex property values one greater than their corresponding labels. If you press the accelerator for a label, focus moves to the next TextBox. For instance, if you press Alt-Z, focus moves to the Zip code TextBox.

Program Accel.

How It Works

Creating accelerators is simple. Just add the ampersand (&) character to the control's Caption property just before the character you want to use as an accelerator. For instance, the <u>O</u>pen button in program Accel has Caption property set to &Open. Visual Basic automatically converts the ampersand into an underscore.

If you want the control to display an ampersand instead of an underscored character, use two ampersands. For instance, to display &Open, set the control's Caption property to &&Open.

Generally, programs should use many accelerators. They are unobtrusive, and they can be quite useful. An experienced user can often manipulate a form much faster using the keyboard instead of the mouse.

Accelerators are also extremely useful when you want to manipulate one program with another. The controlling program can use SendKeys to send character sequences to the other application. Accelerators make moving to specific fields and triggering buttons quick and easy.

When you give a program accelerators, you should make them as unambiguous as possible. Avoid using the same accelerator for more than one control on a form or in the same menu. If the user invokes an accelerator that is used more than once, Visual Basic triggers the accelerator of the next control in the tab sequence. While this works, it can be confusing to the user. The program is simpler if each accelerator means only one thing no matter which control currently has the focus.

108. Save and Restore Control Values

Directory: SaveCtls

A program can save the contents of its controls when it unloads. It can then reload those values when it starts again. This lets a user continue working with the application as if it had never closed. Example program SaveCtls demonstrates this technique. Change the values of the controls, and then exit and restart the program. When the program restarts, the controls contain the values you entered before closing the program.

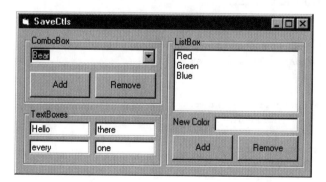

Program SaveCtls.

How It Works

The following code shows how program SaveCtls saves and restores control values. The program's Form_Unload routine calls subroutine SaveData when the form is closing. SaveData uses Visual Basic's Write statement to save the controls' values in a file.

The program's Form_Load routine calls subroutine LoadData when the form is first opened. LoadData uses Visual Basic's Input statement to read the controls' values from the previously saved file.

```
' Save the data for next time.
Private Sub Form_Unload(Cancel As Integer)
    SaveData
End Sub


' Load the data from last time.
Private Sub Form_Load()
    LoadData
End Sub


' Save the current data values into a file.
Private Sub SaveData()
Dim fnum As Integer
Dim txt As String
Dim num_items As Integer
Dim i As Integer

    ' Open the configuration file.
    On Error GoTo NoFile
    fnum = FreeFile
    Open App.Path & "\config.dat" For Output As fnum

    ' Save the cboAnimals data.
    ' Save the number of items.
    Write #fnum, cboAnimals.ListCount
    ' Save the items.
    For i = 0 To cboAnimals.ListCount - 1
        Write #fnum, cboAnimals.List(i)
    Next i
    ' Save the selected item's index.
    Write #fnum, cboAnimals.ListIndex

    ' Read the lstColors data.
    ' Save the number of items.
    Write #fnum, lstColors.ListCount
    ' Save the items.
    For i = 0 To lstColors.ListCount - 1
        Write #fnum, lstColors.List(i)
    Next i
```

```
        ' Save the text boxes.
        Write #fnum, Text1(0).Text
        Write #fnum, Text1(1).Text
        Write #fnum, Text1(2).Text
        Write #fnum, Text1(3).Text

        ' Close the file.
        Close fnum

NoFile:

End Sub

' Load previously saved data from the data file.
Private Sub LoadData()
Dim fnum As Integer
Dim txt As String
Dim num_items As Integer
Dim i As Integer
Dim selected_index As Integer
Dim is_selected As Integer

        ' Clear all controls.
        cboAnimals.Clear
        lstColors.Clear
        For i = 0 To 3
            Text1(i).Text = ""
        Next i

        ' Open the configuration file.
        On Error GoTo NoFile
        fnum = FreeFile
        Open App.Path & "\config.dat" For Input As fnum

        ' Read the cboAnimals data.
        ' Get the number of items.
        Input #fnum, num_items
        ' Get the items.
        For i = 0 To num_items - 1
            Input #fnum, txt
            cboAnimals.AddItem txt
        Next i
        ' Get the selected item index.
        Input #fnum, selected_index
        cboAnimals.ListIndex = selected_index

        ' Read the lstColors data.
        ' Get the number of items.
        Input #fnum, num_items
        ' Get the items.
        For i = 0 To num_items - 1
```

```
        Input #fnum, txt
        lstColors.AddItem txt
    Next i

    ' Get the text boxes.
    Input #fnum, txt
    Text1(0).Text = txt

    Input #fnum, txt
    Text1(1).Text = txt

    Input #fnum, txt
    Text1(2).Text = txt

    Input #fnum, txt
    Text1(3).Text = txt

    ' Close the file.
    Close fnum

NoFile:

End Sub
```

Note that the Input statements in LoadData must exactly match the Write statements in SaveData or the program will not read the saved values correctly.

Also note that the program calls SaveData only when the form is unloaded normally. If the program crashes or if you stop it using the End statement, the Form_Unload event handler does not execute so the data is not saved. If it is important that the data be saved, the program should save it whenever a value changes.

109. Manage Two-Dimensional Control Arrays ④ ⑤ ⑥

Directory: Ctls2D

Control arrays help you manage a group of related controls much as you would manage an array of any other data type. Unfortunately, control arrays are always one-dimensional. When the controls are arranged in rows and columns, a two-dimensional array would be easier to use.

Example program Ctls2D demonstrates a method for managing a two-dimensional array of controls. Run the program and click the ShowValues button to see a list of the controls' values displayed in rows and columns.

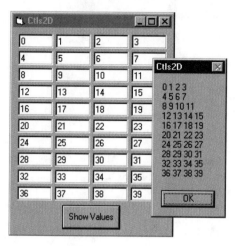

Program Ctls2D.

How It Works

The code that follows shows how program Ctls2D manages its controls. The program declares a two-dimensional array of controls named txtControls. The Form_Load event handler uses the Load statement to create the controls it needs. It saves a reference to each control in the txtControls array. Notice that it handles the first control slightly differently. Because that control is created at design time, Form_Load does not create it, but it does save a reference to that control.

When the user clicks the ShowValues button, the program's cmdShowValues_Click event handler uses the controls in the txtControls array just as if they were in a two-dimensional control array. It builds a list of the controls' values and displays the result in a message box.

```
Option Explicit

Private Const NUM_ROWS = 10
Private Const NUM_COLS = 4

Private txtControls(1 To NUM_ROWS, 1 To NUM_COLS) As TextBox

' Create the controls.
Private Sub Form_Load()
Const GAP = 60
Dim next_index As Integer
Dim X As Single
Dim Y As Single
Dim wid As Single
Dim hgt As Single
Dim r As Integer
Dim c As Integer
```

```vb
    ' Get the first control's position and size.
    wid = txtData(0).Width
    hgt = txtData(0).Height
    X = txtData(0).Left
    Y = txtData(0).Top - hgt - GAP

    ' Create the controls.
    next_index = 0
    For r = 1 To NUM_ROWS
        For c = 1 To NUM_COLS
            If next_index <> 0 Then
                ' If this is not control 0 (which
                ' already exists), load it.
                Load txtData(next_index)
            End If
            Set txtControls(r, c) = txtData(next_index)

            ' Position the control.
            If c = 1 Then
                ' Start a new row.
                X = txtData(0).Left
                Y = Y + hgt + GAP
            Else
                ' Continue this row.
                X = X + wid + GAP
            End If
            txtData(next_index).Move X, Y, wid, hgt
            txtData(next_index).Visible = True
            txtData(next_index).Text = Format$(next_index)
            next_index = next_index + 1
        Next c
    Next r
End Sub

' Show the values in the Debug window.
Private Sub cmdShowValues_Click()
Dim r As Integer
Dim c As Integer
Dim txt As String

    For r = 1 To NUM_ROWS
        For c = 1 To NUM_COLS
            txt = txt & txtControls(r, c).Text & " "
        Next c
        txt = txt & vbCrLf
    Next r
    MsgBox txt
End Sub
```

110. **Build a Splitter**

Directory: **Splitter**

Many Windows programs use a splitter or paned window to separate two form areas. By dragging on the sash between the areas, you can make one larger and the other smaller. Even though this interface has been common in Windows programs for years, Visual Basic does not come with a splitter control. Fortunately, you can build one yourself.

Example program Splitter divides its form into two areas. Click and drag the horizontal area between them to resize the two areas.

Program Splitter.

How It Works

The following code shows how program Splitter works. The program contains two PictureBox controls named picTop and picBottom. These controls occupy the entire form except for a narrow horizontal region between them. The form's MousePointer is set to 7 - Size N S so that it displays an up/down drag arrow when the mouse is over this exposed area.

When the user presses the mouse on the exposed area, the program's Form_Mouse-Down event handler executes. It sets the program's Dragging variable to True, indicating that the user is beginning to drag the splitter bar.

When the program receives a Form_MouseMove event, it first checks the Dragging variable. If Dragging is False, the user is moving the mouse across the exposed area but is not dragging, so the routine exits. If Dragging is True, the event handler calculates the percentage of the distance down the form where the mouse lies. It then invokes the Arrange-Controls subroutine to rearrange the picTop and picBottom controls for the new splitter bar position.

The program's Form_MouseUp event handler simply sets Dragging to False so that future MouseMove events do not make the program drag the splitter bar.

Subroutine ArrangeControls calculates new sizes for the picTop and picBottom controls. It makes picTop the correct height for the splitter bar's current position. It keeps picTop's height between certain minimum and maximum values so that it maintains a reasonable size. It then gives picBottom whatever area is left.

```vb
Option Explicit

Private Const SPLITTER_HEIGHT = 40

' The percentage occupied by the top PictureBox.
Private Percentage1 As Single

' True when we are dragging the splitter.
Private Dragging As Boolean

' Start with the split in the middle.
Private Sub Form_Load()
    Percentage1 = 0.5
End Sub

' Rearrange the splitter areas.
Private Sub Form_Resize()
    ArrangeControls
End Sub

' Start dragging the splitter.
Private Sub Form_MouseDown(Button As Integer, Shift As Integer, _
    X As Single, Y As Single)

    Dragging = True
End Sub

' Continue dragging the splitter.
Private Sub Form_MouseMove(Button As Integer, Shift As Integer, _
    X As Single, Y As Single)

    ' Do nothing if we're not dragging.
    If Not Dragging Then Exit Sub

    Percentage1 = Y / ScaleHeight
    If Percentage1 < 0 Then Percentage1 = 0
    If Percentage1 > 1 Then Percentage1 = 1
    ArrangeControls
End Sub

' Finish dragging the splitter.
Private Sub Form_MouseUp(Button As Integer, Shift As Integer, _
    X As Single, Y As Single)
```

```
        Dragging = False
    End Sub


    ' Arrange the controls on the form.
    Private Sub ArrangeControls()
    Const MIN_HGT1 = 375
    Const MAX_HGT1 = 2535
    Dim hgt1 As Single
    Dim hgt2 As Single

        ' Don't bother if we're iconized.
        If WindowState = vbMinimized Then Exit Sub

        hgt1 = (ScaleHeight - SPLITTER_HEIGHT) * Percentage1
        If hgt1 < MIN_HGT1 Then hgt1 = MIN_HGT1
        If hgt1 > MAX_HGT1 Then hgt1 = MAX_HGT1
        picTop.Move 0, 0, ScaleWidth, hgt1

        hgt2 = (ScaleHeight - SPLITTER_HEIGHT) - hgt1
        picBottom.Move 0, hgt1 + SPLITTER_HEIGHT, ScaleWidth, hgt2
    End Sub
```

This program handles only two vertically arranged splitter areas. You can extend this technique for horizontal splitters and splitters where each area has minimum and maximum sizes. The book *Custom Controls Library* by Rod Stephens (John Wiley & Sons, 1998) shows how to implement some of these improvements in an ActiveX control.

111. Build a Scrolled Window

Directory: Scroller

Many Windows programs use scrolled windows to display objects that are too big to fit on a form all at once. Scroll bars let the user see different parts of the larger object. Even though this interface has been common for many years, Visual Basic does not come with a scrolled window control. Fortunately, you can implement this feature yourself.

Example program Scroller displays a large picture. Resize the form so that the image does not fit vertically, horizontally, or both. Then use the scroll bars to see different parts of the image.

Program Scroller.

How It Works

Program Scroller contains four controls: a vertical scroll bar, a horizontal scroll bar, a PictureBox named picInner, and a PictureBox named picOuter. The picInner control holds the program's picture and is contained within picOuter. The program makes the picture scroll by moving picInner within picOuter. For instance, to display the right portions of the picture, the program moves picInner to the left. The picture is automatically clipped by picOuter so that only those portions that should be visible are shown.

The following code shows how program Scroller manages its controls to produce the scrolling effect. The program's Form_Resize event handler determines how much space the picture needs and how much space is available on the form. Using those values, it determines which scroll bars it needs. For instance, if the form is tall and thin, the program may need only the horizontal scroll bar. After it knows which scroll bars it needs, Form_Resize arranges the picOuter control and the scroll bars. It calls subroutine SetScrollBars to set the scroll bars' properties.

Subroutine SetScrollBars sets each scroll bar's Min property to 0 and its Max property to the difference between the space available and the space required. If the scroll bar is necessary, the space available will be less than the space required and the Max value will be negative. As the user moves the scroll bars, their values indicate the Left and Top properties for picInner within picOuter.

For instance, suppose the picture is 100 units wide and the picOuter control has a ScaleWidth property of 90. Then the horizontal scroll bar's Max property value is 90 – 100 = –10. As the user manipulates the scroll bar, it takes values between 0 and –10. The program sets picInner's Left property to this value, making the picture move from 0 to 10 units to the left. When the Left property is –10, the right edge of the picture will be visible at the right edge of picOuter.

Subroutine SetScrollBars sets the scroll bar's LargeChange property to the picOuter's ScaleWidth value. That makes the control move the picture by the size of picOuter whenever the user clicks on the area between a scroll bar's arrow and its draggable thumb. SetScrollBars sets the scroll bar's SmallChange property to one-fifth this distance. When the user clicks on a scroll bar's arrow, the picture moves one-fifth of picOuter's size.

```
' Position the controls.
Private Sub Form_Resize()
Dim got_wid As Single
Dim got_hgt As Single
Dim need_wid As Single
Dim need_hgt As Single
Dim need_hbar As Boolean
Dim need_vbar As Boolean

    If WindowState = vbMinimized Then Exit Sub

    need_wid = picInner.Width + _
        (picOuter.Width - picOuter.ScaleWidth)
    need_hgt = picInner.Height + _
        (picOuter.Height - picOuter.ScaleHeight)
    got_wid = ScaleWidth
    got_hgt = ScaleHeight

    ' See which scroll bars we need.
    need_hbar = (need_wid > got_wid)
    If need_hbar Then got_hgt = got_hgt - hbarScroller.Height

    need_vbar = (need_hgt > got_hgt)
    If need_vbar Then
        got_wid = got_wid - vbarScroller.Width
        If Not need_hbar Then
            need_hbar = (need_wid > got_wid)
            If need_hbar Then got_hgt = got_hgt - hbarScroller.Height
        End If
    End If

    picOuter.Move 0, 0, got_wid, got_hgt

    If need_hbar Then
        hbarScroller.Move 0, got_hgt, got_wid
        hbarScroller.Visible = True
    Else
        hbarScroller.Visible = False
    End If

    If need_vbar Then
        vbarScroller.Move got_wid, 0, vbarScroller.Width, got_hgt
        vbarScroller.Visible = True
    Else
        vbarScroller.Visible = False
    End If

    ' Set the scroll bar properties.
    SetScrollBars
End Sub
```

```vb
' Set scroll bar properties.
Private Sub SetScrollBars()
    vbarScroller.Min = 0
    vbarScroller.Max = picOuter.ScaleHeight - picInner.Height
    vbarScroller.LargeChange = picOuter.ScaleHeight
    vbarScroller.SmallChange = picOuter.ScaleHeight / 5

    hbarScroller.Min = 0
    hbarScroller.Max = picOuter.ScaleWidth - picInner.Width
    hbarScroller.LargeChange = picOuter.ScaleWidth
    hbarScroller.SmallChange = picOuter.ScaleWidth / 5
End Sub

' Move picInner.
Private Sub vbarScroller_Change()
    picInner.Top = vbarScroller.Value
End Sub

' Move picInner.
Private Sub vbarScroller_Scroll()
    picInner.Top = vbarScroller.Value
End Sub

' Move picInner.
Private Sub hbarScroller_Change()
    picInner.Left = hbarScroller.Value
End Sub

' Move picInner.
Private Sub hbarScroller_Scroll()
    picInner.Left = hbarScroller.Value
End Sub
```

13

Generating Graphics

Forms and PictureBoxes allow a program to display complex graphics. This chapter explains several useful graphics programming techniques such as creating a color gradient, tiling a form with repeating copies of a picture, and allowing the user to select a region using a rubberband box.

Note that several of the programs described in this chapter assume your computer is using more than 256 colors. If it is using 256-color mode, the results may be strange. Areas that should be smoothly shaded may instead be filled with wide bands of distinct colors. If you want the examples to run correctly, you must switch to a higher color resolution.

To change color modes in Windows 95, open the Control Panel's Display tool and select the Settings tab. In the Color Palette list box, select the color mode you want to use, and click the OK button. You must reboot your system before the new values take effect. The Display tool gives you the option to reboot immediately or later.

To change color modes in Windows NT, open the Control Panel's Display tool and select the Settings tab. In the Color Palette list box, select the color mode you want to use, and click the Test button. When the test runs, you should see very smooth red, green, blue, and test gray gradients. If you do, answer Yes when the test asks if you saw the correct result. If the colors appear in broad bands, answer No. Back in the Display tool, click OK, and your screen will darken briefly. When it comes back, you will be running the new color mode.

112. Separate Colors

Directory: UnRGB

Visual Basic's RGB function takes as parameters the red, green, and blue components of a color and returns a long integer that represents the color. Unfortunately, Visual Basic does not include a routine that reverses the process by breaking a color into its red, green, and blue component values.

Normally a color's numeric value is given by the equation:

```
red * 256 * 256 + green * 256 + blue
```

A program can use this equation to break a color into its components, as shown in the following code.

```
' Return the red, green, and blue components of a color.
Private Sub UnRGB(ByVal clr As Long, r As Integer, _
    g As Integer, b As Integer)

    b = clr Mod 256
    g = (clr \ 256) Mod 256
    r = clr \ 256 \ 256
End Sub
```

Example program UnRGB uses the UnRGB subroutine to display color components. Click on the shaded area to select a color. The program displays the color's numeric color value and its red, green, and blue components.

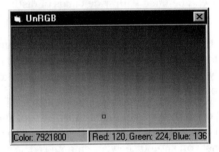

Program UnRGB.

How It Works

The following code shows how program UnRGB responds to mouse clicks. The pic-Shaded control's MouseUp event handler uses the Point method to get the numeric value of the point clicked. It uses then UnRGB to break the color into its components and display the color and components.

The control's DrawMode property was set to vbInvert in the Form_Load event handler. Drawing in invert mode has the useful property that drawing the same thing later erases the previous drawing. After it displays the color and its components, the picShaded_MouseUp event handler draws a small box at the position (SelectedX, SelectedY). This erases the box around the previously selected point. The routine then draws a box around the newly selected point.

```
Option Explicit

' The point just clicked.
Private SelectedX As Single
Private SelectedY As Single

' Display the color and its components.
Private Sub picShaded_MouseUp(Button As Integer, Shift As Integer, _
    X As Single, Y As Single)
Const GAP = 2
Const GAP2 = 2 * GAP
Dim clr As Long
Dim r As Integer
Dim g As Integer
Dim b As Integer

    clr = picShaded.Point(X, Y)
    UnRGB clr, r, g, b
    lblColor.Caption = "Color: " & Format$(clr)
    lblComponents.Caption = _
        "Red: " & Format$(r) & _
        ", Green: " & Format$(g) & _
        ", Blue: " & Format$(b)

    ' Erase the previously selected point.
    picShaded.Line _
        (SelectedX - GAP, SelectedY - GAP)- _
        Step(GAP2, GAP2), , B

    ' Select this point.
    SelectedX = X
    SelectedY = Y
    picShaded.Line _
        (SelectedX - GAP, SelectedY - GAP)- _
        Step(GAP2, GAP2), , B
End Sub
```

113. Draw a Color Gradient

④ ⑤ ⑥

Directory: Gradient

A colorful background can add interest to an otherwise dull application. Example program Gradient displays four areas that are shaded with different color gradients. They begin with one color and gradually fade into another.

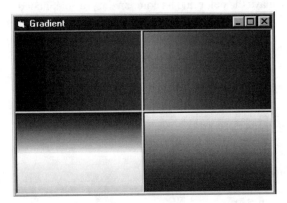

Program Gradient.

How It Works

The most interesting parts of program Gradient are the FadeVertical and FadeHorizontal subroutines. FadeVertical is shown in the following code. FadeHorizontal is similar.

Subroutine FadeVertical draws a vertical color gradient in part of a PictureBox. It starts by saving the PictureBox's ScaleMode property and setting that property to vbPixels. Measuring distances in pixels allows the routine to draw every pixel in the PictureBox quickly and easily with no gaps or duplication.

Next, the routine calculates the amount by which the red, green, and blue color values must change to make the PictureBox's color change from the start color RGB(r1, g1, b1) to the final color RGB(r2, g2, b2) while the Y coordinate ranges from y1 to y2. The values r, g, b, dr, dg, and db are all single-precision variables because the difference in color between Y values will probably be fractional. If these variables were integers, the colors would suffer from roundoff errors and the final color would not be RGB(r2, g2, b2) as desired.

In fact, suppose the difference between r1 and r2 is relatively small and the height of the PictureBox is relatively large. If (r2 - r1) / height is less than 1/2, then an integer dr value would round down to zero. Each time the program added dr to the red component, the color would remain unchanged. Instead of showing a smooth color gradient, the program would display a single color.

Subroutine FadeVertical uses a For loop to examine the Y coordinate values between y1 and y2. For each Y value, the subroutine draws a horizontal line across the width of the area using the current red, green, and blue values to specify the line's color. It then adds the values dr, dg, and db to the color values r, g, and b to calculate the color for the next line.

Finally, when the routine has finished drawing the color gradient, it restores the Picture-Box's original ScaleMode property value.

```
' Fade colors vertically in part of a PictureBox.
Private Sub FadeVertical(ByVal pic As PictureBox, _
    ByVal r1 As Single, ByVal g1 As Single, ByVal b1 As Single, _
    ByVal r2 As Single, ByVal g2 As Single, ByVal b2 As Single, _
    ByVal x1 As Single, ByVal x2 As Single, _
    ByVal y1 As Single, ByVal y2 As Single)
Dim hgt As Single
Dim r As Single
Dim g As Single
Dim b As Single
Dim dr As Single
Dim dg As Single
Dim db As Single
Dim Y As Single
Dim old_scale_mode As Integer

    ' Measure in pixels.
    old_scale_mode = pic.ScaleMode
    pic.ScaleMode = vbPixels

    ' Calculate the change in color for each line.
    hgt = y2 - y1
    If hgt < 1 Then hgt = 1 ' Don't divide by zero.
    dr = (r2 - r1) / hgt
    dg = (g2 - g1) / hgt
    db = (b2 - b1) / hgt
    r = r1
    g = g1
    b = b1

    ' Draw colored vertical lines.
    For Y = y1 To y2
        pic.Line (x1, Y)-(x2, Y), RGB(r, g, b)
        r = r + dr
        g = g + dg
        b = b + db
    Next Y

    ' Restore the original ScaleMode.
    pic.ScaleMode = old_scale_mode
End Sub
```

114. Use Compressed Graphics ⑤ ⑥

Directory: Compact

In version 5, Visual Basic gained the ability to read compressed GIF and JPEG files. When you place one of these files in a Visual Basic program at design time, the program includes a copy of the file's image in its original format. When the program needs to display the image, Visual Basic uncompresses it. That means the resulting executable is smaller than it would be if it included the image in bitmap format.

Example program Compact1 displays an image loaded from the 704KB bitmap file Ivy.bmp. Program Compact2 displays a similar image stored in the 71KB JPEG file Ivy.jpg. The programs look similar, but Compact2 takes much less space.

Program Compact1.

How It Works

The two programs' .vbp, .frm, and .vbw files have roughly the same sizes, but their .frx and .exe files have very different sizes. Compact1's .frx file is 704KB; Compact2's is only 71KB. These sizes are roughly the same as the sizes of the programs' image files. Compact1's .exe file is 720KB; Compact2's is only 88KB.

Using a compressed GIF or JPEG file in a program can save space, but it slows the program down slightly. When it needs to display the image, Visual Basic must decompress the file. Before you decide whether to include images as bitmap files or compressed files, you need to weigh the trade-off between size and speed for your particular application.

115. Resize Using PaintPicture

Directory: Resize

The PaintPicture method lets a program copy parts of an image into a Form, Printer, or PictureBox. PaintPicture takes parameters indicating the source of the image, the coordinates of the part of the image to copy, and coordinates telling where the copy should be placed.

By setting the source and destination coordinates to different values, a program can stretch or resize an image. For instance, if the destination width is twice as big as the source width, PaintPicture makes the resulting image wider than the original.

Example program Resize uses PaintPicture to resize an image. Enter a scale factor and click the Resize button to make the program resize the image.

Program Resize.

How It Works

The following code shows how program Resize works. When the program starts, it sets the destination PictureBox's AutoRedraw property to True. That makes changes to the picture made using PaintPicture become a permanent part of the image.

When you click the Resize button, the program reads the scale factor you entered. It multiplies the height and width of the source image to see how big it should make the destination image. It then resizes the picDest control so that it is big enough to hold the scaled image. It adds the difference between the control's Width and Height properties, and its ScaleWidth and ScaleHeight properties to allow room for the control's borders.

Finally, the program uses PaintPicture to copy the image, specifying the desired source and destination sizes.

```
Option Explicit

' AutoRedraw should be True to make the copied
' picture permanent.
Private Sub Form_Load()
    picDest.AutoRedraw = True
End Sub

' Copy the picture in picSource to picDest using
' the desired scale.
Private Sub cmdResize_Click()
Dim wid1 As Single
Dim hgt1 As Single
Dim wid2 As Single
Dim hgt2 As Single
Dim scale_factor As Single

    ' Get the source dimensions.
    wid1 = picSource.ScaleWidth
    hgt1 = picSource.ScaleHeight

    ' Make picDest the right size.
    scale_factor = CSng(txtScale.Text)
    wid2 = wid1 * scale_factor
    hgt2 = hgt1 * scale_factor
    picDest.Width = _
        picDest.Width - picDest.ScaleWidth + wid2
    picDest.Height = _
        picDest.Height - picDest.ScaleHeight + hgt2

    ' Copy the picture.
    picDest.PaintPicture picSource.Picture, _
        0, 0, wid2, hgt2, _
        0, 0, wid1, hgt1
End Sub
```

Although PaintPicture is fast and easy, it is not perfect. If you enlarge an image too much, the result is blocky. Sometimes when you shrink an image the result can include strange aliasing effects that make it appear rough and jagged. There are techniques for resizing images smoothly, but they fall outside the scope of this book. For information on smooth image scaling, see a graphics book such as *Visual Basic Graphics Programming* by Rod Stephens (John Wiley & Sons, 1997).

116. Tile a Form Using PaintPicture

Directory: Tile

The PaintPicture method lets a program copy parts of an image into a Form, Printer, or PictureBox. Using PaintPicture repeatedly, a program can cover an area with repetitions of an image.

Example program Tile displays two tiled PictureBoxes. The one on the top is covered with copies of a woven pattern. The one on the bottom is covered with a picture of a grainy texture.

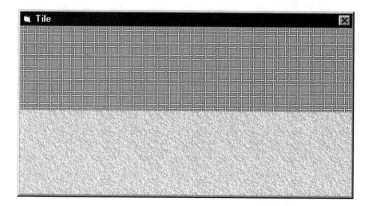

Program Tile.

How It Works

The following code shows how program Tile works. When the program loads, it makes the picTop and picBottom PictureBoxes fill the form. It then sets AutoRedraw to True for these controls and for the PictureBoxes holding the small tile images. Setting AutoRedraw to True makes Visual Basic create permanent copies of the PictureBox images. This step is necessary in many programs that manipulate pictures. Form_Load then calls subroutine TilePicture to tile the PictureBoxes.

TilePicture determines the size of the PictureBox it must cover. It then uses Paint-Picture to copy the tile image repeatedly onto the PictureBox until the PictureBox is completely covered.

```
Option Explicit

' Tile the PictureBoxes.
Private Sub Form_Load()
    ' Make picTop and picBottom as big as possible.
    picTop.Move 0, 0, ScaleWidth, ScaleHeight / 2
    picBottom.Move 0, ScaleHeight / 2, ScaleWidth, ScaleHeight / 2
```

```vb
    ' Set AutoRedraw True so that changes are permanent.
    picTop.AutoRedraw = True
    picBottom.AutoRedraw = True
    picTopTile.AutoRedraw = True
    picBottomTile.AutoRedraw = True

    ' Remove the PictureBox borders.
    picTop.BorderStyle = vbBSNone
    picBottom.BorderStyle = vbBSNone

    ' Make all PictureBoxes work in pixels.
    picTop.ScaleMode = vbPixels
    picBottom.ScaleMode = vbPixels
    picTopTile.ScaleMode = vbPixels
    picBottomTile.ScaleMode = vbPixels

    ' Tile the PictureBoxes.
    TilePicture picTop, picTopTile
    TilePicture picBottom, picBottomTile
End Sub

' Tile the PictureBox with a picture.
Private Sub TilePicture(ByVal pic As PictureBox, _
    ByVal tile As PictureBox)
Dim X As Single
Dim Y As Single
Dim tile_wid As Single
Dim tile_hgt As Single

    ' See how big the tile is.
    tile_wid = tile.ScaleWidth
    tile_hgt = tile.ScaleHeight

    ' Tile the picture.
    For X = 0 To pic.ScaleWidth Step tile_wid
        For Y = 0 To pic.ScaleHeight Step tile_hgt
            ' Copy the picture here.
            pic.PaintPicture tile.Picture, _
                X, Y, tile_wid, tile_hgt, _
                0, 0, tile_wid, tile_hgt
        Next Y
    Next X
End Sub
```

117. View Images

Directory: Viewer

Visual Basic's LoadPicture statement allows a program to load a graphic file. Using DriveListBox, DirectoryListBox, and FileListBox controls, you can build a program that lets you quickly select and view graphic files.

Example program Viewer displays image files. Select a drive, directory, and file to make the program display it.

Program Viewer.

How It Works

The following code shows the most interesting parts of the Viewer program. When it begins, the program uses the AddPattern routine to load patterns for selecting different kinds of files. AddPattern adds a pattern's name to the cboPatterns ComboBox and the value of the pattern to the Patterns array. For instance, the program adds a pattern that appears as "JPG (*.jpg, *.jpeg)" and has value "*.jpg;*.jpeg."

When the user selects a pattern in the ComboBox, the cboPatterns_Click event handler sets the FileListBox control's Pattern property to the corresponding pattern. That makes the FileListBox control select only those files that match the pattern.

When the user picks a drive with the DriveListBox control, the drvSelect_Change event handler notifies the DirectoryListBox that the user has selected a new drive. This routine protects itself with an On Error statement in case the user selects a drive that is not ready. For instance, if the user picks a floppy drive that has no disk in it, the routine enters the error-handling code. That code resets the DriveListBox so that it refers to the drive currently selected by the DirectoryListBox. It uses the static variable ignore_change to prevent itself from updating the DirectoryListBox when the change to the DriveListBox again triggers the drvSelect_Change event handler.

When the user picks a directory in the DirectoryListBox control, the dirSelect_Change event handler notifies the FileListBox that the user has selected a new directory.

Finally, when the user picks a file from the FileListBox control, the filSelect_Click event handler tries to open the file using LoadPicture. If it fails, the routine blanks the picViewer PictureBox and displays an error message in it.

```
Option Explicit

' Patterns for the FileListBox.
Private Patterns() As String

' Make picViewer size to fit its image.
Private Sub Form_Load()
    picViewer.AutoSize = True
    picViewer.AutoRedraw = True

    ' Initialize the filter ComboBox.
    cboPatterns.Clear
    AddPattern "Bitmaps (*.bmp)", "*.bmp"
    AddPattern "GIF (*.gif)", "*.gif"
    AddPattern "JPG (*.jpg, *.jpeg)", "*.jpg;*.jpeg"
    AddPattern "Graphic Files (*.bmp, *.gif, *.jpg, *.jpeg)", _
        "*.bmp;*.gif;*.jpg;*.jpeg"
    AddPattern "All Files (*.*)", "*.*"
    cboPatterns.ListIndex = 0

    ' Select the application's path.
    drvSelect.Drive = App.Path
    dirSelect.Path = App.Path
    filSelect.Path = App.Path
End Sub

' Add a pattern to the ComboBox and pattern list.
Private Sub AddPattern(ByVal pattern_name As String, _
    ByVal pattern_value As String)

    cboPatterns.AddItem pattern_name
    ReDim Preserve Patterns(0 To cboPatterns.NewIndex)
    Patterns(cboPatterns.NewIndex) = pattern_value
End Sub

' The user has selected a pattern. Apply it to
' the FileListBox.
Private Sub cboPatterns_Click()
    filSelect.Pattern = Patterns(cboPatterns.ListIndex)
End Sub
```

```
' The user selected a new drive. Tell the
' directory list.
Private Sub drvSelect_Change()
Static ignore_changes As Boolean

    If ignore_changes Then Exit Sub

    On Error GoTo DriveError
    dirSelect.Path = drvSelect.Drive
    Exit Sub

DriveError:
    ' Reselect the old drive.
    Beep
    ignore_changes = True
    drvSelect.Drive = dirSelect.Path
    ignore_changes = False
    Exit Sub
End Sub


' The user selected a new directory. Tell the
' file list.
Private Sub dirSelect_Change()
    filSelect.Path = dirSelect.Path
End Sub


' The user selected a file. Display it.
Private Sub filSelect_Click()
Dim file_name As String
Dim error_text As String

    On Error GoTo FileOpenError
    file_name = filSelect.Path
    If Right$(file_name, 1) <> "\" Then file_name = file_name & "\"
    file_name = file_name & filSelect.FileName
    picViewer.Picture = LoadPicture(file_name)
    Exit Sub

FileOpenError:
    ' We could not open the file (probably an
    ' invalid format). Display an error message.
    Beep

    ' Remove the current picture.
    Set picViewer.Picture = Nothing
    picViewer.Cls

    ' Display the message.
    error_text = "Error opening file " & file_name
    picViewer.Width = picViewer.Width - picViewer.ScaleWidth + _
        picViewer.TextWidth(error_text) + 240
```

```
    picViewer.Height = picViewer.Height - picViewer.ScaleHeight + _
        picViewer.TextHeight(error_text) + 480
    picViewer.CurrentX = 120
    picViewer.CurrentY = 240
    picViewer.Print error_text
End Sub
```

The Viewer directory includes several graphic files you can use to test program Viewer. If you are using Visual Basic 4, the program will be able to display only bitmap files. If you are using Visual Basic 5 or 6, the program will be able to display GIF and JPEG files as well.

118. Let the User Select Areas

☆ ☆
④ ⑤ ⑥

Directory: DragBox

In many graphical programs, the user must be able to select a rectangular area on a picture. A program can provide this ability using mouse events. When the user clicks and drags, the program draws a box showing the area selected. When the user releases the mouse, the program performs some action using the selected area.

Example program DragBox demonstrates this technique. Click and drag to select an area. When you release the mouse, the program draws the area you selected, enlarged by a factor of four.

Program DragBox.

How It Works

The following code shows how program DragBox works. The variable Dragging indicates whether a drag is in progress. The variables DragX1, DragY1, DragX2, and DragY2 give the coordinates of the currently selected rectangle.

When the program starts, it sets both of its PictureBoxes' AutoRedraw properties to True so that any drawing it does becomes a permanent part of the pictures. It also sets the left PictureBox's DrawMode property to vbInvert. When the program draws a line on the control, the line inverts the colors of the picture beneath. This is important because the inverse of a color's inverse is the original color. That allows the program to erase a line by drawing the line again using the inverted drawing mode.

When the user presses the mouse on the left PictureBox, the program's picSelect_Mouse-Down event handler executes. This routine begins by drawing the currently selected area. If an area was selected before, this erases it because the PictureBox's DrawMode property is vbInvert.

Next, picSelect_MouseDown saves the coordinates where the user has pressed the mouse. It then checks the value of Dragging. If Dragging is True, a region selection is already in progress. The routine cancels the selection by setting Dragging to False and exiting. This is an important step often overlooked by graphics programmers. It allows the user to cancel a region selection. If the user clicks and drags, then presses another mouse button without releasing the first one, the program cancels the selection.

Finally, if Dragging is False, picSelect_MouseDown sets it to True to start the area selection.

When the user moves the mouse over the left PictureBox, the program receives a picSelect_MouseMove event. The event handler first checks to see if an area selection is in progress. If one is not, the event handler exits. This occurs when the user moves the mouse over the PictureBox but has not pressed a mouse button.

Next, the picSelect_MouseMove event handler erases the previously drawn box by redrawing it using invert mode. It saves the new mouse coordinates, adjusting them if necessary so that they remain within the PictureBox's bounds. It then draws another box showing the newly selected area.

Finally, when the user releases the mouse, the program's picSelect_MouseUp event handler executes. This routine first checks to see if an area selection is in progress. If one is not, the routine exits. This occurs when the user begins selecting an area and then cancels by pressing another mouse button.

If a region selection is in progress, picSelect_MouseUp sets Dragging to False to indicate that the operation is finished. It then switches the values of DragX1, DragX2, DragY1, and DragY2 if necessary to ensure that DragX1 < DragX2 and DragY1 < DragY2. Finally, the routine uses PaintPicture to display the selected area enlarged. For more information on enlarging an area with PaintPicture, see Example 115, "Resize Using PaintPicture."

```
Option Explicit

' Dragging variables.
Private Dragging As Boolean
Private DragX1 As Single
Private DragY1 As Single
Private DragX2 As Single
Private DragY2 As Single

' Prepare the PictureBoxes.
Private Sub Form_Load()
    ' Draw boxes in invert mode.
    picSelect.DrawMode = vbInvert
```

```vb
    ' Make changes permanent.
    picSelect.AutoRedraw = True
    picDisplay.AutoRedraw = True

    ' Operations are easier in pixels.
    ScaleMode = vbPixels
    picSelect.ScaleMode = vbPixels
    picDisplay.ScaleMode = vbPixels
End Sub

' Start dragging.
Private Sub picSelect_MouseDown(Button As Integer, Shift As Integer, _
    X As Single, Y As Single)

    ' Erase the previous box, if there is one.
    picSelect.Line (DragX1, DragY1)- _
        (DragX2, DragY2), , B

    ' Save the current coordinates.
    DragX1 = X
    DragY1 = Y
    DragX2 = X
    DragY2 = Y

    ' If we are already dragging, cancel the drag.
    ' Otherwise start a new drag.
    If Dragging Then
        Dragging = False
    Else
        Dragging = True
    End If
End Sub

' Continue dragging.
Private Sub picSelect_MouseMove(Button As Integer, Shift As Integer, _
    X As Single, Y As Single)

    ' Do nothing if we have not started dragging.
    If Not Dragging Then Exit Sub

    ' Erase the previous box.
    picSelect.Line (DragX1, DragY1)- _
        (DragX2, DragY2), , B

    ' Save the new coordinates.
    DragX2 = X
    If DragX2 < 0 Then
        DragX2 = 0
    ElseIf DragX2 > picSelect.ScaleWidth - 1 Then
        DragX2 = picSelect.ScaleWidth - 1
    End If
```

```
        DragY2 = Y
        If DragY2 < 0 Then
            DragY2 = 0
        ElseIf DragY2 > picSelect.ScaleHeight - 1 Then
            DragY2 = picSelect.ScaleHeight - 1
        End If

        ' Draw the new box.
        picSelect.Line (DragX1, DragY1)- _
            (DragX2, DragY2), , B
End Sub

' Finish selecting the area.
Private Sub picSelect_MouseUp(Button As Integer, Shift As Integer, _
    X As Single, Y As Single)
Const SCALE_FACTOR = 4
Dim wid As Single
Dim hgt As Single
Dim tmp As Single

    ' If we are not dragging, do nothing.
    If Not Dragging Then Exit Sub

    Dragging = False

    ' Make sure DragX1 < DragX2 and
    ' DragY1 < DragY2.
    If DragX1 = DragX2 Then
        ' Cannot enlarge an area with no width.
        Beep
        Exit Sub
    ElseIf DragX1 > DragX2 Then
        tmp = DragX1
        DragX1 = DragX2
        DragX2 = tmp
    End If
    If DragY1 = DragY2 Then
        ' Cannot enlarge an area with no height.
        Beep
        Exit Sub
    ElseIf DragY1 > DragY2 Then
        tmp = DragY1
        DragY1 = DragY2
        DragY2 = tmp
    End If

    ' Do something with the selected area. In this
    ' example, enlarge it.
    wid = Abs(DragX1 - DragX2)
    hgt = Abs(DragY1 - DragY2)
    picDisplay.Width = SCALE_FACTOR * wid + _
```

```
        picDisplay.Width - picDisplay.ScaleWidth
    picDisplay.Height = SCALE_FACTOR * hgt + _
        picDisplay.Height - picDisplay.ScaleHeight
    picDisplay.Cls
    picDisplay.PaintPicture picSelect.Picture, _
        0, 0, SCALE_FACTOR * wid, SCALE_FACTOR * hgt, _
        DragX1, DragY1, wid, hgt
End Sub
```

This program lets the user select an arbitrary rectangle within its PictureBox, but some programs may want to require a more restrictive selection. For example, the program might want the selection to always be square. In that case, the program should adjust the coordinates selected in its MouseMove event handler, much as program DragBox adjusts the coordinates so that they remain inside the PictureBox.

119. Simulate Alt-PrntScrn

Directory: AltPrint

Visual Basic does not provide the ability for a program to capture an image of a form or screen and copy it to the clipboard. The Windows operating system, however, lets the user capture an image of the screen by pressing PrntScrn or the image of a form by pressing Alt-PrntScrn. Using this fact, you can capture images by making a program simulate the PrntScrn and Alt-PrntScrn keys.

Example program AltPrint simulates these keys to copy images into the clipboard. Check the Whole Screen box, and click the Copy button to copy an image of the entire screen. Uncheck the check box, and click the Copy button to copy an image of the AltPrint program's form. After you have copied an image to the clipboard, you can paste it into Microsoft Word, Microsoft Paint, other drawing programs, and other programs that can manipulate images.

Program AltPrint.

How It Works

The following code shows how program AltPrint captures images. When you press the Copy button, the program invokes subroutine CopyToClipboard.

If subroutine CopyToClipboard is capturing an image of the form, it must press the Alt key. It begins by using the MapVirtualKey API function to map the VK_MENU virtual key to a scan code. The VK_MENU key represents the Alt key. The routine then uses the keybd_event API function to send the VK_MENU key to the system. It uses DoEvents to give the system time to process the Alt key press.

The program then uses keybd_event to send the system a PrntScrn key.

If the subroutine is capturing an image of the form, it must then release the Alt key. It does this using the keybd_event function again.

```
Option Explicit

#If Win32 Then
    Private Declare Function MapVirtualKey Lib "user32" _
        Alias "MapVirtualKeyA" (ByVal wCode As Long, _
        ByVal wMapType As Long) As Long
    Private Declare Sub keybd_event Lib "user32" ( _
        ByVal bVk As Byte, ByVal bScan As Byte, _
        ByVal dwFlags As Long, ByVal dwExtraInfo As Long)
#End If

Private Const VK_MENU = &H12
Private Const VK_SNAPSHOT = &H2C
Private Const KEYEVENTF_KEYUP = &H2

' Copy an image of the form to the clipboard.
Private Sub cmdCopy_Click()
    CopyToClipboard (chkWholeScreen.Value = vbUnchecked)
End Sub

' Simulate Alt-PrntScrn to copy an image of the
' form to the clipboard.
Private Sub CopyToClipboard(ByVal form_only As Boolean)
Dim alt_scan_code As Long

    If form_only Then
        ' Get the scan code for Alt.
        alt_scan_code = MapVirtualKey(VK_MENU, 0)

        ' Press Alt.
        keybd_event VK_MENU, alt_scan_code, 0, 0
        DoEvents
    End If

    ' Press Print Scrn.
```

```
        If form_only Then
            keybd_event VK_SNAPSHOT, 0, 0, 0
        Else
            keybd_event VK_SNAPSHOT, 1, 0, 0
        End If
        DoEvents

        If form_only Then
            ' Release Alt.
            keybd_event VK_MENU, alt_scan_code, KEYEVENTF_KEYUP, 0
            DoEvents
        End If
    End Sub
```

120. Use BitBlt and StretchBlt

☆ ☆
④ ⑤ ⑥

Directory: BitBlt

Visual Basic's PaintPicture method allows a program to copy pictures from one control to another easily. The BitBlt and StretchBlt API functions provide similar capabilities. Because they are API functions, they are harder to use correctly, but they provide better performance. In an extremely graphics-intensive application, the extra speed may be worth the increased difficulty.

Example program BitBlt compares the performance of PaintPicture, BitBlt, and StretchBlt. Enter the number of times you want the program to repeat a test, and click a button to make the program run the corresponding test.

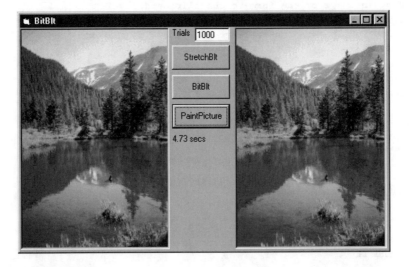

Program BitBlt.

How It Works

The BitBlt API function copies part of an image from one control to another, keeping the image its original size and shape. StretchBlt also copies part of an image from one control to another, but it lets the program stretch and resize the image.

Visual Basic's PaintPicture method does basically the same thing as StretchBlt, so you should use it whenever possible. Using PaintPicture is simpler and less likely to cause errors. The consequences of a mistake are also less severe. If you pass PaintPicture the wrong arguments, the program will fail and the Visual Basic debugger will point out your mistake. If you pass BitBlt or StretchBlt the wrong arguments, they will probably crash the program and the Visual Basic development environment as well. They may even crash the entire Windows operating system.

These routines are slightly faster than PaintPicture, however, so sometimes the extra inconvenience is justified. The performance gains are not huge, though, so be certain you need the extra speed before you reject PaintPicture.

The following code shows how program BitBlt works. Notice how many more arguments are required by BitBlt and StretchBlt.

```
Option Explicit

' Declare the API functions.
#If Win32 Then
    Private Declare Function BitBlt Lib "gdi32" ( _
        ByVal hDestDC As Long, ByVal X As Long, ByVal Y As Long, _
        ByVal nWidth As Long, ByVal nHeight As Long, _
        ByVal hSrcDC As Long, ByVal XSrc As Long, ByVal YSrc As Long, _
        ByVal dwRop As Long) As Long
    Private Declare Function StretchBlt Lib "gdi32" ( _
        ByVal hDC As Long, ByVal X As Long, ByVal Y As Long, _
        ByVal nWidth As Long, ByVal nHeight As Long, _
        ByVal hSrcDC As Long, ByVal XSrc As Long, ByVal YSrc As Long, _
        ByVal nSrcWidth As Long, ByVal nSrcHeight As Long, _
        ByVal dwRop As Long) As Long
#Else
    Private Declare Function BitBlt Lib "GDI" ( _
        ByVal hDestDC As Integer, ByVal X As Integer, _
        ByVal Y As Integer, ByVal nWidth As Integer, _
        ByVal nHeight As Integer, ByVal hSrcDC As Integer, _
        ByVal XSrc As Integer, ByVal YSrc As Integer, _
        ByVal dwRop As Long) As Integer
    Private Declare Function StretchBlt Lib "GDI" ( _
        ByVal hDC As Integer, ByVal X As Integer, ByVal Y As Integer, _
        ByVal nWidth As Integer, ByVal nHeight As Integer, _
        ByVal hSrcDC As Integer, ByVal XSrc As Integer, _
        ByVal YSrc As Integer, ByVal nSrcWidth As Integer, _
        ByVal nSrcHeight As Integer, ByVal dwRop&) As Integer
#End If
```

```vb
Private Const SRCCOPY = &HCC0020

' Make the destination picture the same size as
' the source picture.
Private Sub Form_Load()
    picTo.Width = picFrom.Width
    picTo.Height = picFrom.Height
End Sub

' Copy using PaintPicture.
Private Sub cmdPaintPicture_Click()
Dim num_trials As Integer
Dim trial As Integer
Dim start_time As Single
Dim wid As Single
Dim hgt As Single

    num_trials = CInt(txtTrials.Text)
    wid = picFrom.ScaleWidth
    hgt = picFrom.ScaleHeight

    lblTime.Caption = ""
    MousePointer = vbHourglass
    start_time = Timer
    For trial = 1 To num_trials
        picTo.PaintPicture picFrom.Picture, 0, 0
        DoEvents
    Next trial
    MousePointer = vbDefault

    lblTime.Caption = _
        Format$(Timer - start_time, "0.00") & _
        " secs"
End Sub

' Copy using BitBlt.
Private Sub cmdBitBlt_Click()
Dim num_trials As Integer
Dim trial As Integer
Dim start_time As Single
Dim wid As Single
Dim hgt As Single

    num_trials = CInt(txtTrials.Text)
    wid = picFrom.ScaleWidth
    hgt = picFrom.ScaleHeight

    lblTime.Caption = ""
    MousePointer = vbHourglass
    start_time = Timer
    For trial = 1 To num_trials
```

```
        BitBlt picTo.hDC, 0, 0, wid, hgt, _
            picFrom.hDC, 0, 0, _
            SRCCOPY
        DoEvents
    Next trial
    MousePointer = vbDefault

    lblTime.Caption = _
        Format$(Timer - start_time, "0.00") & _
        " secs"
End Sub

' Copy using StretchBlt.
Private Sub cmdStretchBlt_Click()
Dim num_trials As Integer
Dim trial As Integer
Dim start_time As Single
Dim wid As Single
Dim hgt As Single

    num_trials = CInt(txtTrials.Text)
    wid = picFrom.ScaleWidth
    hgt = picFrom.ScaleHeight

    lblTime.Caption = ""
    MousePointer = vbHourglass
    start_time = Timer
    For trial = 1 To num_trials
        StretchBlt picTo.hDC, 0, 0, wid, hgt, _
            picFrom.hDC, 0, 0, wid, hgt, _
            SRCCOPY
        DoEvents
    Next trial
    MousePointer = vbDefault

    lblTime.Caption = _
        Format$(Timer - start_time, "0.00") & _
        " secs"
End Sub
```

The exact amount of time you may save depends on your particular system configuration. Table 13.1 shows the times in seconds needed to copy an image 1000 times on two different systems. On the Windows 95 system, the difference in speed is small. On the Windows NT system, PaintPicture takes more than three times as long as BitBlt or StretchBlt.

Table 13.1 Seconds to Copy Images

SYSTEM	BITBLT	STRETCHBLT	PAINTPICTURE
Windows 95 90 MHz Pentium Visual Basic 4	4.56	4.56	4.72
Windows NT 133 MHz Pentium Visual Basic 6	2.08	2.12	6.70

121. Center an Image

④ ⑤ ⑥

Directory: Center

When you assign a picture to the background of a Form or PictureBox, Visual Basic displays the image in the upper left corner. A program often looks better if the image is centered. Visual Basic will not do this for you, but you can center an image using the PaintPicture method.

Example program Center displays an image centered on its form. When you resize the form, the program recenters the image. If you make the form too small for the image to fit, the program shrinks the image so it fits.

Program Center.

How It Works

The following code shows how program Center works. The key is the Form_Resize event handler. This routine uses PaintPicture to copy the image in the picHidden PictureBox onto the form. It begins by comparing the image's size to the size of the form. If the image is too big to fit, the routine decreases its width and height appropriately.

For instance, suppose the image is too wide to fit. Then the routine reduces the image's width to the width available on the form. It reduces the image's height correspondingly so the image has the same width-to-height ratio as it did originally. This makes the image as large as possible while still fitting on the form and still keeping its original shape.

After it has corrected the image's size, the Form_Resize event handler determines where to place the image to center it. It then uses PaintPicture to display the image.

```
Option Explicit

' Prepare the form and hidden PictureBox control.
Private Sub Form_Load()
    AutoRedraw = True

    picHidden.Visible = False
    picHidden.AutoSize = True
    picHidden.BorderStyle = vbBSNone
End Sub

' Center the image.
Private Sub Form_Resize()
Dim to_x As Single
Dim to_y As Single
Dim wid As Single
Dim hgt As Single

    ' Clear the form.
    Cls

    ' See if the image is too big to fit.
    wid = picHidden.ScaleWidth
    hgt = picHidden.ScaleHeight
    If wid > ScaleWidth Then
        hgt = hgt * ScaleWidth / wid
        wid = ScaleWidth
    End If
    If hgt > ScaleHeight Then
        wid = wid * ScaleHeight / hgt
        hgt = ScaleHeight
    End If

    ' See where we need to put the picture to center it.
    to_x = (ScaleWidth - wid) / 2
    to_y = (ScaleHeight - hgt) / 2
```

```
' Copy the picture centered on the form.
Me.PaintPicture picHidden.Picture, _
    to_x, to_y, wid, hgt
End Sub
```

122. Use FloodFill

Directory: Flood

Filling complex shapes can be difficult using Visual Basic. For instance, suppose you want to fill the area where two polygons overlap. This would be difficult using Visual Basic alone. You would need to find the area contained in both polygons and explicitly fill it yourself. Even if you can find the boundary of the area easily, filling it is awkward because Visual Basic does not provide routines that fill polygons.

The FloodFill API function lets a program fill an irregular area quickly and easily. Example program Flood demonstrates the FloodFill function. Click on an area, and the program fills it with a random color.

Program Flood.

How It Works

The following code shows how program Flood works. When the program starts, it draws a star with some text over it. This creates a number of irregularly shaped areas.

When you click on the form, the program's Form_MouseDown event handler executes. This routine uses the Rnd function to pick a random number between 1 and 15. It uses Visual Basic's QBColor function to convert that value into a color. It repeats this process until it generates a color different from the color currently used by the point clicked. QBColor also provides a color with index 0, but the subroutine ignores it. That color is black and produces a poor result in this program.

The routine then uses the FloodFill API function to fill the area where the mouse has touched using the chosen color. The first parameter to FloodFill gives the device context (hDC) of the form so the function knows on which form to draw. The second and third parameters give the coordinates in pixels of the point where the function should start filling. The last parameter indicates the area's border color. FloodFill colors pixels in all directions until it reaches pixels with this color.

In this program, the fill area boundary color is black, so FloodFill colors pixels until it reaches black pixels. In particular, if you click on a black pixel such as those that make up the text, FloodFill immediately finds a black pixel so it colors nothing.

```
Option Explicit

#If Win32 Then
    Private Declare Function FloodFill Lib "gdi32" ( _
        ByVal hDC As Long, ByVal X As Long, ByVal Y As Long, _
        ByVal crColor As Long) As Long
#Else
    Private Declare Function FloodFill Lib "GDI" ( _
        ByVal hDC As Integer, ByVal X As Integer, ByVal Y As Integer, _
        ByVal crColor As Long) As Integer
#End If

' Draw a star shape and some text.
Private Sub Form_Load()
    Randomize

    ' Draw a star.
    Line (100, 20)-(25, 150)
    Line -(180, 30)
    Line -(25, 60)
    Line -(190, 130)
    Line -(100, 20)

    ' Draw some text.
    CurrentX = 20
    CurrentY = 30
    Font.Name = "Times New Roman"
    Font.Size = 80
    Print "Star"

    ' The control ignores FillColor if FillStyle
    ' is vbFSTransparent.
    FillStyle = vbFSSolid

    ' Measure in pixels.
    ScaleMode = vbPixels
End Sub

' Flood the clicked area using a random color.
Private Sub Form_MouseDown(Button As Integer, Shift As Integer, _
    X As Single, Y As Single)
Dim color As Long
```

```
' Pick a random QBColor other than black and
' the point's current color.
Do
    color = QBColor(Int(15 * Rnd + 1))
Loop While color = Point(X, Y)
FillColor = color

' Fill the area.
FloodFill hDC, X, Y, vbBlack
End Sub
```

123. Use Polygon

Directory: Polygon

By repeatedly using Visual Basic's Line method, a program can draw complex polygons. Because the Line method can draw only a single line segment at a time, this can be tedious and slow. The Polygon API function makes drawing polygons easier. It is also much faster than using Line, particularly if the polygon contains many line segments.

Example program Polygon demonstrates the Polygon API function. When the program starts, it calculates the coordinates of the points defining a star and connects them using the Polygon function.

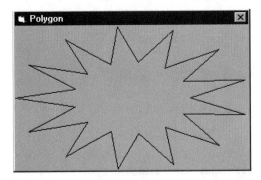

Program Polygon.

How It Works

The following code shows how program Polygon works. The interesting code is contained in the Form_Resize event handler. When the form is resized, the program calculates the coordinates of the points it needs and places them in an array of the POINTAPI user-defined type.

It then passes the first element of the array to the Polygon function. Because this parameter is passed by reference, this effectively gives the function the address of the first element in the array. The function uses that address to find the other elements in the array. Form_Resize also passes Polygon the number of items in the array so that it knows how many points to draw. If the first and last points are not the same, Polygon automatically connects them to close the polygon.

```
Option Explicit

#If Win32 Then
    Private Type POINTAPI
        x As Long
        y As Long
    End Type
    Private Declare Function Polygon Lib "gdi32" ( _
        ByVal hDC As Long, lpPoint As POINTAPI, _
        ByVal nCount As Long) As Long
#Else
    Private Type POINTAPI
        x As Integer
        y As Integer
    End Type
    Private Declare Function Polygon Lib "GDI" ( _
        ByVal hDC As Integer, lpPoints As POINTAPI, _
        ByVal nCount As Integer) As Integer
#End If

' Draw a star.
Private Sub Form_Resize()
Const NUM_STAR_POINTS = 13
Const NUM_POINTS = 2 * NUM_STAR_POINTS
Dim pts(1 To NUM_POINTS) As POINTAPI
Dim rx1 As Single
Dim rx2 As Single
Dim ry1 As Single
Dim ry2 As Single
Dim theta As Single
Dim dtheta As Single
Dim cx As Single
Dim cy As Single
Dim i As Integer

    Cls
    rx2 = ScaleWidth * 0.5
    ry2 = ScaleHeight * 0.5
    rx1 = rx2 * 0.5
    ry1 = ry2 * 0.5
    cx = ScaleWidth / 2
    cy = ScaleHeight / 2
```

```
    ' Calculate points' coordinates.
    dtheta = 2 * 3.14159265 / NUM_POINTS
    theta = 0
    For i = 1 To NUM_POINTS Step 2
        pts(i).x = cx + rx1 * Cos(theta)
        pts(i).y = cy + ry1 * Sin(theta)
        theta = theta + dtheta
        pts(i + 1).x = cx + rx2 * Cos(theta)
        pts(i + 1).y = cy + ry2 * Sin(theta)
        theta = theta + dtheta
    Next i

    Polygon hDC, pts(1), NUM_POINTS
End Sub
```

The Polygon API function obeys Visual Basic's drawing properties. For instance, if you set a form's FillStyle property to 0 - Solid and its FillColor property to red, the Polygon function fills the polygon it draws with red.

124. Stretch a Picture

Directory: Stretch

A program can use the PaintPicture method to stretch an image to fill a PictureBox or form. Example program Stretch demonstrates this technique. When you resize the form, the program stretches a PictureBox to fill the form. It then uses PaintPicture to stretch an image to fill the PictureBox.

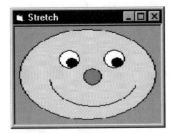

Program Stretch.

How It Works

The following code shows how program Stretch works. The most interesting code is in the picVisible_Resize event handler. There the program calls PaintPicture to copy the image in picHidden onto picVisible, making the new image fit picVisible.

```
Option Explicit

' Prepare the controls.
Private Sub Form_Load()
    picVisible.AutoRedraw = True
    picHidden.Visible = False
End Sub

' Make picVisible fill the form.
Private Sub Form_Resize()
    picVisible.Move 0, 0, ScaleWidth, ScaleHeight
End Sub

' Copy the image into picVisible.
Private Sub picVisible_Resize()
    picVisible.PaintPicture picHidden.Picture, _
        0, 0, picVisible.ScaleWidth, _
        picVisible.ScaleHeight, _
        0, 0, picHidden.ScaleWidth, _
        picHidden.ScaleHeight, vbSrcCopy
End Sub
```

Note that the result given by this program is less than perfect. Some of the thin lines at the top and bottom of the face have breaks in them, and some near the left and right sides are blocky. These effects often occur when a program resizes an image using PaintPicture or StretchBlt. More complicated techniques can resize an image smoothly, but they are outside the scope of this book. For more information, consult an advanced graphics book.

CHAPTER 14

Implementing Animation

This chapter explains some simple methods for producing animation in Visual Basic. It also explains how a program can let the user drag complicated images around a form. Using a similar technique, a program can move complex objects programmatically.

125. Bounce a Ball

Directory: Bounce1

The easiest way for a program to animate an object is to clear its form and then redraw the object in a new position. Example program Bounce1 uses this approach to draw a moving ball that bounces off the sides of the form. When its Timer controls fires, the program clears its form and redraws the ball, repositioned slightly. If the program does this quickly enough, the ball appears to move.

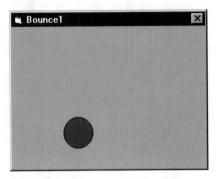

Program Bounce1.

How It Works

The following code shows how program Bounce1 works. The Form_Load event handler calculates the minimum and maximum coordinates the ball's center must have to keep the ball on the form. It then randomly selects an initial position and velocity for the ball. The ball's velocity components VelX and VelY give the distance the ball is moved each time the Timer event occurs.

When the program receives a tmrBounce_Timer event, it adds the velocity components VelX and VelY to the ball's position (CurX, CurY). If one of the coordinates lies outside the allowed boundaries, the program adjusts the ball's position and reverses the corresponding velocity.

For instance, suppose the ball is moving to the left so the X component of its velocity VclX is negative. When the tmrBounce_Timer event occurs, the program adds this negative X value to CurX. Now suppose CurX < Xmin. In that case, the ball has reached the left edge of the form. The program sets CurX = Xmin so the ball lies at the edge of the form. It also sets VelX = -VelX. This reverses the direction of the ball's velocity component in the X direction so the ball moves to the right. This has the effect of making the ball seem to bounce off the left edge of the form.

The last piece of interesting code in program Bounce1 is the MoveBall routine. MoveBall uses the Cls method to clear the form. It then updates the ball's position and redraws it in its new location.

```
Option Explicit

' Variables for positioning the ball.
Private Const BallR = 10            ' Radius.
Private CurX As Single              ' Position.
Private CurY As Single
Private VelX As Single              ' Velocity.
Private VelY As Single
Private Xmin As Single              ' Edge of canvas.
Private Ymin As Single
Private Xmax As Single
```

```
Private Ymax As Single

' Initialize the ball.
Private Sub Form_Resize()
    ' Measure in pixels.
    ScaleMode = vbPixels
    FillStyle = vbFSSolid
    FillColor = vbRed
    AutoRedraw = True

    ' Set the ball's center limits.
    Xmin = BallR
    Ymin = BallR
    Xmax = ScaleWidth - BallR
    Ymax = ScaleHeight - BallR

    ' Set initial position and velocity.
    Randomize
    CurX = Int((Xmax - Xmin + 1) * Rnd + Xmin)
    CurY = Int((Ymax - Ymin + 1) * Rnd + Ymin)
    VelX = Int((10 - 5 + 1) * Rnd + 5)
    VelY = Int((10 - 5 + 1) * Rnd + 5)

    MoveBall CurX, CurY
End Sub

' Move the ball.
Private Sub tmrBounce_Timer()
Dim new_x As Single
Dim new_y As Single

    new_x = CurX + VelX
    If (new_x > Xmax) Then
        new_x = Xmax
        VelX = -VelX
    ElseIf (new_x < Xmin) Then
        new_x = Xmin
        VelX = -VelX
    End If

    new_y = CurY + VelY
    If (new_y > Ymax) Then
        new_y = Ymax
        VelY = -VelY
    ElseIf (new_y < Ymin) Then
        new_y = Ymin
        VelY = -VelY
    End If

    MoveBall new_x, new_y
End Sub
```

```
' Erase the ball at (CurX, CurY) and redraw it at
' (new_x, new_y).
Private Sub MoveBall(ByVal new_x As Single, ByVal new_y As Single)
    ' Erase the form.
    Cls

    ' Draw the ball in its new position.
    CurX = new_x
    CurY = new_y
    Circle (CurX, CurY), BallR

    ' Update the display.
    Refresh
End Sub
```

126. Bounce a Ball Faster ④ ⑤ ⑥

Directory: Bounce2

Program Bounce1 is fast enough on many computers. If you make the form larger, however, you will find that the program slows down. The Cls statement takes longer to clear a large form than a small one. On some computers, Bounce1 may not be able to move the ball quickly enough to produce smooth animation when the form is very large.

The problem with Bounce1 is that it uses Cls to erase the ball even though the ball takes up a relatively small part of the form. Instead of using Cls, a program can erase the ball by drawing a box over it using the Line statement. If the program fills the box with the form's background color, it will erase the box. The program can then redraw the ball in its new position.

Example program Bounce2 uses this approach. When its timer event fires, the program erases the ball and redraws it, repositioned slightly.

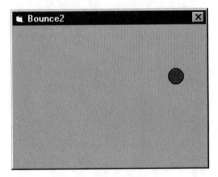

Program Bounce2.

How It Works

Program Bounce2 is very similar to program Bounce1. The main difference is in the MoveBall subroutine so only it is shown here. See the previous section for information about the other parts of the program.

The change to MoveBall is in how the routine erases the ball. Program Bounce2 uses a Line statement to cover the ball with a box filled using the form's background color.

```
Option Explicit

' Variables for positioning the ball.
Private Const BallR = 10          ' Radius.
Private Const BallD = 2 * BallR + 2 ' Diameter.
    :


' Erase the ball at (CurX, CurY) and redraw it at
' (new_x, new_y).
Private Sub MoveBall(ByVal new_x As Single, ByVal new_y As Single)
    ' Erase the ball at its current position.
    Line (CurX - BallR, CurY - BallR)- _
        Step(BallD, BallD), BackColor, BF

    ' Draw the ball in its new position.
    CurX = new_x
    CurY = new_y
    Circle (CurX, CurY), BallR

    ' Update the display.
    Refresh
End Sub
```

☆ ☆
④ ⑤ ⑥

127. Bounce a Ball on a Background

Directory: Bounce3

Programs Bounce1 and Bounce2, described in the previous sections, show how a program can animate a bouncing ball over a blank background. When it moves the ball, these programs erase the ball from its current position and then redraw it in a new position. That approach does not work if the form has a nonblank background. In that case, erasing some or all of the background would erase the background picture.

Instead of erasing the ball, the program can save the contents of the background picture behind the ball before drawing it. To erase the ball, the program restores the image it saved.

Example program Bounce3 demonstrates this technique. To move the ball, the program first restores the background behind the ball's current position. It then saves the background behind the ball's new position and draws the ball there.

Program Bounce3.

How It Works

The following code shows how program Bounce3 works. It is similar to programs Bounce1 and Bounce2, so only the new code is described here.

The program stores the image behind the ball in the hidden PictureBox control picHidden. The Form_Resize event handler makes this control big enough to cover the ball. In addition to the tasks it performs for program Bounce1, Form_Resize also uses the PaintPicture method to copy the background behind the ball's initial position into the picHidden control.

The program's tmrBounce_Timer event handler is the same as the one used by program Bounce1. The only other new code is in the MoveBall subroutine. This routine uses PaintPicture to restore the background where the ball currently lies. It then uses Paint-Picture to save an image of the background beneath the ball's new location so that it can erase the ball later. It finishes by drawing the ball in its new position.

```
Option Explicit

' Variables for positioning the ball.
Private Const BallR = 10             ' Radius.
Private Const BallD = 2 * BallR + 2  ' Diameter.
Private CurX As Single               ' Position.
Private CurY As Single
Private VelX As Single               ' Velocity.
Private VelY As Single
Private Xmin As Single               ' Edge of canvas.
Private Ymin As Single
Private Xmax As Single
Private Ymax As Single

' Initialize the ball.
Private Sub Form_Resize()
    ' Measure in pixels.
    ScaleMode = vbPixels
    FillStyle = vbFSSolid
```

```
        FillColor = vbBlue
        AutoRedraw = True

        ' Set the ball's center limits.
        Xmin = BallR
        Ymin = BallR
        Xmax = ScaleWidth - BallR
        Ymax = ScaleHeight - BallR

        ' Make picHidden big enough to hold what's
        ' behind the ball.
        picHidden.Visible = False
        picHidden.ScaleMode = vbPixels
        picHidden.Width = BallD
        picHidden.Height = BallD

        ' Set initial position and velocity.
        Randomize
        CurX = Int((Xmax - Xmin + 1) * Rnd + Xmin)
        CurY = Int((Ymax - Ymin + 1) * Rnd + Ymin)
        VelX = Int((10 - 5 + 1) * Rnd + 5)
        VelY = Int((10 - 5 + 1) * Rnd + 5)

        ' Copy what's behind the ball's position.
        picHidden.PaintPicture Picture, _
            0, 0, BallD, BallD, _
            CurX - BallR, CurY - BallR, BallD, BallD
        picHidden.Picture = picHidden.Image

        ' Display the ball.
        MoveBall CurX, CurY
End Sub

' Move the ball.
Private Sub tmrBounce_Timer()
Dim new_x As Single
Dim new_y As Single

    new_x = CurX + VelX
    If (new_x > Xmax) Then
        new_x = Xmax
        VelX = -VelX
    ElseIf (new_x < Xmin) Then
        new_x = Xmin
        VelX = -VelX
    End If

    new_y = CurY + VelY
    If (new_y > Ymax) Then
        new_y = Ymax
        VelY = -VelY
```

```
        ElseIf (new_y < Ymin) Then
            new_y = Ymin
            VelY = -VelY
        End If

        MoveBall new_x, new_y
    End Sub


' Erase the ball at (CurX, CurY) and redraw it at
' (new_x, new_y).
Private Sub MoveBall(ByVal new_x As Single, ByVal new_y As Single)
        ' Erase the ball at its current position.
        PaintPicture picHidden.Picture, _
            CurX - BallR, CurY - BallR, BallD, BallD, _
            0, 0, BallD, BallD

        ' Copy what's behind the ball's new position.
        CurX = new_x
        CurY = new_y
        picHidden.PaintPicture Picture, _
            0, 0, BallD, BallD, _
            CurX - BallR, CurY - BallR, BallD, BallD
        picHidden.Picture = picHidden.Image

        ' Draw the ball in its new position.
        Circle (CurX, CurY), BallR

        ' Update the display.
        Refresh
    End Sub
```

☆ ☆ ☆
④ ⑤ ⑥

128. Drag a Picture

Directory: DragPic

Over the last several years, direct manipulation interfaces have become common. One of the most basic tasks for a direct manipulation interface is to allow the user to drag something from one position to another. Moving rectangular images is not too difficult using PaintPicture, but moving irregularly shaped objects can be challenging.

Example program DragPic lets the user drag an irregularly shaped caption to different locations on a picture. Click and drag the caption to reposition it.

Program DragPic.

How It Works

The code that follows shows how program DragPic works. The program uses two PictureBoxes named picMeow and picMask to define the picture to be dragged. The control picMeow contains the image of the caption that is overlaid on the background picture. The control picMask contains a mask image for the picture stored in picMeow. The mask's pixels are black where they correspond to locations in picMeow that should be shown on the background picture. The mask's other pixels are white. In this case, picMask's image looks like a black speech balloon. In practice, the mask is usually created by taking a copy of the picture and then coloring all of the interesting pixels black.

The program also uses a hidden PictureBox named picHidden. The program's Form_Load event handler copies the form's picture into this control. That lets the program repair the background behind the caption when the user drags it aside.

The Form_Load event handler also calculates the size of the picture and stores the width and height in the variables PicWid and PicHgt. It then computes the largest X and Y coordinates the picture can have for its upper left corner while still appearing completely on the form. It stores these values in variables Xmax and Ymax. It uses these values later to ensure that the user does not drag the caption off the form.

The form's mouse event handlers deal with the dragging process. The MouseDown event handler starts the drag. It first examines the point in the mask that corresponds to the point the user is clicking. If the upper left corner of the picture is at (CurX, CurY) and the mouse is at (X, Y), then the point corresponds to the coordinates (X - CurX, Y - CurY) in the mask.

If this point in the mask is black, the user is pressing over a part of the picture that should be visible over the background. In that case, the program begins dragging the picture. It sets Dragging to True so that it later knows a drag is in progress. It also saves the difference in coordinates between the mouse's position and the upper left corner of the picture. It will use these values to position the image as it is dragged.

If the point lies outside the interesting part of the mask, the program ignores the MouseDown event.

The program's Form_MouseMove routine continues the drag. First, this subroutine checks Dragging to see if a drag is in progress, and, if one is not, the routine exits. The routine then updates the picture's position based on the current mouse position and the difference between the picture's original upper left corner and the mouse position when the user first clicked on the picture. If the new coordinates are so big or small that the picture would not lie completely within the form, the routine corrects them. It then calls subroutine DrawPicture to display the picture in its new location.

The Form_MouseUp event handler stops the drag by simply setting Dragging to False.

Probably the most interesting code in this program lies in the DrawPicture subroutine. It begins by using the BitBlt API function to copy part of the image stored in picHidden over the picture's old location. That erases the cartoon caption and restores the form's background to its unobscured appearance.

DrawPicture then uses BitBlt to copy the mask onto the form using the MERGEPAINT operator. This operator makes BitBlt combine the image stored in picMask with the image on the form in a special way. Pixels that correspond to black positions in the mask are set to white in the result. Pixels that correspond to white pixels in the mask are left unchanged. The result is a white cut-out hole where the overlaid picture belongs.

Next, DrawPicture uses BitBlt to copy the picture in picMeow onto the form using the SRCAND operator. Pixels in the cut-out area take on the values of the pixels in picMeow. The other pixels are left unchanged. The final result is that the picture in picMeow is dropped onto the background.

```
Option Explicit

#If Win32 Then
    Private Declare Function BitBlt Lib "gdi32" ( _
        ByVal hDestDC As Long, ByVal X As Long, ByVal Y As Long, _
        ByVal nWidth As Long, ByVal nHeight As Long, _
        ByVal hSrcDC As Long, ByVal XSrc As Long, _
        ByVal YSrc As Long, ByVal dwRop As Long) As Long
#Else
    Private Declare Function BitBlt Lib "GDI" ( _
        ByVal hDestDC As Integer, ByVal X As Integer, _
        ByVal Y As Integer, ByVal nWidth As Integer, _
        ByVal nHeight As Integer, ByVal hSrcDC As Integer, _
        ByVal XSrc As Integer, ByVal YSrc As Integer, _
        ByVal dwRop As Long) As Integer
#End If

Private Const MERGEPAINT = &HBB0226
Private Const SRCAND = &H8800C6
Private Const SRCCOPY = &HCC0020
```

```
' Variables for positioning the image.
Dim OldX As Single
Dim OldY As Single
Dim CurX As Single
Dim CurY As Single
Dim OffsetX As Single
Dim OffsetY As Single
Dim PicWid As Single
Dim PicHgt As Single
Dim Xmax As Single
Dim Ymax As Single
Dim Dragging As Boolean

' Get the picture's size and initialize things.
Private Sub Form_Load()
    picHidden.Picture = Picture
    picHidden.Visible = False

    ScaleMode = vbPixels
    picMeow.ScaleMode = vbPixels
    picMask.ScaleMode = vbPixels

    PicWid = picMeow.ScaleWidth
    PicHgt = picMeow.ScaleHeight
    Xmax = ScaleWidth - PicWid
    Ymax = ScaleHeight - PicHgt
    OldX = 30
    OldY = 30
    CurX = 30
    CurY = 30


    DrawPicture
End Sub

' Start dragging the picture.
Private Sub Form_MouseDown(Button As Integer, Shift As Integer, _
    X As Single, Y As Single)

    ' See if this point corresponds to
    ' a black point on the mask.
    If picMask.Point(X - CurX, Y - CurY) <> vbBlack Then Exit Sub

    ' Start dragging.
    Dragging = True
    OffsetX = CurX - X
    OffsetY = CurY - Y
End Sub

' Continue dragging.
Private Sub Form_MouseMove(Button As Integer, Shift As Integer, _
    X As Single, Y As Single)
```

```
    If Not Dragging Then Exit Sub

    CurX = X + OffsetX
    CurY = Y + OffsetY

    If CurX < 0 Then CurX = 0
    If CurX > Xmax Then CurX = Xmax
    If CurY < 0 Then CurY = 0
    If CurY > Ymax Then CurY = Ymax

    DrawPicture
End Sub

' Stop dragging.
Private Sub Form_MouseUp(Button As Integer, Shift As Integer, _
    X As Single, Y As Single)

    Dragging = False
End Sub

' Draw the picture at (CurX, CurY).
Private Sub DrawPicture()
    ' Fix the part of the image that was covered.
    BitBlt hDC, _
        OldX, OldY, PicWid, PicHgt, _
        picHidden.hDC, OldX, OldY, SRCCOPY
    OldX = CurX
    OldY = CurY

    ' Paint on the new image.
    BitBlt hDC, _
        CurX, CurY, PicWid, PicHgt, _
        picMask.hDC, 0, 0, MERGEPAINT
    BitBlt hDC, _
        CurX, CurY, PicWid, PicHgt, _
        picMeow.hDC, 0, 0, SRCAND

    ' Update the display.
    Refresh
End Sub
```

Note that this program could have used PaintPicture to copy images instead of the BitBlt API function. Even though PaintPicture would work, BitBlt provides better performance. This program must update its picture extremely quickly as the user drags the mouse. If the program is not as fast as possible, the image will not keep up, and the result will be unsatisfying. The program uses BitBlt to get the best performance possible.

CHAPTER 15

Using Fonts

Most controls display text of some kind. A control's font determines the text's typeface, size, orientation, and special features such as italics or underlining. The examples in this chapter show to how examine and manipulate the fonts available on computer monitors and printers.

129. List Available Fonts

Directory: ListFont

Before you can work with fonts, it helps to know what fonts are available. Visual Basic's Screen and Printer objects each provide FontCount and Fonts properties that a program can use to see what fonts are available. Example program ListFont uses these properties to list the fonts available to the Screen and Printer objects. To the right of a font name is an S if the font is a screen font and a P if it is a printer font. Click on a screen font's name to see a sample of text using that font.

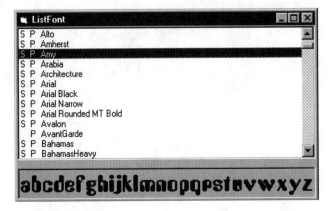

Program ListFont.

How It Works

The following code shows how program ListFonts works. When the program starts, it calls subroutine SetListTabs to set two tabs in the program's ListBox control. For more information on setting tabs in a ListBox, see Example 83, "Set Tabs in a ListBox."

The program then calls LoadFontNames twice to load the font names for the Screen and Printer objects. Subroutine LoadFontNames uses the Screen and Printer objects' Font-Count and Fonts properties to load the appropriate font names. It then calls subroutine Quicksort to sort the array of font names. For more information on Quicksort, see Example 22, "Sort a List."

After it has loaded and sorted the font lists, the program merges the two lists. While either the screen or printer font list has unused entries, the program selects the name from the list that is alphabetically smallest. It adds an S for screen fonts and a P for printer fonts. It places the result in the ListBox control.

When you click on the ListBox, the program's lstFonts_Click event handler executes. This routine sets the lblSample control's font name and size so that you can see a sample of some text using the selected font.

Note that the program may not be able to display exactly the font selected. For example, some fonts come only in certain sizes, and some printer fonts may not be available on the computer's screen. In cases like these, the operating system's font mapper automatically selects a font that is as close as possible to the desired font.

```
Option Explicit

#If Win32 Then
    Private Declare Function SendMessage Lib "user32" _
        Alias "SendMessageA" (ByVal hWnd As Long, ByVal wMsg As Long, _
        ByVal wParam As Long, lParam As Any) As Long
#End If

Private Const LB_SETTABSTOPS = &H192
```

```
' The size in points of the sample font.
Private Const FONT_SIZE = 20

' List the fonts.
Private Sub Form_Load()
Dim tabs(1 To 2) As Long
Dim screen_fonts() As String
Dim printer_fonts() As String
Dim screen_count As Integer
Dim printer_count As Integer
Dim i1 As Integer
Dim i2 As Integer
Dim entry As String

    #If Win32 = False Then
        MsgBox "This program works only in 32-bit Visual Basic."
        End
    #End If

    Show
    Screen.MousePointer = vbHourglass
    lstFonts.Visible = False
    DoEvents

    ' Make lblSample tall enough to display the samples.
    lblSample.Height = 1.5 * ScaleY(FONT_SIZE, vbPoints, ScaleMode)

    ' Define the tabs (in pixels).
    tabs(1) = 10
    tabs(2) = 20

    ' Set the tabs.
    SetListTabs lstFonts, 2, tabs

    ' Load the font name arrays.
    lblSample.Caption = "Reading screen fonts."
    lblSample.Refresh
    LoadFontNames Screen, screen_fonts, screen_count

    lblSample.Caption = "Reading printer fonts."
    lblSample.Refresh
    LoadFontNames Printer, printer_fonts, printer_count

    ' Merge the lists.
    lblSample.Caption = "Merging font lists."
    lblSample.Refresh
    i1 = 1
    i2 = 1
    Do While (i1 <= screen_count) Or _
            (i2 <= printer_count)
        ' Pick the smaller entry.
        If i1 > screen_count Then
```

```vb
            ' We're out of screen fonts. Use a printer font.
            entry = " " & vbTab & "P" & vbTab & printer_fonts(i2)
            i2 = i2 + 1
        ElseIf i2 > printer_count Then
            ' We're out of printer fonts. Use a screen font.
            entry = "S" & vbTab & " " & vbTab & screen_fonts(i1)
            i1 = i1 + 1
        Else
            ' Use whichever is alphabetically first.
            If screen_fonts(i1) <= printer_fonts(i2) Then
                ' Use a screen font.
                entry = "S" & vbTab
                If screen_fonts(i1) = printer_fonts(i2) Then
                    entry = entry & "P"
                    i2 = i2 + 1
                Else
                    entry = entry & " "
                End If
                entry = entry & vbTab & screen_fonts(i1)
                i1 = i1 + 1
            Else
                ' Use a printer font.
                entry = " " & vbTab & "P" & vbTab & printer_fonts(i2)
                i2 = i2 + 1
            End If
        End If
        lstFonts.AddItem entry
    Loop

    ' Free the font name arrays.
    Erase screen_fonts
    Erase printer_fonts

    lblSample.Caption = _
        "abcdefghijklmnopqrstuvwxyz" & _
        "ABCDEFGHIJKLMNOPQRSTUVWXYZ"
    lstFonts.Visible = True
    lstFonts.ListIndex = 0
    Screen.MousePointer = vbDefault
End Sub

' Set the ListBox's tabs.
Private Sub SetListTabs(ByVal lst As ListBox, ByVal num As Long, _
    tabs() As Long)

    SendMessage lstFonts.hWnd, LB_SETTABSTOPS, 2, tabs(1)
End Sub

' Load and sort the font names for this object.
Private Sub LoadFontNames(ByVal obj As Object, _
    ByRef font_names() As String, ByRef font_count As Integer)
Dim i As Integer
```

```
    ' Get the font names.
    font_count = obj.FontCount
    ReDim font_names(1 To font_count)
    For i = 1 To font_count
        font_names(i) = obj.Fonts(i - 1)
    Next i

    ' Sort the font names.
    QuickSort font_names, 1, font_count
End Sub

' Sort this part of the array using QuickSort.
Private Sub QuickSort(ByRef List() As String, _
    ByVal min As Integer, ByVal max As Integer)
Dim med_value As String
Dim hi As Integer
Dim lo As Integer
Dim i As Integer

    ' If the list has no more than CutOff elements,
    ' finish it off with SelectionSort.
    If max <= min Then Exit Sub

    ' Pick the dividing value.
    i = Int((max - min + 1) * Rnd + min)
    med_value = List(i)

    ' Swap it to the front.
    List(i) = List(min)

    lo = min
    hi = max
    Do
        ' Look down from hi for a value < med_value.
        Do While List(hi) >= med_value
            hi = hi - 1
            If hi <= lo Then Exit Do
        Loop
        If hi <= lo Then
            List(lo) = med_value
            Exit Do
        End If

        ' Swap the lo and hi values.
        List(lo) = List(hi)

        ' Look up from lo for a value >= med_value.
        lo = lo + 1
        Do While List(lo) < med_value
            lo = lo + 1
            If lo >= hi Then Exit Do
```

```
        Loop
        If lo >= hi Then
            lo = hi
            List(hi) = med_value
            Exit Do
        End If

        ' Swap the lo and hi values.
        List(hi) = List(lo)
    Loop

    ' Sort the two sublists.
    QuickSort List(), min, lo - 1
    QuickSort List(), lo + 1, max
End Sub

' Display a sample of the selected font.
Private Sub lstFonts_Click()
    lblSample.Font.Name = Mid$(lstFonts.List(lstFonts.ListIndex), 5)
    lblSample.Font.Size = FONT_SIZE
End Sub
```

130. Use Superscripts and Subscripts

Directory: SScripts

Visual Basic's Label control does not provide a method for displaying superscripts or subscripts. Using the Print method, you can add this capability to a program. Example program SScripts uses the Print method to display equations with superscripts and subscripts. Enter text using ^ to indicate a shift upward and v to indicate a shift downward. To display a ^ or v character, precede it with a backslash (\). To display a backslash, precede it with another backslash. When you have entered the formula you want to display, click the Display button to see the result.

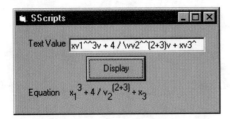

Program SScripts.

How It Works

Program SScripts uses the following code to display subscripts and superscripts. The most interesting code is in the PrintEquation subroutine. This routine examines each of the characters in its input string. If ignore_shift is True, the routine displays the next character without trying to interpret it as a special character.

If ignore_shift is False and if the next character is a backslash, the routine sets ignore_shift to True. This indicates that it should display the next character without trying to interpret it as a special character.

If the next character is ^, the routine subtracts an offset value from the form's CurrentY value. This makes subsequent text print at the distance OFFSET closer to the top of the form. This makes the following text superscripted.

Similarly, if the next character is v, the routine adds an offset value to the program's CurrentY value. That moves subsequent text distance OFFSET farther from the top of the form so that the text is subscripted.

Finally, if none of the previous conditions hold, the routine displays the character using the Print method normally. The semi-colon in the code after the Print statement makes Visual Basic start the next Print command at the end of the current character instead of starting a new line.

```
Option Explicit

' Make the form preserve what we draw.
Private Sub Form_Load()
    AutoRedraw = True
End Sub

' Format the equation.
Private Sub cmdDisplay_Click()
    Cls
    CurrentX = txtVBStyle.Left
    CurrentY = Label1(1).Top
    PrintEquation Me, txtVBStyle.Text
End Sub

' Display an equation with superscripting. Set
' the form's CurrentX and CurrentY before
' calling this routine.
Private Sub PrintEquation(frm As Form, equation As String)
Const OFFSET = 90
Dim ignore_shift As Integer
Dim i As Integer
Dim ch As String

    For i = 1 To Len(equation)
        ch = Mid$(equation, i, 1)
        If ignore_shift Then
```

```
            ' Display the character.
            frm.Print ch;
            ignore_shift = False
        ElseIf ch = "\" Then
            ' Display the next character as it is.
            ignore_shift = True
        ElseIf ch = "^" Then
            ' Raise the following characters.
            frm.CurrentY = frm.CurrentY - OFFSET
        ElseIf ch = "v" Then
            ' Lower the following characters.
            frm.CurrentY = frm.CurrentY + OFFSET
        Else
            ' Display the character.
            frm.Print ch;
        End If
    Next i
End Sub
```

This version of the PrintEquation subroutine was designed to display strings that use ^, v, and \ to indicate formatting. With some extra work, you could make the routine parse normal Visual Basic equations and superscript them accordingly. For instance, the routine would display the Visual Basic equation x ^ 3 + y ^ (a + b) / z ^ 1.23E-47 as $x^3 + y^{a+b} / z^{1.23E-47}$.

☆ ☆ ☆
④ ⑤ ⑥

131. Create New Fonts

Directory: TallFont

The CreateFont API function allows a program to modify certain kinds of fonts to create new ones at run time. For instance, a program can use CreateFont to display a TrueType font that is stretched, compressed, or tilted at an angle. Example program TallFont uses CreateFont to display text that is tall and thin, short and wide, bold, italic, underlined, and stricken out.

Program TallFont.

How It Works

CreateFont is one of the more complex API functions. It takes 14 parameters that describe the font you want to create. The CreateFont function is declared by the following code:

```
Declare Function CreateFont Lib "gdi32" Alias "CreateFontA" ( _
    ByVal Height As Long, ByVal Width As Long, _
    ByVal Escapement As Long, ByVal Orientation As Long, _
    ByVal Weight As Long, ByVal Italic As Long, _
    ByVal Underline As Long, ByVal StrikeOut As Long, _
    ByVal CharSet As Long, ByVal OutputPrecision As Long, _
    ByVal ClipPrecision As Long, ByVal Quality As Long, _
    ByVal PitchAndFamily As Long, ByVal Face As String) _
    As Long
```

This function returns the handle of a logical font that describes the font specified in the parameters. The font mapper selects a physical font that matches this logical font as closely as possible. How close the match is depends on the parameters specified in CreateFont and on the fonts available on the system.

After a program has a logical font handle, it can use the SelectObject API function to make a form or PictureBox use the font. After the call to SelectObject, text printed on the Form or PictureBox uses the new font.

A program usually specifies at least the Height and Face parameters to define the size and name of the font. It can set many of the other parameters to zero to tell the font mapper to use default values. The CreateFont parameters are described briefly in the following list. For more detailed information, consult the online API documentation.

Height. This parameter gives the height for the font in logical units. If this parameter is greater than zero, it specifies the cell height of the font. The cell height may include some empty space above the characters. If Height is less than zero, it specifies the character height of the font. The character height does not include the empty space above the characters. If the Height parameter is zero, the font mapper uses a default value.

Width. This parameter specifies the average width of characters in the font. If Width is zero, the font mapper picks a default width that matches the height specified in the Height parameter.

Escapement. The font's escapement is the angle of slope of the text in tenths of degrees measured counterclockwise from the x-axis.

Orientation. This parameter specifies the orientation angle of the characters in tenths of degrees. Windows assumes that Escapement and Orientation are the same, so it ignores Orientation.

Weight. This parameter specifies the boldness of the font. The most useful values are FW_NORMAL (400) and FW_BOLD (700). The exact result depends on the font. If you set the weight to FW_DONTCARE (0), the font mapper uses a default weight.

Italic. If this value is not zero, the font mapper selects a font that is *italic.*

Underline. If this value is not zero, the font mapper selects a font that is underlined.

StrikeOut. If this value is not zero, the font mapper selects a font with ~~strikeout~~.

CharSet. This parameter specifies the font's character set. Usually, a program should set this to ANSI_CHARSET (0). If the program specifies the value DEFAULT_CHARSET (1), the font mapper uses the name and size parameters to select the logical font.

OutputPrecision. This parameter specifies how closely the selected font must match the specified height, width, escapement, character orientation, and pitch.

ClipPrecision. This parameter determines how characters that are partially outside the clipping region are drawn. When Escapement is not zero, this value should include CLIP_LH_ANGLES (16). For example, to have rotated text clipped one character at a time, the program would set ClipPrecision to CLIP_LH_ANGLES Or CLIP_CHARACTER_PRECIS (1).

Quality. This parameter tells the font manager how hard it should try to match the logical font specified with the physical font eventually displayed.

PitchAndFamily. This parameter gives the pitch and family of the font combined using the Or operator. These values tell the font mapper generally what kind of font to use if it cannot find exactly the font specified.

Face. This parameter specifies the typeface name of the font such as Times New Roman. This is generally what you think of when you think of a font. Table 15.1 lists some fonts that are available on most Windows systems.

Table 15.1 Fonts Available on Most Windows Systems

FONT FAMILY	FONT NAME
Arial	Arial
	Arial Bold
	Arial Italic
	Arial Bold Italic
Courier New	Courier New
	Courier New Bold
	Courier New Italic
	Courier New Bold Italic
Symbol	Symbol (ABCDEFabcdef)
Times New Roman	Times New Roman
	Times New Roman Bold
	Times New Roman Italic
	Times New Roman Bold Italic

The following code shows how program TallFont uses the CreateFont API function to produce different fonts. The form's Load event handler calls the DrawText subroutine to display several lines of text using different fonts.

Subroutine DrawText uses CreateFont to create a font with the parameters passed to it. It uses SelectObject to select the font and then it draws the text. The routine then uses SelectObject to reselect the original font and DeleteObject to free the customized font's graphic resources. This step is extremely important. If the routine does not free the new font, it may eventually use up all of the graphic resources on the computer and prevent other programs from running properly.

```
Option Explicit

#If Win32 Then
    Private Declare Function CreateFont Lib "gdi32" _
        Alias "CreateFontA" (ByVal H As Long, ByVal W As Long, _
        ByVal E As Long, ByVal O As Long, ByVal W As Long, _
        ByVal i As Long, ByVal U As Long, ByVal S As Long, _
        ByVal C As Long, ByVal OP As Long, ByVal CP As Long, _
        ByVal Q As Long, ByVal PAF As Long, ByVal F As String) As Long
    Private Declare Function SelectObject Lib "gdi32" ( _
        ByVal hDC As Long, ByVal hObject As Long) As Long
    Private Declare Function DeleteObject Lib "gdi32" ( _
        ByVal hObject As Long) As Long
#Else
    Private Declare Function CreateFont Lib "GDI" ( _
        ByVal H As Integer, ByVal W As Integer, ByVal E As Integer, _
        ByVal O As Integer, ByVal W As Integer, ByVal i As Integer, _
        ByVal U As Integer, ByVal S As Integer, ByVal C As Integer, _
        ByVal OP As Integer, ByVal CP As Integer, ByVal Q As Integer, _
        ByVal PAF As Integer, ByVal F As String) As Integer
    Private Declare Function SelectObject Lib "GDI" ( _
        ByVal hDC As Integer, ByVal hObject As Integer) As Integer
    Private Declare Function DeleteObject Lib "GDI" ( _
        ByVal hObject As Integer) As Integer
#End If


' Draw some text samples.
Private Sub Form_Load()
Const FW_NORMAL = 400       ' Normal weight.
Const FW_BOLD = 700         ' Bold weight.
Dim X As Single

    AutoRedraw = True

    X = 240
    DrawText Me, "Tall Thin Text", X, 240, _
        "Arial Bold", 60, 10, _
        FW_BOLD, False, False, False
    DrawText Me, "Short", X, 1200, _
```

```
                "Times New Roman", 20, 40, _
                FW_BOLD, False, False, False
        DrawText Me, "Wide", X, 1560, _
                "Times New Roman", 20, 40, _
                FW_BOLD, False, False, False
        DrawText Me, "Text", X, 1920, _
                "Times New Roman", 20, 40, _
                FW_BOLD, False, False, False


        X = 3600
        DrawText Me, "Bold", X, 240, _
                "Arial", 30, 0, _
                FW_BOLD, False, False, False
        DrawText Me, "Italic", X, 840, _
                "Arial", 30, 0, _
                FW_NORMAL, True, False, False
        DrawText Me, "Underline", X, 1440, _
                "Arial", 30, 0, _
                FW_NORMAL, False, True, False
        DrawText Me, "Strikeout", X, 2040, _
                "Arial", 30, 0, _
                FW_NORMAL, False, False, True
End Sub

' Draw the text in the indicated style at the
' position (X, Y).
Private Sub DrawText(ByVal obj As Object, ByVal txt As String, _
    ByVal X As Single, ByVal Y As Single, ByVal font_name As String, _
    ByVal hgt As Long, ByVal wid As Long, ByVal wgt As Long, _
    ByVal use_italic As Boolean, ByVal use_underline As Boolean, _
    ByVal use_strikeout As Boolean)
Const ANSI_CHARSET = 0      ' ANSI character set.
Dim new_font As Long
Dim old_font As Long

    ' Create the font.
    new_font = CreateFont(hgt, wid, 0, 0, _
        wgt, use_italic, use_underline, _
        use_strikeout, ANSI_CHARSET, 0, _
        0, 0, 0, font_name)

    ' Select the new font.
    old_font = SelectObject(obj.hDC, new_font)

    ' Draw the text.
    obj.CurrentX = X
    obj.CurrentY = Y
    obj.Print txt

    ' Restore the original font.
    SelectObject obj.hDC, old_font
```

```
     ' Free font resources (important!).
        DeleteObject new_font
    End Sub
```

132. Create Rotated Fonts

Directory: RotFont

A program can also use the CreateFont API function to display rotated text. Example program RotFont uses a font rotated 45 degrees to display column headers for a matrix of values.

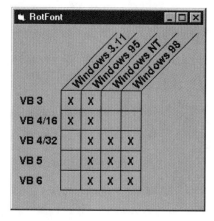

Program RotFont.

How It Works

The following code shows how program RotFont uses the CreateFont API function to produce rotated text. The declarations of the CreateFont, SelectObject, and DeleteObject API functions are the same as those used by program TallFont described in the previous section, so they are omitted here.

```
    ' Draw the grid.
    Private Sub Form_Load()
    Const CLIP_LH_ANGLES = 16  ' Needed for tilted fonts.
    Const FW_NORMAL = 400      ' Normal weight.
    Const FW_BOLD = 700        ' Bold weight.
    Const ANSI_CHARSET = 0     ' ANSI character set.
    Const PI = 3.14159625
    Const PI_180 = PI / 180#
    Const ANGLE = 45
    Const FONT_SIZE = 16
```

```vb
Const FONT_NAME = "Arial"

Dim row_hgt As Single
Dim col_wid As Single
Dim old_font As Long
Dim new_font As Long
Dim cur_x As Single
Dim cur_y As Single
Dim start_x As Single
Dim start_y As Single
Dim col_headers As New Collection
Dim i As Integer

    AutoRedraw = True

    ' *****************************
    ' * Work with the rotated font *
    ' *****************************
    ' Create a rotated font.
    new_font = CreateFont(FONT_SIZE, 0, _
        ANGLE * 10, ANGLE * 10, _
        FW_BOLD, 0, 0, 0, ANSI_CHARSET, 0, _
        CLIP_LH_ANGLES, 0, 0, FONT_NAME)

    ' Select the new font.
    old_font = SelectObject(hDC, new_font)

    ' See how big text is in this font.
    col_wid = 3 * TextWidth("X")
    row_hgt = 2 * TextHeight("X")

    ' Find the biggest column header.
    col_headers.Add "Windows 3.11"
    col_headers.Add "Windows 95"
    col_headers.Add "Windows NT"
    col_headers.Add "Windows 98"
    start_y = TextWidth(col_headers(1))
    For i = 2 To col_headers.Count
        cur_y = TextWidth(col_headers(i))
        If start_y < cur_y Then start_y = cur_y
    Next i
    start_y = start_y / Sqr(2) + 120

    ' Find the biggest row header.
    start_x = TextWidth("VB 4/32") + 120

    ' Draw the column headers.
    cur_x = start_x + 120 + col_wid / 3
    cur_y = start_y
    For i = 1 To col_headers.Count
        DrawText cur_x, cur_y, col_headers(i), col_wid, 0
    Next i
```

```
' Restore the original font.
SelectObject hDC, old_font

' Free font resources (important!).
DeleteObject new_font

' ***************************
' * Work with a normal font *
' ***************************
' Create a font rotated 360 degrees. This makes
' the font match the rotated font more closely.
new_font = CreateFont(FONT_SIZE, 0, _
    3600, 3600, FW_BOLD, 0, 0, 0, ANSI_CHARSET, 0, _
    CLIP_LH_ANGLES, 0, 0, FONT_NAME)

' Select the new font.
old_font = SelectObject(hDC, new_font)

' Draw the row headers.
cur_y = start_y + 240

cur_x = 120
DrawText cur_x, cur_y, "VB 3", 0, 0
cur_x = start_x + 60 + col_wid / 3
DrawText cur_x, cur_y, "X", col_wid, 0
DrawText cur_x, cur_y, "X", col_wid, row_hgt

cur_x = 120
DrawText cur_x, cur_y, "VB 4/16", 0, 0
cur_x = start_x + 60 + col_wid / 3
DrawText cur_x, cur_y, "X", col_wid, 0
DrawText cur_x, cur_y, "X", col_wid, row_hgt

cur_x = 120
DrawText cur_x, cur_y, "VB 4/32", 0, 0
cur_x = start_x + 60 + col_wid / 3
DrawText cur_x, cur_y, "", col_wid, 0
DrawText cur_x, cur_y, "X", col_wid, 0
DrawText cur_x, cur_y, "X", col_wid, 0
DrawText cur_x, cur_y, "X", col_wid, row_hgt

cur_x = 120
DrawText cur_x, cur_y, "VB 5", 0, 0
cur_x = start_x + 60 + col_wid / 3
DrawText cur_x, cur_y, "", col_wid, 0
DrawText cur_x, cur_y, "X", col_wid, 0
DrawText cur_x, cur_y, "X", col_wid, 0
DrawText cur_x, cur_y, "X", col_wid, row_hgt

cur_x = 120
DrawText cur_x, cur_y, "VB 6", 0, 0
```

```
    cur_x = start_x + 60 + col_wid / 3
    DrawText cur_x, cur_y, "", col_wid, 0
    DrawText cur_x, cur_y, "X", col_wid, 0
    DrawText cur_x, cur_y, "X", col_wid, 0
    DrawText cur_x, cur_y, "X", col_wid, row_hgt

    ' Restore the original font.
    SelectObject hDC, old_font

    ' Free font resources (important!).
    DeleteObject new_font

    ' *****************
    ' * Draw the grid *
    ' *****************
    ' Draw the vertical and diagonal lines.
    cur_x = start_x + 60
    cur_y = start_y + 240 - row_hgt / 4 + 5 * row_hgt
    For i = 0 To 4
        Line (cur_x + i * col_wid, cur_y)- _
            Step(0, -5 * row_hgt)
        Line -Step(start_y, -start_y)
    Next i

    ' Draw the horizontal lines.
    cur_x = start_x + 60
    cur_y = start_y + 240 - row_hgt / 4
    For i = 0 To 5
        Line (cur_x, cur_y + i * row_hgt)- _
            Step(4 * col_wid, 0)
    Next i
End Sub

' Draw some text at the given position.
' Increase X by dx.
Private Sub DrawText(X As Single, Y As Single, ByVal txt As String,
ByVal dx As Single, ByVal dy As Single)
    CurrentX = X
    CurrentY = Y
    Print txt;
    X = X + dx
    Y = Y + dy
End Sub
```

Rotated text usually looks best when the font is large and the angle of rotation is a multiple of 45 degrees.

☆ ☆ ☆
④ ⑤ ⑥

133. Draw Curved Text

Directory: CurvFont

Once a program can display angled text using CreateFont, it is just a short step to creating text that lies along a curve. Example program CurvFont draws text that follows a spiral path.

Program CurvFont.

How It Works

The following code shows how program CurvFont works. The declarations of the CreateFont, SelectObject, and DeleteObject API functions are the same as those used by the examples in the previous sections, so they are omitted here.

The program uses the variable curve_radians to keep track of the point along the spiral in radians. For each character in the text, the program converts the angle in radians into an angle in degrees. That gives the angle of rotation for the character. The program uses CreateFont to make a font rotated at that angle, and it displays the character. It then increases curve_radians by an amount large enough to leave room for the character, and it draws the next character. It continues this process until it runs out of text to display.

```
' Draw text following a spiral path.
Private Sub Form_Load()
Const CLIP_LH_ANGLES = 16 ' Needed for tilted fonts.
Const FW_BOLD = 700        ' Boldweight.
Const ANSI_CHARSET = 0     ' ANSI character set.
Const PI = 3.14159625
Const PI_180 = PI / 180#
Const FONT_SIZE = 16
```

```
Const FONT_NAME = "Times New Roman"
Const QUOTE = " To be or not to be, that is the question. " & _
    "Whether 'tis nobler in the mind to suffer the slings and " & _
    "arrows of outrageous fortune, or to take arms against a " & _
    "sea of troubles, and by opposing end them? "
Const DRAW_SPIRAL = False

Dim old_font As Long
Dim new_font As Long
Dim c_x As Single
Dim c_y As Single
Dim last_x As Single
Dim last_y As Single
Dim new_x As Single
Dim new_y As Single
Dim curve_radians As Single
Dim font_degrees As Single
Dim r As Single
Dim wid As Single
Dim ch As String
Dim i As Integer

    AutoRedraw = True
    c_x = ScaleWidth / 2
    c_y = ScaleHeight / 2

    curve_radians = -1.5 * PI
    For i = 1 To Len(QUOTE)
        ch = Mid$(QUOTE, i, 1)

        ' Create a rotated font.
        font_degrees = curve_radians * 180 / PI - 90
        new_font = CreateFont(FONT_SIZE, 0, _
            font_degrees * 10, font_degrees * 10, _
            FW_BOLD, 0, 0, 0, ANSI_CHARSET, 0, _
            CLIP_LH_ANGLES, 0, 0, FONT_NAME)
        old_font = SelectObject(hDC, new_font)

        ' Draw the text.
        r = -curve_radians * 100
        new_x = c_x + r * Cos(curve_radians)
        new_y = c_y - r * Sin(curve_radians)
        CurrentX = new_x
        CurrentY = new_y
        Print ch

        ' Draw this part of the spiral.
        If DRAW_SPIRAL Then
            new_x = c_x + r * Cos(curve_radians)
            new_y = c_y - r * Sin(curve_radians)
            If last_x > 0 Then Line (last_x, last_y)-(new_x, new_y)
```

```
            last_x = new_x
            last_y = new_y
        End If

        ' Increase curve_radians by enough for
        ' this letter.
        curve_radians = curve_radians - _
            1.5 * TextWidth(ch) / r

        ' Restore the original font.
        SelectObject hDC, old_font
        DeleteObject new_font
    Next i
End Sub
```

16

Making Menus

Menus are one of the most ubiquitous features in Windows. Almost every Windows application provides menus that stop, control, and configure it. Visual Basic's Menu Editor makes creating simple menus easy, but providing sophisticated menus requires a little extra work. The examples in this chapter explain some of the more advanced ways you can use menus in your programs.

---

134. Use Popup Menus

Directory: PopUp

Displaying a popup menu is relatively easy in Visual Basic. Example program PopUp displays a popup menu when you right-click on its form. The form has a fixed border so you can resize it only by using the Big Form and Small Form popup menu items.

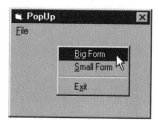

Program PopUp.

How It Works

To use a popup menu, first create the menu as you would any other using the Menu Editor. Set the main popup menu's Visible property to False so that the menu does not appear in the form's menu bar. Give the menu whatever items you want it to display when it is presented at run time.

The program displays the popup menu using the PopupMenu statement. For instance, if the top-level popup menu is named mnuPopup, the following code displays it as a popup menu.

```
PopupMenu mnuPopup
```

When the user selects an item from the menu, the corresponding menu event handler executes just as if the menu were displayed in the program's menu bar.

The following code shows how program PopUp manages its popup menu. The program has a File menu with one menu item named mnuFileExit. The popup menu is named mnuPopup, and it contains menu items named mnuPopupBig, mnuPopupSmall, and mnuPopupExit. The first two items change the form's size, and the third unloads the form.

When the form receives a MouseDown event, it checks whether the mouse button pressed is the right button. If it is, the program presents the popup menu using the PopupMenu statement.

```
Option Explicit

' Start with the small size.
Private Sub Form_Load()
    mnuPopupSmall_Click
End Sub

' If this is the right mouse button, display
' the popup menu.
Private Sub Form_MouseDown(Button As Integer, Shift As Integer, _
    X As Single, Y As Single)

    If Button = vbRightButton _
        Then PopupMenu mnuPopup
End Sub

' Unload the form.
Private Sub mnuFileExit_Click()
    Unload Me
End Sub

' Make the form big.
Private Sub mnuPopupBig_Click()
    Width = 4 * 1440
    Height = 3 * 1440
End Sub
```

```
' Invoke the File menu's Exit command.
Private Sub mnuPopupExit_Click()
    mnuFileExit_Click
End Sub


' Make the form small.
Private Sub mnuPopupSmall_Click()
    Width = 2 * 1440
    Height = 1.5 * 1440
End Sub
```

Different controls can display menu items that are appropriate for their own needs. This allows the program to prevent the clutter that would result if every possible command were placed in the program's menu bar. Popup menus also save space by remaining hidden until the user needs them.

135. Make Menu Items at Run Time

Directory: MakeMenu

Visual Basic's Load and Unload statements allow a program to create and remove controls in a control array at run time. Many programmers are unaware that Load and Unload apply to menu items as well as other kinds of controls. A program can create and remove menu items at run time using the Load and Unload statements.

Open the Menu Editor and create menus as usual. Create an item in the menu where you will later want to add more items. Set that item's Index property to 0. You can also set its Visible property to False if you do not want that item to be visible.

At run time, the program can use Load and Unload to create and remove new items with the same name as the one you created.

Example program MakeMenu uses this approach. When you click the Make Item button, the program creates a new menu item. Click the Remove Item button to remove the last item created.

Program MakeMenu.

How It Works

The following code shows how program MakeMenu works. When you click the Create Item button, the cmdMakeItem_Click event handler creates the new menu item. If this is the first item in the menu, the program uses the menu item that was created at design time with Index property set to 0. Otherwise, it uses the Load statement to create a new item.

When you click the Remove Item button, the cmdRemoveItem_Click event handler removes the last menu item created. If this is the first item in the menu, the program cannot unload it because that item was created at design time. Instead it sets the menu's Visible property to False.

```vb
Option Explicit

Private NextMenuIndex As Integer

' Create a new menu item.
Private Sub cmdMakeItem_Click()
    ' If this is not the first item, load the
    ' new item. Otherwise use the item we created
    ' at design time.
    If NextMenuIndex > 0 Then _
        Load mnuCommandsSub(NextMenuIndex)

    ' Set the item's caption.
    mnuCommandsSub(NextMenuIndex).Caption = _
        "Command &" & Format$(NextMenuIndex)

    ' If this is the first item, enable the menu.
    If NextMenuIndex = 0 Then mnuCommands.Enabled = True

    ' Set NextMenuIndex to the index of the next item.
    NextMenuIndex = NextMenuIndex + 1
End Sub

' Remove a menu item.
Private Sub cmdRemoveItem_Click()
    ' If this is the first item, disable the menu
    ' (we cannot unload a control created at design time).
    NextMenuIndex = NextMenuIndex - 1
    If NextMenuIndex = 0 Then
        mnuCommands.Enabled = False
    Else
        ' Unload the last item.
        Unload mnuCommandsSub(NextMenuIndex)
    End If
End Sub

' Respond to a dynamically created menu command.
Private Sub mnuCommandsSub_Click(Index As Integer)
    MsgBox "Execute command number " & Format$(Index)
```

```
End Sub

' Unload the form.
Private Sub mnuFileExit_Click()
    Unload Me
End Sub
```

Example 66, "Make a RichTextBox Editor," shows how to build a most recently used (MRU) file list that lists the four files most recently used by the program. You can apply the techniques described here to that example to provide an MRU list that lists any number of previously used files.

136. Disable the Close Command

Directory: NoClose

There are many ways to close a form. The user can click on the X in the form's upper right corner, select the Close command from the system menu in the upper left corner, double-click on the system menu, right-click on the form's icon and select the Close command, or press Alt-F4.

You can disable these methods by setting the form's ControlBox property to False. Unfortunately, this also prevents the user from invoking the form's Minimize and Maximize buttons. Using API functions, a program can disable the close features without removing the Minimize, Maximize, and other system menu commands.

Example program NoClose demonstrates this technique. The X in the upper right of the form is disabled and the system menu contains no Close command. The form does not respond to Alt-F4 or double-clicking on its system menu. The only way to exit the program normally is to click its Close button.

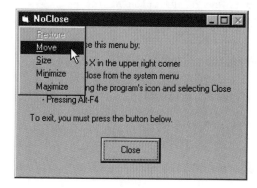

Program NoClose.

How It Works

The following code shows how program NoClose works. When the program starts, it calls the RemoveMenu subroutine, indicating that it should remove the system menu's Close item and its menu separator.

RemoveMenu uses the DeleteMenu API function to remove the indicated menu items. Notice that it uses the items' positions in the menu to remove them. For example, the Close item has index 6 in the menu (they are numbered starting with 0), so Remove-Menu indicates that DeleteMenu should remove item number 6. These numbers will not work if the arrangement of the system menu changes in future versions of Windows. In that case, the routine should be modified to search for specific item names using the GetMenuString API function.

Removing the Close item from the system menu disables the X in the form's upper right corner. It does not prevent the user from closing the form with Alt-F4. To do that, the program uses the Boolean variable ReadyToClose. This value is initially False. If the user presses Alt-F4, the form's QueryUnload event handler sees that ReadyToClose is False and it cancels the close. When the user clicks the form's Close button, the cmdClose_Click event handler sets ReadyToClose to True and then unloads the form.

```
Option Explicit

#If Win32 Then
    Private Declare Function GetSystemMenu Lib "user32" ( _
        ByVal hWnd As Long, ByVal bRevert As Long) As Long
    Private Declare Function DeleteMenu Lib "user32" ( _
        ByVal hMenu As Long, ByVal nPosition As Long, _
        ByVal wFlags As Long) As Long
#Else
    Private Declare Function GetSystemMenu Lib "User" ( _
        ByVal hWnd As Integer, ByVal bRevert As Integer) As Integer
    Private Declare Function DeleteMenu Lib "User" ( _
        ByVal hMenu As Integer, ByVal nPosition As Integer, _
        ByVal wFlags As Integer) As Integer
#End If

Private Const MF_BYPOSITION = &H400&

Private ReadyToClose As Boolean

' Remove the Close system menu item and the
' menu separator.
Private Sub Form_Load()
    RemoveMenus False, False, False, False, _
        False, True, True
End Sub
```

```
' Remove the indicated system menus.
Private Sub RemoveMenus( _
    remove_restore As Boolean, _
    remove_move As Boolean, _
    remove_size As Boolean, _
    remove_minimize As Boolean, _
    remove_maximize As Boolean, _
    remove_separator As Boolean, _
    remove_close As Boolean)
Dim hMenu As Long

    ' Get the form's system menu handle.
    hMenu = GetSystemMenu(hwnd, False)

    If remove_close Then DeleteMenu hMenu, 6, MF_BYPOSITION
    If remove_separator Then DeleteMenu hMenu, 5, MF_BYPOSITION
    If remove_maximize Then DeleteMenu hMenu, 4, MF_BYPOSITION
    If remove_minimize Then DeleteMenu hMenu, 3, MF_BYPOSITION
    If remove_size Then DeleteMenu hMenu, 2, MF_BYPOSITION
    If remove_move Then DeleteMenu hMenu, 1, MF_BYPOSITION
    If remove_restore Then DeleteMenu hMenu, 0, MF_BYPOSITION
End Sub

' Set ReadyToClose so the QueryUnload event handler
' will let the unload continue.
Private Sub cmdClose_Click()
    ReadyToClose = True
    Unload Me
End Sub

' Cancel if ReadyToClose is false. This happens
' when the user presses Alt-F4 even though the
' Close item is gone from the system menu.
Private Sub Form_QueryUnload(Cancel As Integer, UnloadMode As Integer)
    Cancel = Not ReadyToClose
End Sub
```

The system menu does not always interact with Visual Basic in the ways you might expect. For instance, you can use subroutine RemoveMenus to remove the Minimize and Maximize items from the system menu. That will prevent the Minimize and Maximize buttons from working, but it does not disable them. They will not work, but the user can still click them. If you want to disable these functions, you should set the form's MinButton and MaxButton properties to False. That removes them from the system menu automatically.

137. List a Form's Menus

④ ⑤ ⑥

Directory: ListMenu

Visual Basic does not provide an easy method for examining a form's menu structure at run time, but a program can use API functions to examine its menus. Example program ListMenu does just that. When the program starts, it displays a list of its menus using indentation to show which items are contained in each menu.

Program ListMenu.

How It Works

The following code shows how program ListMenu works. The key to the program is the GetMenuInfo subroutine. This routine takes as parameters a menu's handle, the number of spaces it should indent the menu's information, and a string to hold this menu's information.

GetMenuInfo uses the GetMenuItemCount API function to see how many items are contained in the menu it is examining. Then, for each item in the menu, the subroutine uses the GetSubMenu API function to get the item's menu handle. It passes the handle to the GetMenuString API function to get the item's caption, and it adds the caption to the result string text.

Subroutine GetMenuInfo then calls itself recursively to get the information for its menu items. It increases the spaces parameter so the menu information is indented properly. If the item is a command item and not a submenu, the GetMenuItemCount API function returns 0 in the recursive call to GetMenuInfo. That routine will not loop over any items because it contains none, so it does not call itself again and the recursion ends.

```
Option Explicit

#If Win32 Then
```

```
        Private Declare Function GetMenu Lib "user32" _
            (ByVal hWnd As Long) As Long
        Private Declare Function GetMenuItemCount Lib "user32" _
            (ByVal hMenu As Long) As Long
        Private Declare Function GetSubMenu Lib "user32" ( _
            ByVal hMenu As Long, ByVal nPos As Long) As Long
        Private Declare Function GetMenuString Lib "user32" _
            Alias "GetMenuStringA" (ByVal hMenu As Long, _
            ByVal wIDItem As Long, ByVal lpString As String, _
            ByVal nMaxCount As Long, ByVal wFlag As Long) As Long
#Else
        Private Declare Function GetMenu Lib "User" _
            (ByVal hWnd As Integer) As Integer
        Private Declare Function GetMenuItemCount Lib "User" _
            (ByVal hMenu As Integer) As Integer
        Private Declare Function GetSubMenu Lib "User" ( _
            ByVal hMenu As Integer, ByVal nPos As Integer) As Integer
        Private Declare Function GetMenuString Lib "User" ( _
            ByVal hMenu As Integer, ByVal wIDItem As Integer, _
            ByVal lpString As String, ByVal nMaxCount As Integer, _
            ByVal wFlag As Integer) As Integer
#End If

Private Const MF_BYPOSITION = &H400&

' Make the TextBox as large as possible.
Private Sub Form_Resize()
    txtMenus.Move 0, 0, ScaleWidth, ScaleHeight
End Sub

' Display the form's menu information.
Private Sub Form_Load()
Dim txt As String

    GetMenuInfo GetMenu(hWnd), 0, txt
    txtMenus.Text = txt
End Sub

' Get the information about the form's menus.
Private Sub GetMenuInfo(hMenu As Long, spaces As Integer, txt As String)
Dim num As Integer
Dim i As Integer
Dim length As Long
Dim sub_hmenu As Long
Dim sub_name As String

    num = GetMenuItemCount(hMenu)
    For i = 0 To num - 1
        ' Save this menu's caption.
        sub_hmenu = GetSubMenu(hMenu, i)
        sub_name = Space$(256)
        length = GetMenuString(hMenu, i, _
```

```
                    sub_name, Len(sub_name), MF_BYPOSITION)
            sub_name = Left$(sub_name, length)

            txt = txt & Space$(spaces) & sub_name & vbCrLf

            ' Get its child menu's names.
            GetMenuInfo sub_hmenu, spaces + 4, txt
        Next i
    End Sub
```

This program starts its search for menu information using the form's hWnd property. The program could use the FindWindow API function to obtain the hWnd property of a form used by another application. It could then use the method demonstrated here to learn about that form's menus.

138. Hide a Form's Menus

Directory: HideMnu

A program can hide its menu bar by setting the Visible properties for each of its top-level menus to False. When the last menu is hidden, the menu bar disappears. To restore the menu bar, the program sets one or more of its menus' Visible properties to True.

Program HideMnu uses this method to hide and restore its menu bar. Check the Show Menu Bar box to make the menu bar visible. Uncheck the box to make the menu bar disappear.

Program HideMnu.

How It Works

Program HideMnu uses the following code to manage its menu bar. When it starts, the program fills a collection with the form's top-level menu objects. When the user clicks the Show Menu Bar checkbox, the chkShowMenuBar_Click event handler displays or hides these objects.

```
Option Explicit

Private Menus As New Collection

' Fill a collection with the main menu objects.
Private Sub Form_Load()
    Menus.Add mnuFile
    Menus.Add mnuCommands
    Menus.Add mnuHelp

    chkShowMenuBar.Value = vbChecked
End Sub

' Display or hide the menu bar.
Private Sub chkShowMenuBar_Click()
Dim obj As Menu
Dim show_menu As Boolean

    show_menu = (chkShowMenuBar.Value = vbChecked)
    For Each obj In Menus
        obj.Visible = show_menu
    Next obj
End Sub
```

139. Hide a Form's Menus Using the API

④ ⑤ ⑥

Directory: HideMnu2

The previous example shows how to hide a form's menu bar by setting the Visible properties of its top-level menus. Although this is effective, it is a bit cumbersome. The program must keep track of the top-level menus. If you later change the menu structure, you must update the menu collection.

A program can accomplish the same thing using API functions. Program HideMnu2 demonstrates this method. Check the Show Menu Bar box to make the menu bar visible. Uncheck the box to make the menu bar disappear.

Program HideMnu2.

How It Works

The HideMnu2 program uses the following code to make its menus appear and disappear. When you click the Show Menu Bar check box, the chkShowMenuBar_Click event handler executes. This routine checks its static hMenu variable to see if it currently holds the handle for a menu. If hMenu is 0, the routine does not have a menu handle so the menu must currently be displayed. The routine uses the GetMenu API function to get and save the menu bar's handle. It then uses the SetMenu API function to set the menu bar's handle to 0. That makes the menu bar disappear.

If the hMenu variable is not 0, it contains a menu handle. The routine uses the SetMenu API function to restore the form's menu bar. It then sets hMenu to 0 so that it will know that the menu bar is visible the next time it executes.

```
Option Explicit

#If Win32 Then
    Private Declare Function GetMenu Lib "user32" _
        (ByVal hWnd As Long) As Long
    Private Declare Function SetMenu Lib "user32" _
        (ByVal hWnd As Long, ByVal hMenu As Long) As Long
#Else
    Private Declare Function GetMenu Lib "User" _
        (ByVal hWnd As Integer) As Integer
    Private Declare Function SetMenu Lib "User" _
        (ByVal hWnd As Integer, ByVal hMenu As Integer) As Integer
#End If

' Display or hide the menu bar.
Private Sub chkShowMenuBar_Click()
Static hMenu As Long

    If hMenu = 0 Then
        ' Get the menu handle and hide the menu.
        hMenu = GetMenu(hWnd)
        SetMenu hWnd, 0
    Else
        ' Restore the old menu.
        SetMenu hWnd, hMenu
        hMenu = 0
    End If
End Sub
```

140. Add to the System Menu

Directory: SysAbout

Some Windows programs have an About command in their system menus. Visual Basic itself does not provide access to the system menu, but you can add commands using API functions. Example program SysAbout adds a menu separator and an About command to the system menu. When you select the command, the program presents a dialog box.

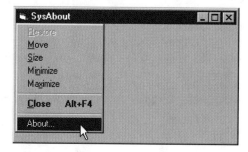

Program SysAbout.

How It Works

Adding a new item to the system menu is not hard. Detecting when the user invokes that item is a bit more difficult. It requires that the program subclass to intercept Windows messages and look for the message sent by the new menu item. Because subclassing requires the program to pass the address of a function to the SetWindowLong API function, the program must use the AddressOf operator. AddressOf was introduced in Visual Basic 5, so this method does not work with earlier versions of Visual Basic.

The following code is contained in program SysAbout's main form. All it does is call subroutine AddAboutCommand. That routine is contained in the module SysAbout.bas.

```
Option Explicit

' Create the About command.
Private Sub Form_Load()
    AddAboutCommand hWnd
End Sub
```

Module SysAbout.bas contains the following code. Subroutine AddAboutCommand uses the GetSystemMenu API function to get the system menu's handle. It uses the AppendMenu API function to add a separator and the About command to the menu. It assigns the value of the IDM_ABOUT constant to the About command. When the user selects this item from the system menu, the form receives the WM_SYSCOMMAND

Windows message with the parameter IDM_ABOUT. Subroutine AddAboutCommand finishes by replacing the old WindowProc with a new one that looks for this message.

The AboutWindowProc function watches for the WM_SYSCOMMAND message with the parameter IDM_ABOUT. When it receives that message, it presents the program's About dialog.

```
Option Explicit

' The original WindowProc.
Private OldWindowProc As Long

Private Declare Function CallWindowProc Lib "user32" _
    Alias "CallWindowProcA" (ByVal lpPrevWndFunc As Long, _
    ByVal hWnd As Long, ByVal msg As Long, ByVal wParam As Long, _
    ByVal lParam As Long) As Long
Private Declare Function SetWindowLong Lib "user32" _
    Alias "SetWindowLongA" (ByVal hWnd As Long, ByVal nIndex As Long, _
    ByVal dwNewLong As Long) As Long
Private Const GWL_WNDPROC = (-4)

Private Declare Function GetSystemMenu Lib "user32" ( _
    ByVal hWnd As Long, ByVal bRevert As Long) As Long
Private Declare Function AppendMenu Lib "user32" _
    Alias "AppendMenuA" (ByVal hMenu As Long, ByVal wFlags As Long, _
    ByVal wIDNewItem As Long, ByVal lpNewItem As String) As Long
Private Const WM_SYSCOMMAND = &H112
Private Const MF_SEPARATOR = &H800&
Private Const MF_BYPOSITION = &H400&
Private Const MF_ENABLED = &H0&
Private Const MF_STRING = &H0&

' The ID we are assigning to the About command.
Private Const IDM_ABOUT = 1999

' Create the About command and replace the WindowProc
' with one that looks for it.
Public Sub AddAboutCommand(ByVal hWnd As Long)
Dim hSystemMenu As Long

    ' Get the system menu's handle.
    hSystemMenu = GetSystemMenu(hWnd, False)

    ' Add a separator to the end of the system menu.
    AppendMenu hSystemMenu, MF_SEPARATOR, 0, ""

    ' Add "About" to the end of the system menu.
    AppendMenu hSystemMenu, MF_STRING + MF_ENABLED, _
        IDM_ABOUT, "About..."
```

```
    ' Install the WindowProc to handle it.
    OldWindowProc = SetWindowLong( _
        hWnd, GWL_WNDPROC, _
        AddressOf AboutWindowProc)
End Sub

' Pass along all messages except the one that
' makes the context menu appear.
Public Function AboutWindowProc(ByVal hWnd As Long, ByVal msg As Long, _
    ByVal wParam As Long, ByVal lParam As Long) As Long

    If msg = WM_SYSCOMMAND And _
        wParam = IDM_ABOUT _
    Then
        frmAbout.Show vbModal
        Exit Function
    End If

    AboutWindowProc = CallWindowProc( _
        OldWindowProc, hWnd, msg, wParam, _
        lParam)
End Function
```

Using this technique, you can add other items to the system menu. Most users will not expect items here, however, so you should not get carried away with this. You should probably not put items in this menu that are important and not available elsewhere.

Managing Forms

Forms are the basic unit of Windows programming in Visual Basic. Almost all of a program's user interface is displayed on forms. This chapter describes special ways a program can manipulate forms. It tells how to keep one form on top of another, manage wait cursors, and create irregularly shaped forms.

---

141. Size a Form in Inches ④ ⑤ ⑥

Directory: Inches

A form's Width and Height properties give the form's size in twips (1/1440 inch). To specify a form's size in inches, a program needs to convert from inches to twips. Program Inches sets its form's interior size in inches. Note that these are logical inches and the exact dimensions of the form will depend on your computer's monitor.

Program Inches.

How It Works

Program Inches uses the following code to size its form. Subroutine SetFormSizeIn-Inches sets the form's size. It multiplies the desired dimensions by 1440 to convert them from inches into twips. It also adjusts the dimensions to allow room for the form's borders. It uses the ScaleX and ScaleY methods to translate the form's current interior dimensions into twips.

```
Option Explicit

' Set the form to the indicated size.
Private Sub cmdResize_Click()
    SetFormSizeInInches Me, _
        CSng(txtWidth.Text), CSng(txtHeight.Text)
End Sub

' Set the form's interior size in inches.
Public Sub SetFormSizeInInches(ByVal frm As Form, _
    ByVal wid As Single, ByVal hgt As Single)

    frm.Width = wid * 1440 + frm.Width - _
        frm.ScaleX(frm.ScaleWidth, frm.ScaleMode, vbTwips)
    frm.Height = hgt * 1440 + frm.Height - _
        frm.ScaleY(frm.ScaleHeight, frm.ScaleMode, vbTwips)
End Sub
```

142. Keep a Form on Top of Another ⑤ ⑥

Directory: OnTop

Sometimes it is useful to make one form remain above another. For instance, a drawing program might display a tool box or color palette that should remain above the drawing area.

Starting with Visual Basic 5, a program can make one form the child of another. The child form must always remain on top of its parent. Example program OnTop demonstrates this technique. The two frmChild forms must always remain on top of the main parent form, no matter which of the three has the input focus. The parent-child relationship makes the child forms automatically unload when their parent does.

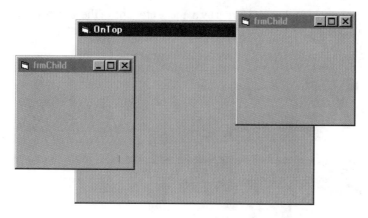

Program OnTop.

How It Works

The following code shows how program OnTop works. When it starts, the program simply displays two child forms modelessly specifying itself as their parent.

```
Option Explicit

' Display two child forms.
Private Sub Form_Load()
Dim child As frmChild

    Set child = New frmChild
    child.Show vbModeless, Me

    Set child = New frmChild
    child.Show vbModeless, Me
End Sub
```

Unfortunately, a child window in an MDI application cannot be the parent of other windows. That means this method will not allow you to create an MDI application where one MDI child must remain above all of the others.

143. Display a Form by Name

Directory: ByName

Occasionally, it is convenient for a program to open a form using its name. For instance, the program might know that it needs to open a form named "Person" but not that this is an instance of the form type frmPerson. A program can implement this kind of behavior using a Select Case statement.

Example program ByName displays forms by name. Enter one of the strings Person, Place, or Thing in the TextBox, and click the Open button. The program creates and displays the corresponding form.

Program ByName.

How It Works

Program ByName uses the following code to display forms. When you click the Open button, the program reads the form name you entered. It uses a Select statement to create a form of the correct type. It then displays the form.

```
Option Explicit

' Open the named form.
Private Sub cmdOpen_Click()
Dim frm As Form

    ' Assign frm to the right kind of form.
    Select Case LCase$(txtFormName.Text)
        Case "person"
            Set frm = New frmPerson
        Case "place"
            Set frm = New frmPlace
        Case "thing"
            Set frm = New frmThing
        Case Else
            MsgBox "There is no form named '" & _
                txtFormName.Text & "'"
            Exit Sub
    End Select
```

```
' Show the form.
    frm.Show
End Sub
```

144. Display a Single Form by Name

Directory: ByName2

Some programs may need to specify a form by its name but display only one instance of each type of form. One approach to creating the forms would be to modify the previous example's Select Case statement so that it displays the unique instance of each form instead of creating a new instance using the Set frm = New statement. The following code shows the previous example's cmdOpen_Click event handler modified in this way.

```
Private Sub cmdOpen_Click()
    ' Display the right form.
    Select Case LCase$(txtFormName.Text)
        Case "person"
            frmPerson.Show
        Case "place"
            frmPlace.Show
        Case "thing"
            frmThing.Show
        Case Else
            MsgBox "There is no form named '" & _
                txtFormName.Text & "'"
    End Select
End Sub
```

Another approach is to store the forms in a collection using their names as keys. Then the program can quickly access and display the forms when it needs them. Example program ByName2 demonstrates this approach. Enter one of the strings Person, Place, or Thing in the TextBox, and click the Open button. The program creates and displays the corresponding form.

Program ByName2.

How It Works

When program ByName2 starts, it fills a collection with references to its forms using the forms' names as keys. Later, when you click the Open button, the program uses the name you entered to quickly locate and display the form. This method is faster than the Select Case statement used in the previous example, particularly if the program contains many forms.

```
Option Explicit

' A collection of the forms to display.
Private FormInstances As Collection

' Save the forms in the FormInstances collection.
Private Sub Form_Load()
    Set FormInstances = New Collection

    FormInstances.Add frmPerson, "person"
    FormInstances.Add frmPlace, "place"
    FormInstances.Add frmThing, "thing"
End Sub

' Open the named form.
Private Sub cmdOpen_Click()
Dim frm As Form

    ' Trap the error if the form name is not in
    ' the collection.
    On Error Resume Next
    Set frm = FormInstances(LCase$(txtFormName.Text))
    If Err.Number <> 0 Then
        ' There must not be a form with this name.
```

```
            MsgBox "There is no form named '" & _
                txtFormName.Text & "'"
        Else
            ' Show the form.
            frm.Show
        End If
    End Sub
```

145. Manage Hourglass Cursors

☆ ☆
④ ⑤ ⑥

Directory: Waits

When a program performs a long operation, it should display an hourglass cursor so the user knows it is doing something time-consuming. Unfortunately, this can sometimes be confusing for the programmer. If several complex subroutines that call one another each display the hourglass cursor, it can be hard to decide when to restore the cursor to normal. This can be especially tricky if one or more of the subroutines ends prematurely due to an error. The result can be a rapidly flickering hourglass cursor, a cursor that resets before the long operation finishes, or a cursor that never resets so that the user is stuck with an hourglass cursor forever.

If a program uses a single subroutine to manage the hourglass cursor, that routine can keep track of the cursor's desired value. The subroutine keeps a count of the long routines that are currently executing. When a routine starts, it calls this subroutine to increase the hourglass cursor count. When it finishes, it calls the subroutine again to reduce the count. When the count reaches 0, the subroutine restores the default cursor.

Example Waits demonstrates this technique. Click the Start Wait button to increase the wait count. Click the End Wait button to reduce the count. Click the Clear Waits button to reset the count to 0. While the count is greater than 0, the program displays an hourglass cursor.

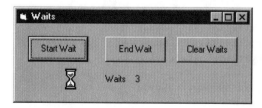

Program Waits.

How It Works

Program Waits uses the following code to manage its cursor. The Hourglass subroutine keeps track of the number of routines that want the cursor set to an hourglass. The program passes this routine the value 1 to increase the wait count and -1 to decrease it. Subroutine Hourglass determines whether the cursor's state should change and updates it accordingly. By comparing the cursor's previous and new states, the routine avoids causing a flickering cursor when the program repeatedly sets the cursor to an hourglass.

A subroutine can protect itself from errors within the routines it calls by passing Hourglass a large negative number such as -10,000 to clear the wait count. For instance, suppose the user clicks a button that starts a long process. The button starts by calling Hourglass with the parameter 1 to display the hourglass cursor. One of the routines the button's code invokes may also call subroutine Hourglass. If it then fails, it may exit prematurely without reducing the wait count properly. If the button click event handler simply decreases the wait count by 1, the count will still be greater than 0 so the cursor will remain an hourglass forever. The event handler can prevent this by passing subroutine Hourglass the value -10,000 to clear the wait count.

```
Option Explicit

' Add 1 to the wait count.
Private Sub cmdStartWait_Click()
    Hourglass 1
End Sub

' Subtract 1 from the wait count.
Private Sub cmdEndWait_Click()
    Hourglass -1
End Sub

' Clear all the waits.
Private Sub cmdClearWaits_Click()
    Hourglass -10000
End Sub

' Add or subtract the value from wait_counter. If
' wait_counter = 0, display the default cursor.
' Otherwise display the hourglass cursor.
'
' Use +1 to start waiting, -1 to stop waiting,
' -10000 to clear all waits.
Private Sub Hourglass(ByVal add_to_count As Integer)
Static wait_counter As Integer

Dim was_hourglass As Boolean
Dim now_hourglass As Boolean

    ' Record the current cursor state.
    was_hourglass = (wait_counter > 0)
```

```
        ' Update start_wait.
        wait_counter = wait_counter + add_to_count
        If wait_counter < 0 Then wait_counter = 0

        ' See if the cursor's status has changed.
        ' We set it only if it has. Otherwise
        ' repeatedly resetting the cursor with the
        ' same value will make it flicker.
        now_hourglass = (wait_counter > 0)
        If now_hourglass <> was_hourglass Then
            If wait_counter = 0 Then
                Screen.MousePointer = vbDefault
            Else
                Screen.MousePointer = vbHourglass
            End If
        End If

        ' Update the wait counter display.
        ' Remove this in a real application.
        lblWaits = wait_counter
    End Sub
```

146. Make an Elliptical Form

④ ⑤ ⑥

Directory: Ellipse

Normally windows are rectangular. Using API functions, a program can make a form that has an interesting and unusual shape. Example program Ellipse displays an elliptical form.

Program Ellipse.

How It Works

Program Ellipse uses the CreateEllipticRgn API function to define an elliptical region. The region is measured in pixels from the upper left corner of the window. The program then uses the SetWindowRgn API function to confine its form to the region.

Any part of the form that lies outside the region is clipped off by windows. It is not merely transparent; it is as good as gone. If you click in a position that would be part of the form if it were rectangular but has been clipped off, the mouse click passes through to whatever window lies below.

In this program, the elliptical region chops off the program's Close button and system menu in the corners of its menu bar. Without those buttons, it is hard for the user to close the form so the program includes a Close button to make exiting easy. The region also excludes the form's resizable border so the user cannot easily resize it. If the region had chopped off all of the title bar, the user would also have difficulty moving the form.

```vb
Option Explicit

#If Win32 Then
    Private Declare Function CreateEllipticRgn Lib "gdi32" ( _
        ByVal X1 As Long, ByVal Y1 As Long, ByVal X2 As Long, _
        ByVal Y2 As Long) As Long
    Private Declare Function SetWindowRgn Lib "user32" ( _
        ByVal hWnd As Long, ByVal hRgn As Long, ByVal bRedraw As Long) _
        As Long
    Private Declare Function DeleteObject Lib "gdi32" ( _
        ByVal hObject As Long) As Long
#Else
    Private Declare Function CreateEllipticRgn Lib "GDI" ( _
        ByVal X1 As Integer, ByVal Y1 As Integer, ByVal X2 As Integer, _
        ByVal Y2 As Integer) As Integer
    Private Declare Function SetWindowRgn Lib "user" ( _
        ByVal hWnd As Integer, ByVal hRgn As Integer, _
        ByVal bRedraw As Integer) As Integer
    Private Declare Function DeleteObject Lib "GDI" ( _
        ByVal hObject As Integer) As Integer
#End If

Private WindowRegion As Long

' Confine the form to an elliptical region.
Private Sub Form_Resize()
Static done_before As Boolean

Dim wid As Long
Dim hgt As Long
Dim rgn As Long

    ' Do nothing if we have done this before
    ' or we are minimized.
    If WindowState = vbMinimized Then Exit Sub
    If done_before Then Exit Sub
    done_before = True

    ' Create the elliptical region.
    wid = ScaleX(Width, vbTwips, vbPixels) - 20
```

```
    hgt = ScaleY(Height, vbTwips, vbPixels) - 20
    rgn = CreateEllipticRgn(10, 10, wid, hgt)

    ' Restrict the window to the region.
    SetWindowRgn hWnd, rgn, True

    ' Center the Close button.
    cmdClose.Move _
        (ScaleWidth - cmdClose.Width) / 2, _
        (ScaleHeight - cmdClose.Height) / 2
End Sub

' Unload the form.
Private Sub cmdClose_Click()
    Unload Me
End Sub
```

147. Make a Polygonal Form

Directory: PolyForm

The previous example shows how to create an elliptical form. Example program Poly-Form uses API functions to create a polygonal form.

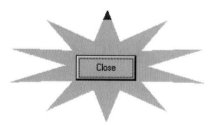

Program PolyForm.

How It Works

Program PolyForm uses the CreatePolygonRgn API function to define a polygonal region. It uses the SetWindowRgn API function to confine its form to the region. As is the case in the previous example, the region removes the form's system menu, Close button, and resizable borders. The program includes a Close button to make ending the program easier.

```
Option Explicit

#If Win32 Then
    Private Declare Function CreatePolygonRgn Lib "gdi32" ( _
        lpPoint As POINTAPI, ByVal nCount As Long, _
```

```
            ByVal nPolyFillMode As Long) As Long
        Private Declare Function SetWindowRgn Lib "user32" ( _
            ByVal hWnd As Long, ByVal hRgn As Long, ByVal bRedraw As Long) _
            As Long
        Private Declare Function DeleteObject Lib "gdi32" ( _
            ByVal hObject As Long) As Long
        Private Type POINTAPI
            x As Long
            y As Long
        End Type
#Else
        Private Declare Function CreatePolygonRgn Lib "GDI" ( _
            lpPoints As POINTAPI, ByVal nCount As Integer, _
            ByVal nPolyFillMode As Integer) As Integer
        Private Declare Function SetWindowRgn Lib "user" ( _
            ByVal hWnd As Integer, ByVal hRgn As Integer, _
            ByVal bRedraw As Integer) As Integer
        Private Declare Function DeleteObject Lib "GDI" ( _
            ByVal hObject As Integer) As Integer
        Type POINTAPI
            x As Integer
            y As Integer
        End Type
#End If


' Confine the form to a star-shaped region.
Private Sub Form_Resize()
Const ALTERNATE = 1
Const NUM_POINTS = 20
Const PI = 3.14159265


Static done_before As Boolean

Dim wid As Single
Dim hgt As Single
Dim theta As Single
Dim dtheta As Single
Dim i As Integer
Dim w(0 To 1) As Single
Dim h(0 To 1) As Single
Dim cx As Single
Dim cy As Single
Dim points() As POINTAPI
Dim rgn As Long

    ' Do nothing if we have done this before
    ' or we are minimized.
    If WindowState = vbMinimized Then Exit Sub
    If done_before Then Exit Sub
    done_before = True

    ' Create the points for the polygon.
```

```
' This example makes a many-pointed star.
wid = ScaleX(Width, vbTwips, vbPixels) - 20
hgt = ScaleY(Height, vbTwips, vbPixels) - 20
cx = wid / 2
cy = hgt / 2
w(0) = wid * 0.2
w(1) = wid * 0.5
h(0) = hgt * 0.2
h(1) = hgt * 0.5
dtheta = 2 * PI / NUM_POINTS
theta = PI / 2
ReDim points(1 To NUM_POINTS)
For i = 1 To NUM_POINTS
    With points(i)
        .x = cx + w(i Mod 2) * Cos(theta)
        .y = cy + h(i Mod 2) * Sin(theta)
        theta = theta + dtheta
    End With
Next i

' Create the polygonal region.
rgn = CreatePolygonRgn(points(1), _
    NUM_POINTS, ALTERNATE)

' Restrict the window to the region.
SetWindowRgn hWnd, rgn, True

' Position the Close button.
cmdClose.Move _
    cx - cmdClose.Width / 2 - _
        ScaleX(5, vbPixels, ScaleMode), _
    cy - cmdClose.Height / 2 - _
        ScaleY(20, vbPixels, ScaleMode)
End Sub


' Unload the form.
Private Sub cmdClose_Click()
    Unload Me
End Sub
```

148. Make a Form with a Hole in It

Directory: HoleForm

Like the previous two examples, this example shows how to confine a form to a region. In this case, the region is a rectangle containing the entire form, minus a rectangular region in the middle. The result is a form with a hole in it.

Example program HoleForm demonstrates this technique. In the figure, you can see the Notepad application showing through the hole. If you click on a window through the hole, that application pops to the top and receives the input focus.

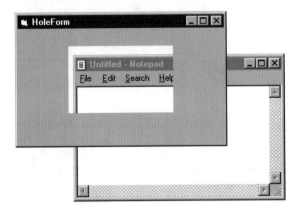

Program HoleForm.

How It Works

Program HoleForm uses the CreateRectRgn API function to define two rectangular regions. The first is the size of the form. The second is only half as large and is centered on the form.

The program then uses the CombineRgn API function to combine the two regions. The program passes the RGN_DIFF flag to CombineRgn to subtract the smaller region from the larger one. It then uses SetWindowRgn to confine the form to the resulting region.

```
Option Explicit

#If Win32 Then
    Private Declare Function CreateRectRgn Lib "gdi32" ( _
        ByVal X1 As Long, ByVal Y1 As Long, ByVal X2 As Long, _
        ByVal Y2 As Long) As Long
    Private Declare Function CombineRgn Lib "gdi32" ( _
        ByVal hDestRgn As Long, ByVal hSrcRgn1 As Long, _
        ByVal hSrcRgn2 As Long, ByVal nCombineMode As Long) As Long
    Private Declare Function SetWindowRgn Lib "user32" ( _
        ByVal hWnd As Long, ByVal hRgn As Long, ByVal bRedraw As Long) _
        As Long
    Private Declare Function DeleteObject Lib "gdi32" ( _
        ByVal hObject As Long) As Long
#Else
    Private Declare Function CreateRectRgn Lib "GDI" ( _
        ByVal X1 As Integer, ByVal Y1 As Integer, ByVal X2 As Integer, _
        ByVal Y2 As Integer) As Integer
    Private Declare Function CombineRgn Lib "GDI" ( _
        ByVal hDestRgn As Integer, ByVal hSrcRgn1 As Integer, _
```

```
        ByVal hSrcRgn2 As Integer, ByVal nCombineMode As Integer) _
        As Integer
    Private Declare Function SetWindowRgn Lib "user" ( _
        ByVal hWnd As Integer, ByVal hRgn As Integer, _
        ByVal bRedraw As Integer) As Integer
    Private Declare Function DeleteObject Lib "GDI" ( _
        ByVal hObject As Integer) As Integer
#End If

' Confine the form to a region with a hole in it.
Private Sub Form_Resize()
Static done_before As Boolean

Const RGN_DIFF = 4

Dim outer_rgn As Long
Dim inner_rgn As Long
Dim combined_rgn As Long
Dim wid As Single
Dim hgt As Single
Dim border_width As Single
Dim title_height As Single

    ' Do nothing if we have done this before
    ' or we are minimized.
    If WindowState = vbMinimized Then Exit Sub
    If done_before Then Exit Sub
    done_before = True

    ' Create the regions.
    wid = ScaleX(Width, vbTwips, vbPixels)
    hgt = ScaleY(Height, vbTwips, vbPixels)
    outer_rgn = CreateRectRgn(0, 0, wid, hgt)

    border_width = (wid - ScaleWidth) / 2
    title_height = hgt - border_width - ScaleHeight
    inner_rgn = CreateRectRgn( _
        wid * 0.25, hgt * 0.25, _
        wid * 0.75, hgt * 0.75)

    ' Subtract the inner region from the outer.
    combined_rgn = CreateRectRgn(0, 0, 0, 0)
    CombineRgn combined_rgn, outer_rgn, _
        inner_rgn, RGN_DIFF

    ' Restrict the window to the combined region.
    SetWindowRgn hWnd, combined_rgn, True

    ' Delete the regions we no longer need.
    DeleteObject inner_rgn
    DeleteObject outer_rgn
End Sub
```

149. Center a Form

Directory: CentFrm

The positioning of a form when it is created depends on how it is built. Normally, a form is positioned where it was created at design time. For some forms such as splash screens and about dialogs, it is better to display the form centered on the screen. Example program CentFrm centers its form when it loads.

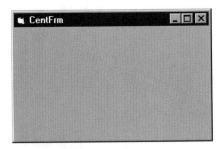

Program CentFrm.

How It Works

The following few lines of code are all that program CentFrm needs to center its form.

```
' Center the form on the screen.
Private Sub Form_Load()
    Left = (Screen.Width - Width) / 2
    Top = (Screen.Height - Height) / 2
End Sub
```

150. Read Windows Messages

Directory: SubClass

The Windows operating systems manage controls by sending them messages. The control interprets the messages and takes whatever action it must. For instance, when a TextBox control receives the message WM_SETTEXT, it sets its text to a value specified with the message.

Normally, Visual Basic programs handle messages automatically. Sometimes, however, it is useful to see what messages a control receives. Example program SubClass displays information about the messages its form receives.

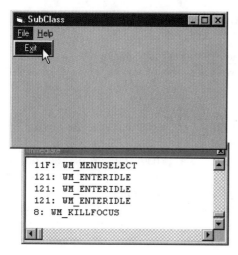

Program SubClass.

How It Works

The following code is contained in the main form used by program SubClass. The most important part is the call to the InstallWatchWindowProc subroutine contained in Sub-Class.bas. The form's menus exist only so the program can display the Windows messages that it receives when the user selects menu items.

```
Option Explicit

' Install the WatchWindowProc routine.
Private Sub Form_Load()
    InstallWatchWindowProc Me
End Sub

' Unload the form.
Private Sub mnuFileExit_Click()
    Unload Me
End Sub

' Display an about dialog.
Private Sub mnuHelpAbout_Click()
    MsgBox "Display an about dialog here."
End Sub
```

The following code is contained in the SubClass.bas module. The main program calls subroutine InstallWatchWindowProc to prepare to watch for Windows messages. InstallWatchWindowProc calls the LoadMsgNames routine to initialize a collection of message names. The list of names is quite long, so only a tiny part of it is shown here.

InstallWatchWindowProc then calls the SetWindowLong API function to install the subroutine WatchWindowProc as the form's new WindowProc. The WindowProc routine is called by Windows when it needs to send a message to the window. Installing a new WindowProc is called subclassing in Visual Basic.

The AddressOf statement used in the call to SetWindowLong was introduced in Visual Basic 5, so this procedure will not work in earlier versions of Visual Basic. Note that AddressOf works with functions declared in .bas modules, so function WatchWindow-Proc is defined in a .bas module.

When Windows sends a message to the form, the WatchWindowProc subroutine receives it. That routine calls MsgName to display the message's name. It then uses the Call-WindowProc API function to process the message using the form's original WindowProc routine. This is extremely important. If the subroutine does not process the form's messages normally, it will be unable to perform normal Windows tasks such as refreshing itself, drawing itself on the screen, resizing itself, and so forth. A new WindowProc routine such as this one should always pass any messages it does not handle completely by itself on to the original WindowProc routine.

```vb
Option Explicit

Private OldWindowProc As Long

Private Declare Function CallWindowProc Lib "user32" Alias _
    "CallWindowProcA" (ByVal lpPrevWndFunc As Long, _
    ByVal hwnd As Long, ByVal msg As Long, ByVal wParam As Long, _
    ByVal lParam As Long) As Long
Private Declare Function SetWindowLong Lib "user32" Alias _
    "SetWindowLongA" (ByVal hwnd As Long, ByVal nIndex As Long, _
    ByVal dwNewLong As Long) As Long

Private Const GWL_WNDPROC = (-4)
Private Const WM_USER = &H400

Private MsgNames As New Collection

' Install the WatchWindowProc routine.
Public Sub InstallWatchWindowProc(ByVal frm As Form)
    ' Load the message name collection.
    LoadMsgNames

    ' Install the WindowProc.
    OldWindowProc = SetWindowLong( _
        frm.hwnd, GWL_WNDPROC, _
        AddressOf WatchWindowProc)

    ' Display a marker in the Debug window.
    Debug.Print "********************"
End Sub

' Fill the MsgNames collection with windows
' message names.
Private Sub LoadMsgNames()
```

```
        MsgNames.Add "WM_NULL", "0"
        MsgNames.Add "WM_CREATE", "1"
            :
    ' <Lots of values omitted>
            :
End Sub


' Return the name of a message.
Private Function MsgName(ByVal num As Long) As String
    ' Be careful in case a message is not present.
    On Error Resume Next
    MsgName = MsgNames(Hex$(num))
    If Err.Number = 0 Then Exit Function

    If num >= 0 And num < WM_USER Then
        MsgName = "Range 1 message reserved for Windows"
    ElseIf num >= WM_USER And num <= &H7FFF Then
        MsgName = "Reserved for private window classes"
    ElseIf num >= &H8000 And num <= &HBFFF Then
        MsgName = "Range 3 message reserved for Windows"
    ElseIf num >= &H8000 And num <= &HBFFF Then
        MsgName = "String message for use by applications"
    Else
        MsgName = "Unknown message" & Str$(num)
    End If
End Function


' Display and process the message.
Private Function WatchWindowProc(ByVal hwnd As Long, _
    ByVal msg As Long, ByVal wParam As Long, ByVal lParam As Long) _
    As Long

    ' Display this message's name.
    Debug.Print Hex$(msg) & ": " & MsgName(msg)

    ' Call the original WindowProc so we process
    ' the message as usual.
    WatchWindowProc = CallWindowProc( _
        OldWindowProc, hwnd, msg, wParam, _
        lParam)
End Function
```

Visual Basic does not work properly while a WindowProc routine processes a Windows message. Break points within the WindowProc do not behave normally. The program also cannot shut down properly if you stop it using the Run menu's End command or the End button on the development environment's toolbars. If you stop the program in this way, the entire Visual Basic development environment crashes, and you lose any changes you have made since the last time you saved. The program can end safely if you end it in the normal way by closing all of its forms.

Subclassing in Visual Basic is very dangerous. If you make any mistakes, you are likely to crash the development environment and lose any unsaved changes. For that reason, you should save every time you run a program that subclasses.

151. Fix a Form's Width

Directory: FixWidth

The previous section explains how to subclass a form to examine Windows messages. Once you can examine these messages, it is a simple matter to take action when a form receives a particular message.

Example program FixWidth examines its form's messages looking for the message WM_WINDOWPOSCHANGING. That message indicates the window is changing size or position. When it sees this message, the program resets the form's width to its original value. This prevents the form from changing width and results in a fixed width form.

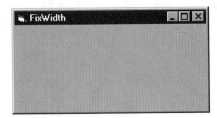

Program FixWidth.

How It Works

The main form used by program FixWidth does nothing more than call the Install-FixWidthWindowProc subroutine contained in module FixWidth.bas.

```
Option Explicit

' Install the FixWidthWindowProc.
Private Sub Form_Load()
    InstallFixWidthWindowProc Me
End Sub
```

The following code is contained in module FixWidth.bas. Subroutine InstallFixWidth-WindowProc subclasses the form to install function FixWidthWindowProc as the form's new WindowProc. When the window receives a message, FixWidthWindowProc checks to see if it is the WM_WINDOWPOSCHANGING message that could indicate a change in the form's size.

The first time the function detects this message, it saves the form's width. This is the form's original width. Subsequently, the function resets the width field cx in the message's size and position data structure to the original value.

```
Option Explicit

Private OldWindowProc As Long
Private Declare Function CallWindowProc Lib "user32" _
    Alias "CallWindowProcA" (ByVal lpPrevWndFunc As Long, _
    ByVal hwnd As Long, ByVal msg As Long, ByVal wParam As Long, _
    lParam As WINDOWPOS) As Long
Private Declare Function SetWindowLong Lib "user32" _
    Alias "SetWindowLongA" (ByVal hwnd As Long, ByVal nIndex As Long, _
    ByVal dwNewLong As Long) As Long
Private Const GWL_WNDPROC = (-4)

Private Type WINDOWPOS
    hwnd As Long
    hWndInsertAfter As Long
    x As Long
    y As Long
    cx As Long
    cy As Long
    flags As Long
End Type

Private Const WM_WINDOWPOSCHANGING = &H46

' Install the FixWidthWindowProc.
Public Sub InstallFixWidthWindowProc(ByVal frm As Form)
    OldWindowProc = SetWindowLong( _
        frm.hwnd, GWL_WNDPROC, _
        AddressOf FixWidthWindowProc)
End Sub

' Process messages looking for size changes.
Private Function FixWidthWindowProc(ByVal hwnd As Long, _
    ByVal msg As Long, ByVal wParam As Long, lParam As WINDOWPOS) _
    As Long

Static done_before As Boolean
Static orig_wid As Long

    If msg = WM_WINDOWPOSCHANGING Then
        ' Don't bother unless width > 0.
        If lParam.cx > 0 Then
            ' The first time, save the original width.
            If Not done_before Then
                done_before = True
                orig_wid = lParam.cx
            End If
```

```
            ' Force the form to have the original width.
            lParam.cx = orig_wid
        End If
    End If

    ' Process the message as usual.
    FixWidthWindowProc = CallWindowProc( _
        OldWindowProc, hwnd, msg, wParam, _
        lParam)
End Function
```

Using similar techniques you can control other aspects of the form's geometry. For instance, by setting the size and position data structure's x and y values, you can control the form's position. By forcing cx and cy to lie between minimum and maximum values, you can give the form a minimum and maximum size. If you set cx = cy, you can make the form square.

152. Display an Icon in the System Tray

☆ ☆ ☆
⑤ ⑥

Directory: SysTray

The right side of the Windows task bar contains a small box called the system tray. Many systems display a clock and other special icons here. Using API functions, a program can place its icon in the system tray, too.

Example program SysTray does this. When the program is minimized, you can left-click on the tray icon to restore the form. You can also right-click on the tray icon to open a menu allowing you to minimize, maximize, or close the program.

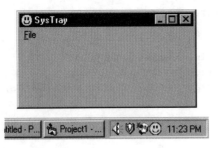

Program SysTray.

How It Works

The following code is contained in the SysTray program's main form module. When the form loads, it calls the AddToTray and SetTrayTip subroutines defined in module SysTray.bas. AddToTray adds the form's icon to the system tray and prepares the application to receive tray messages. SetTrayTip sets the text that is displayed when the user rests the mouse over the tray icon. These routines are described in more detail shortly.

When the form resizes, it calls subroutine SetTrayMenuItems to enable the appropriate popup menu items. For instance, when the form is minimized, SetTrayMenuItems disables the menu's Minimize item and enables the Restore and Maximize items.

When the form unloads, the program calls the RemoveFromTray subroutine. This routine removes the program's icon from the system tray. If the routine is not called, the icon remains in the system tray even after the program exits.

The main form used by program SysTray provides the menu displayed by the tray icon. When you right-click on the icon, the program displays the form's mnuTray popup menu. Its mnuTrayMaximize, mnuTrayMinimize, and mnuTrayRestore items provide the functionality of the menu. These menu items send the application Windows messages to make it maximize, minimize, and restore itself.

```
Option Explicit

' Enable the appropriate tray menu items.
Public Sub SetTrayMenuItems(window_state As Integer)
    Select Case window_state
        Case vbMinimized
            mnuTrayMaximize.Enabled = True
            mnuTrayMinimize.Enabled = False
            mnuTrayRestore.Enabled = True
        Case vbMaximized
            mnuTrayMaximize.Enabled = False
            mnuTrayMinimize.Enabled = True
            mnuTrayRestore.Enabled = True
        Case vbNormal
            mnuTrayMaximize.Enabled = True
            mnuTrayMinimize.Enabled = True
            mnuTrayRestore.Enabled = False
    End Select
End Sub


' Install the program's icon in the system tray.
Private Sub Form_Load()
    ' Prepare to receive tray messages.
    AddToTray Me, mnuTray

    ' Set the system tray tool tip.
    SetTrayTip "VB Helper tray icon program"
End Sub
```

```
' Enable the correct tray menu items.
Private Sub Form_Resize()
    SetTrayMenuItems WindowState
End Sub


' Important! Remove the tray icon before exiting.
Private Sub Form_Unload(Cancel As Integer)
    RemoveFromTray
End Sub


' Unload the form.
Private Sub mnuFileExit_Click()
    Unload Me
End Sub


' Unload the form.
Private Sub mnuTrayClose_Click()
    Unload Me
End Sub


' Maximize the form.
Private Sub mnuTrayMaximize_Click()
    SendMessage hwnd, WM_SYSCOMMAND, _
        SC_MAXIMIZE, 0&
End Sub


' Minimize the form.
Private Sub mnuTrayMinimize_Click()
    SendMessage hwnd, WM_SYSCOMMAND, _
        SC_MINIMIZE, 0&
End Sub


' Restore the form.
Private Sub mnuTrayRestore_Click()
    SendMessage hwnd, WM_SYSCOMMAND, _
        SC_RESTORE, 0&
End Sub
```

The following code is contained in the SysTray.bas module. Subroutine AddToTray saves references to the form and its system tray popup menu for later use. It subclasses the form so that the TrayWindowProc function can examine Windows messages. It then uses the Shell_NotifyIcon API function to install the form's icon in the system tray.

The TrayWindowProc function looks for TRAY_CALLBACK messages. When it finds one, it determines whether the event is a left or right mouse button click. If the event is a left-button click, the routine restores the form. If the event is a right-button click, the routine presents the form's popup menu.

If the message represents a minimize or restore command, the program handles it. This is necessary so that the program can call the SetTrayMenuItems subroutine to enable the appropriate menu commands. It also allows the program to hide its form instead of shrinking it to an icon as the minimize command normally would. Note that the form's ShowInTaskBar property must be set to False at design time for this to work.

After all this special processing, the TrayWindowProc function passes any remaining messages to the form's original WindowProc for further processing.

The SetTrayTip subroutine uses the Shell_NotifyIcon API function to set the system tray icon's tool tip text. If the user lets the mouse hover over the icon, this text is displayed.

Subroutine RemoveFromTray uses the Shell_NotifyIcon API function to remove the form's icon from the system tray. It then uses SetWindowLong to restore the form's original WindowProc function. At this point, the program is back to normal with no special tray icon or message processing.

```
Option Explicit

Private OldWindowProc As Long
Private TheForm As Form
Private TheMenu As Menu

Private Declare Function CallWindowProc Lib "user32" _
    Alias "CallWindowProcA" (ByVal lpPrevWndFunc As Long, _
    ByVal hwnd As Long, ByVal Msg As Long, ByVal wParam As Long, _
    ByVal lParam As Long) As Long
Private Declare Function SetWindowLong Lib "user32" _
    Alias "SetWindowLongA" (ByVal hwnd As Long, ByVal nIndex As Long, _
    ByVal dwNewLong As Long) As Long
Private Declare Function Shell_NotifyIcon Lib "shell32.dll" _
    Alias "Shell_NotifyIconA" (ByVal dwMessage As Long, _
    lpData As NOTIFYICONDATA) As Long

Private Const WM_USER = &H400
Private Const WM_LBUTTONUP = &H202
Private Const WM_MBUTTONUP = &H208
Private Const WM_RBUTTONUP = &H205
Private Const TRAY_CALLBACK = (WM_USER + 1001&)
Private Const GWL_WNDPROC = (-4)
Private Const GWL_USERDATA = (-21)
Private Const NIF_ICON = &H2
Private Const NIF_TIP = &H4
Private Const NIM_ADD = &H0
Private Const NIF_MESSAGE = &H1
Private Const NIM_MODIFY = &H1
Private Const NIM_DELETE = &H2

Private Type NOTIFYICONDATA
    cbSize As Long
    hwnd As Long
    uID As Long
    uFlags As Long
    uCallbackMessage As Long
    hIcon As Long
```

```vb
        szTip As String * 64
End Type


Private TheData As NOTIFYICONDATA


Public Declare Function SendMessage Lib "user32" _
    Alias "SendMessageA" (ByVal hwnd As Long, ByVal wMsg As Long, _
    ByVal wParam As Long, lParam As Any) As Long


Public Const WM_SYSCOMMAND = &H112
Public Const SC_RESTORE = &HF120&
Public Const SC_MINIMIZE = &HF020&
Public Const SC_MAXIMIZE = &HF030&


' Add the form's icon to the system tray.
Public Sub AddToTray(frm As Form, mnu As Menu)
    ' Save references to the form and menu for later.
    Set TheForm = frm
    Set TheMenu = mnu


    ' Install the new WindowProc.
    OldWindowProc = SetWindowLong(frm.hwnd, _
        GWL_WNDPROC, AddressOf TrayWindowProc)


    ' Install the form's icon in the tray.
    With TheData
        .uID = 0
        .hwnd = frm.hwnd
        .cbSize = Len(TheData)
        .hIcon = frm.Icon.Handle
        .uFlags = NIF_ICON
        .uCallbackMessage = TRAY_CALLBACK
        .uFlags = .uFlags Or NIF_MESSAGE
        .cbSize = Len(TheData)
    End With
    Shell_NotifyIcon NIM_ADD, TheData
End Sub


' Look for system tray messages.
Public Function TrayWindowProc(ByVal hwnd As Long, ByVal Msg As Long, _
    ByVal wParam As Long, ByVal lParam As Long) As Long
Const WM_SYSCOMMAND = &H112


    If Msg = TRAY_CALLBACK Then
        ' The user clicked on the tray icon.
        ' Look for click events.
        If lParam = WM_LBUTTONUP Then
            ' On left click, show the form.
            TheForm.Show
            SendMessage hwnd, WM_SYSCOMMAND, _
                SC_RESTORE, 0&
            TheForm.SetFocus
```

```vb
                Exit Function
            End If


            If lParam = WM_RBUTTONUP Then
                ' On right click, show the popup menu.
                TheForm.PopupMenu TheMenu
                Exit Function
            End If
        End If


        ' Handle the minimize and restore commands.
        If Msg = WM_SYSCOMMAND Then
            If wParam = SC_MINIMIZE Then
                TheForm.Hide
                TheForm.SetTrayMenuItems vbMinimized
                Exit Function
            ElseIf wParam = SC_RESTORE Then
                If Not TheForm.Visible Then
                    TheForm.Show
                    TheForm.SetTrayMenuItems vbNormal
                End If
            End If
        End If


        ' Send other messages to the original
        ' window proc.
        TrayWindowProc = CallWindowProc( _
            OldWindowProc, hwnd, Msg, _
            wParam, lParam)
End Function


' Set a new tray tip.
Public Sub SetTrayTip(tip As String)
    With TheData
        .szTip = tip & vbNullChar
        .uFlags = NIF_TIP
    End With
    Shell_NotifyIcon NIM_MODIFY, TheData
End Sub


' Remove the icon from the system tray.
Public Sub RemoveFromTray()
    ' Remove the icon from the tray.
    With TheData
        .uFlags = 0
    End With
    Shell_NotifyIcon NIM_DELETE, TheData

    ' Restore the original window proc.
    SetWindowLong TheForm.hwnd, GWL_WNDPROC, _
        OldWindowProc
End Sub
```

```
' Set a new tray icon.
Public Sub SetTrayIcon(pic As Picture)
    ' Do nothing if the picture is not an icon.
    If pic.Type <> vbPicTypeIcon Then Exit Sub

    ' Update the tray icon.
    With TheData
        .hIcon = pic.Handle
        .uFlags = NIF_ICON
    End With
    Shell_NotifyIcon NIM_MODIFY, TheData
End Sub
```

☆ ☆
④ ⑤ ⑥

153. Move a Form without a Title Bar

Directory: MoveForm

If a form's caption is blank and its MinButton, MaxButton, and ControlBox properties are all set to False, the form does not display a title bar. That may sometimes be convenient for the program, but it removes the user's normal method for moving the form.

The program can use a small PictureBox and some API functions to let the user move the form without a title bar. Example program MoveForm does this. Click and drag on the small colored PictureBox in the upper left corner to move the form.

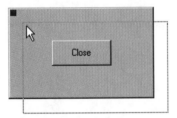

Program MoveForm.

How It Works

The following code shows how program MoveForm works. When the form loads, the program sets its Caption property to a blank string. The form's MinButton, MaxButton, and ControlBox properties were set to False at design time, so this removes the form's title bar.

Because this also removes the usual methods for closing the form, the program includes a Close button. The cmdClose_Click event handler simply unloads the form.

The program's most interesting code is in the picGrab_MouseDown event handler. When the user presses the mouse button over the picGrab PictureBox, this event handler calls the ReleaseCapture API function. That releases the mouse capture that was initiated by the mouse button press.

The routine then uses the SendMessage API function to start the form move. The following code sends the form a WM_NCLBUTTONDOWN message with the HTCAPTION parameter to simulate a button press over the title bar. Alternatively, the program could send the WM_SYSCOMMAND message with the parameter &HF012 to tell Windows to let the user move the form. This method is included and is commented out in the code.

```vb
Option Explicit

#If Win32 Then
    Private Declare Function ReleaseCapture Lib "user32" () As Long
    Private Declare Function SendMessage Lib "user32" _
        Alias "SendMessageA" (ByVal hWnd As Long, ByVal wMsg As Long, _
        ByVal wParam As Long, lParam As Any) As Long
#Else
    Private Declare Sub ReleaseCapture Lib "User" ()
    Private Declare Function SendMessage Lib "User" _
        (ByVal hWnd As Integer, ByVal wMsg As Integer, _
        ByVal wParam As Integer, lParam As Any) As Long
#End If

Private Const HTCAPTION = 2
Private Const WM_NCLBUTTONDOWN = &HA1
Private Const WM_SYSCOMMAND = &H112

' Set the form's caption = "" to remove the
' title bar. MinButton, MaxButton, and ControlBox
' must all be set to False at design time.
Private Sub Form_Load()
    Caption = ""
End Sub

' Unload the form.
Private Sub cmdClose_Click()
    Unload Me
End Sub

' Start the move operation.
Private Sub picGrab_MouseDown(Button As Integer, Shift As Integer, _
    X As Single, Y As Single)

    ' Relase the mouse click's capture.
    ReleaseCapture

    ' Start the move.
    SendMessage hWnd, WM_NCLBUTTONDOWN, _
        HTCAPTION, 0&

    ' Or use:
'    SendMessage hwnd, WM_SYSCOMMAND, _
'        &HF012&, 0&
End Sub
```

CHAPTER 18

Using Files and Directories

M any programs manipulate files and directories. This chapter demonstrates powerful file management techniques including ways to determine if a file exists, read text files and arrays, search a directory hierarchy for a file, and copy selected files in a directory hierarchy.

154. See If a File Exists

Directory: Exists

Before a program tries to work with a file, it should determine whether the file actually exists. If the file is missing, the program can present the user with a meaningful message instead of crashing.

Example program Exists compares three techniques for checking a file's existence. Enter the name of the file and the number of times you want the program to repeat the tests. The tests are fast so you may need to repeat them many times to get meaningful results. When you click the Find button, the program executes the tests and displays the amount of time it took for each.

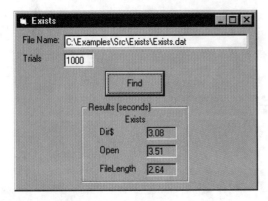

Program Exists.

How It Works

This program uses three methods to determine whether a file exists. Function FileExistsWithDir uses Visual Basic's Dir$ statement. Dir$ returns the name of the file if it exists and a blank string if it does not.

The FileExistsWithOpen function tries to open the file using Visual Basic's Open statement. If the file does not exist, the Open statement raises an error. The function uses an error handler to catch the error and set its return value to False.

Function FileExistsWithFileLen uses the FileLen statement to try to get the file's length. If the file does not exist, FileLen raises an error. The function uses an error handler to catch the error and set its return value to False.

```
Option Explicit

' Initialize the file name.
Private Sub Form_Load()
Dim file_path As String

    file_path = App.Path
    If Right$(file_path, 1) <> "\" Then _
        file_path = file_path & "\"
    txtFileName.Text = file_path & "Exists.dat"
End Sub

' Try three different methods for determining
' whether the file exists.
Private Sub cmdFind_Click()
Dim trial As Long
Dim num_trials As Long
Dim start_time As Single
Dim file_exists As Boolean
```

```
Dim txt As String

    Screen.MousePointer = vbHourglass
    DoEvents

    num_trials = CLng(txtTrials.Text)
    txt = txtFileName.Text

    ' Try using Dir$.
    start_time = Timer
    For trial = 1 To num_trials
        file_exists = FileExistsWithDir(txt)
    Next trial
    lblDir.Caption = Format$(Timer - start_time, "0.00")
    DoEvents

    ' Try using Open.
    start_time = Timer
    For trial = 1 To num_trials
        file_exists = FileExistsWithOpen(txt)
    Next trial
    lblOpen.Caption = Format$(Timer - start_time, "0.00")
    DoEvents

    ' Try using FileLen.
    start_time = Timer
    For trial = 1 To num_trials
        file_exists = FileExistsWithFileLen(txt)
    Next trial
    lblFileLen.Caption = Format$(Timer - start_time, "0.00")
    DoEvents

    If file_exists Then
        lblExists.Caption = "Exists"
    Else
        lblExists.Caption = "Does not exist"
    End If

    Screen.MousePointer = vbDefault
End Sub

' Use the Dir$ statement to see if the file exists.
Private Function FileExistsWithDir(ByVal filename As String)
Dim file_name As String

    file_name = Dir$(filename)
    FileExistsWithDir = (file_name <> "")
End Function

' Use the Open statement to see if the file exists.
```

```
Private Function FileExistsWithOpen(ByVal filename As String)
Dim fnum As String

    fnum = FreeFile
    On Error GoTo FileDoesntExist
    Open filename For Input As fnum
    Close fnum
    FileExistsWithOpen = True
    Exit Function

FileDoesntExist:
    FileExistsWithOpen = False
End Function

' Use the FileLen statement to see if the file exists.
Private Function FileExistsWithFileLen(ByVal filename As String)
Dim length As Long

    On Error GoTo FileDoesntExist
    length = FileLen(filename)
    FileExistsWithFileLen = True
    Exit Function

FileDoesntExist:
    FileExistsWithFileLen = False
End Function
```

The three methods tested by this program are very similar in speed. In one set of tests, they took between 2.6 and 3.5 milliseconds per test. Given that none of the methods is significantly faster, the best choice is probably FileExistsWithDir because it is small and simple, and does not rely on an error handler.

155. Read a File's Contents

Directory: ReadFile

Visual Basic provides several methods for reading files including the Input$, Input #, Get, and Line Input statements. To read the entire contents of a file quickly and easily, a program can use the Input$ statement specifying the length of the file. Example program ReadFile demonstrates this technique. Enter the name of a file, and click the Open button to make the program read and display the file's contents.

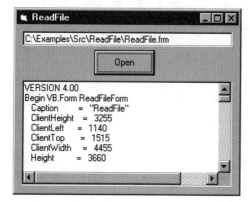

Program ReadFile.

How It Works

Program ReadFile's FileContents function reads the file. It opens the file and uses the Input$ statement to read the entire file in a single operation. The function uses the LOF statement to determine the length of the file so that it can pass that length to Input$. Function FileContents simply returns the contents retrieved by the Input$ statement.

```
Option Explicit

' Initialize the file name.
Private Sub Form_Load()
Dim file_path As String

    file_path = App.Path
    If Right$(file_path, 1) <> "\" Then _
        file_path = file_path & "\"
    txtFileName.Text = file_path & "ReadFile.frm"
End Sub

' Return the file's contents. Display errors.
Private Function FileContents(ByVal filename As String) As String
Dim fnum As Integer

    On Error GoTo OpenError
    fnum = FreeFile
    Open filename For Input As fnum
    FileContents = Input$(LOF(fnum), #fnum)
    Close fnum
    Exit Function
```

```
OpenError:
    MsgBox "Error " & Format$(Err.Number) & _
        " reading file." & vbCrLf & _
        Err.Description
    Exit Function
End Function
```

156. Read and Write Arrays

Directory: Arrays

The previous example shows how a program can use the Input$ statement to read text data from a file. Visual Basic's Get and Put statements let a program read and write array data from a file. A program that does not use Get and Put carefully, however, may take far longer to process array data than necessary.

Example program Arrays demonstrates two ways for reading and writing array data. When you run the program, you will find that one method is much faster than the other.

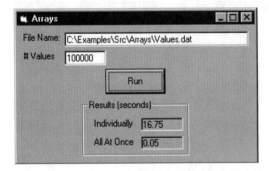

Program Arrays.

How It Works

When the user clicks the Run button in program Arrays, the cmdRun_Click event handler executes. This routine initializes an array with sequential values. It calls subroutine Put-ValuesIndividually to save the values into a file and then subroutine GetValuesIndividually to read the values back out of the file. After displaying the time it needed, the routine repeats these steps using the PutValuesAtOnce and GetValuesAtOnce subroutines.

Subroutine PutValuesIndividually loops through the array's values using Put to write each into the output file one at a time. Similarly GetValuesIndividually loops through the array's values using Get to read each value from the file one at a time.

Subroutine PutValuesAtOnce calls Put, passing it the array itself. That allows Put to write the entire array into the file in a single step. Subroutine GetValuesAtOnce calls

Get, passing it the array, so Get reads the entire array at once. Writing and reading the array in a single step allows Put and Get to access the disk only once instead of hundreds or thousands of times. Because disk access is extremely slow compared to other computer operations, this makes a huge difference. In one test, subroutines PutValuesIndividually and GetValuesIndividually took more than 300 times as long as subroutines PutValuesAtOnce and GetValuesAtOnce.

```
Option Explicit

' Initialize the file name.
Private Sub Form_Load()
Dim file_path As String

    file_path = App.Path
    If Right$(file_path, 1) <> "\" Then _
        file_path = file_path & "\"
    txtFileName.Text = file_path & "Values.dat"
End Sub

' Create some data. Write it to the file and then
' read it back using the two different methods.
Private Sub cmdRun_Click()
Dim values() As Long
Dim num_values As Long
Dim i As Long
Dim start_time As Single
Dim file_name As String

    Screen.MousePointer = vbHourglass
    lblIndividual.Caption = ""
    lblAtOnce.Caption = ""
    DoEvents

    ' Create the values.
    num_values = CLng(txtNumValues.Text)
    ReDim values(1 To num_values)
    For i = 1 To num_values
        values(i) = i
    Next i

    ' Save and read the values individually.
    file_name = txtFileName.Text
    start_time = Timer
    PutValuesIndividually file_name, values
    GetValuesIndividually file_name, values
    lblIndividual.Caption = Format$(Timer - start_time, "0.00")
    DoEvents

    ' Verify that the numbers are correct.
    For i = 1 To num_values
```

```
        If values(i) <> i Then Stop
    Next i

    ' Save and read the values with Put and Get.
    start_time = Timer
    PutValuesAtOnce file_name, values
    GetValuesAtOnce file_name, values
    lblAtOnce.Caption = Format$(Timer - start_time, "0.00")
    DoEvents

    ' Verify that the numbers are correct.
    For i = 1 To num_values
        If values(i) <> i Then Stop
    Next i

    Screen.MousePointer = vbDefault
End Sub

' Save the values in the array one at a time.
Private Sub PutValuesIndividually(ByVal file_name As String, _
    val() As Long)
Dim fnum As Integer
Dim i As Long

    fnum = FreeFile
    Open file_name For Binary As fnum
    For i = 1 To UBound(val)
        Put #fnum, , val(i)
    Next i
    Close fnum
End Sub

' Get the values in the array one at a time.
Private Sub GetValuesIndividually(ByVal file_name As String, _
    val() As Long)
Dim fnum As Integer
Dim i As Long

    fnum = FreeFile
    Open file_name For Binary As fnum
    For i = 1 To UBound(val)
        Get #fnum, , val(i)
    Next i
    Close fnum
End Sub

' Save the values in the array all at once.
Private Sub PutValuesAtOnce(ByVal file_name As String, val() As Long)
Dim fnum As Integer

    fnum = FreeFile
    Open file_name For Binary As fnum
```

```
        Put #fnum, , val
        Close fnum
    End Sub


' Get the values in the array all at once.
Private Sub GetValuesAtOnce(ByVal file_name As String, val() As Long)
Dim fnum As Integer

    fnum = FreeFile
    Open file_name For Binary As fnum
    Get #fnum, , val
    Close fnum
End Sub
```

157. Count the Lines in a File

Directory: CountLns

Visual Basic's Line Input statement reads one line at a time from a file. Using this command, it is easy to count the number of lines in a file. Example program CountLns does just that. Enter the name of a file, and click the Count Lines button to make the program count the lines in the file.

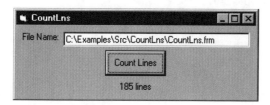

Program CountLns.

How It Works

When the user clicks the Count Lines button, the cmdCountLines_Click event handler executes. This routine opens the file and uses the Line Input statement to read lines from the file until it reaches the end of the file.

```
Option Explicit

' Initialize the file name.
Private Sub Form_Load()
Dim file_path As String

    file_path = App.Path
    If Right$(file_path, 1) <> "\" Then _
```

```
        file_path = file_path & "\"
    txtFileName.Text = file_path & "CountLns.frm"
End Sub


' Count the line in the file.
Private Sub cmdCountLines_Click()
Dim fnum As Integer
Dim lines As Long
Dim one_line As String

    Screen.MousePointer = vbHourglass
    DoEvents

    ' Open the fle.
    fnum = FreeFile
    Open txtFileName.Text For Input As fnum

    ' Read the lines one at a time.
    Do While Not EOF(fnum)
        Line Input #fnum, one_line
        lines = lines + 1
    Loop
    Close fnum

    lblLines.Caption = Format$(lines) & " lines"

    Screen.MousePointer = vbDefault
End Sub
```

---

158. Filter a File ☆ ☆ ④ ⑤ ⑥

Directory: Filter

The previous example shows how to examine a file one line at a time. Using a similar technique, a program can modify the lines in a file. Example program Filter demonstrates this method by removing lines from a file that contain a target string.

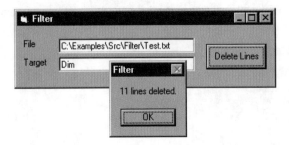

Program Filter.

How It Works

The most interesting part of program Filter is the cmdDeleteLines_Click event handler. This routine uses the GetTempPath API function to learn which directory is used for temporary files on the system. It uses the GetTempFileName API function to get the name of a file it can use as a temporary file. The program opens the temporary file and the input file.

Next, for each of the lines in the input file, cmdDeleteLines_Click uses InStr to see if the line contains the target string. If it does, the program skips the line and increments the deleted counter. If the target is not contained in the line, the program writes the line into the temporary file.

When it has finished reading the input file, the program closes both files and uses Visual Basic's Kill command to delete the original input file. It finishes by using the Name statement to rename the temporary file with the input file's name. The result looks to the user as if the program has edited the file and removed the target lines.

```
Option Explicit

#If Win32 Then
    Private Declare Function GetTempPath Lib "kernel32" _
        Alias "GetTempPathA" (ByVal nBufferLength As Long, _
        ByVal lpBuffer As String) As Long
    Private Declare Function GetTempFileName Lib "kernel32" _
        Alias "GetTempFileNameA" (ByVal lpszPath As String, _
        ByVal lpPrefixString As String, ByVal wUnique As Long, _
        ByVal lpTempFileName As String) As Long
#End If


' Initialize the file name.
Private Sub Form_Load()
Dim file_path As String

    #If Win32 = False Then
        MsgBox "This program only runs in 32-bit Visual Basic."
        Unload Me
        Exit Sub
    #End If

    file_path = App.Path
    If Right$(file_path, 1) <> "\" Then _
        file_path = file_path & "\"
    txtFileName.Text = file_path & "Test.txt"
End Sub

' Delete the lines that contain the target.
Private Sub cmdDeleteLines_Click()
Const MAX_PATH = 260
Const NAME_LEN = MAX_PATH + 80

Dim inname As String
```

```vb
Dim strlen As Integer
Dim outpath As String
Dim outname As String
Dim infile As Integer
Dim outfile As Integer
Dim one_line As String
Dim target As String
Dim deleted As Integer

    On Error GoTo DeleteLineError

    ' Get the temporary file directory.
    outpath = Space$(NAME_LEN)
    strlen = GetTempPath(NAME_LEN, outpath)
    If strlen = 0 Then
        MsgBox "Error getting temporary file path."
        Exit Sub
    Else
        outpath = Left$(outpath, strlen)
    End If

    ' Get a temporary file name.
    outname = Space$(NAME_LEN)
    If GetTempFileName(outpath, "tmp", _
        0, outname) = 0 _
    Then
        MsgBox "Error getting temporary file name."
        Exit Sub
    End If
    strlen = InStr(outname, vbNullChar) - 1
    If strlen > 0 Then _
        outname = Left$(outname, strlen)

    ' Open the output file.
    outfile = FreeFile
    Open outname For Output As outfile

    ' Open the input file.
    inname = txtFileName.Text
    infile = FreeFile
    Open inname For Input As infile

    MousePointer = vbHourglass
    DoEvents

    ' Copy the file skipping lines containing the
    ' target.
```

```
deleted = 0
target = txtTarget.Text
Do While Not EOF(infile)
    Line Input #infile, one_line
    If InStr(one_line, target) = 0 Then
        ' Target not found. Save this line.
        Print #outfile, one_line
    Else
        ' Target found. Do not save this line.
        deleted = deleted + 1
    End If
Loop

' Close the files.
Close infile
Close outfile

' Delete the original file.
Kill inname

' Give the new file the old name.
Name outname As inname
MsgBox Format$(deleted) & " lines deleted."
MousePointer = vbDefault
Exit Sub

DeleteLineError:
    MsgBox "Error " & Format$(Err.Number) & _
        vbCrLf & Err.Description
    MousePointer = vbDefault
    Exit Sub
End Sub
```

159. List a Directory's Subdirectories

Directory: SubDirs

Visual Basic's Dir$ statement returns information about files. Using Dir$ and the GetAttr function, a program can list the subdirectories beneath a directory. Example program SubDirs does this. Enter the name of a starting directory, and click the Search button to make the program search for subdirectories beneath that directory.

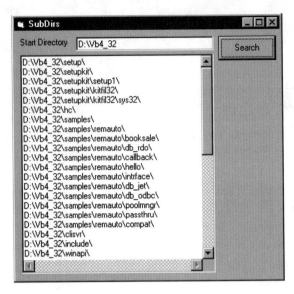

Program SubDirs.

How It Works

When the user clicks the Search button, the cmdSearch_Click event handler executes. That routine calls the FindSubdirs function to retrieve a list of the selected directory's subdirectories.

Function FindSubdirs uses the Dir$ function to retrieve a list of the subdirectories within the indicated directory. When it is called with a search pattern as its first argument, the Dir$ function returns the name of the first file it finds that matches the pattern. In subsequent calls with the first parameter omitted, the Dir$ function returns the next file that matches the original pattern. Function FindSubdirs calls Dir$ repeatedly until it returns a blank string indicating that it has returned the names of all the matching files in the directory.

FindSubdirs must now search the subdirectories for subdirectories of their own. Unfortunately, the Dir$ function is not safe for recursive use. That means when it finds one subdirectory, FindSubdirs cannot immediately call Dir$ to search that subdirectory. If it calls Dir$ again specifying the first parameter, the previous round of calls to Dir$ is disrupted.

To avoid this problem, function FindSubdirs calls Dir$ until it has read every subdirectory in the directory it is searching. It saves these subdirectory names in its dirs array. When it has all the names, it recursively calls itself to find the information for those subdirectories. It combines the results with the subdirectory names to generate its result.

As the function calls the Dir$ function, it ignores files named ., .., and PAGEFILE.SYS. The file . represents the current directory. The file .. represents the directory's parent directory. The file PAGEFILE.SYS is the system paging file. All of these files have special meaning that is not useful to the program and listing these files could cause problems. For instance, if the program examined the . directory, it would repeat the search of the current directory. It would find the file . again, search it again, and repeat the search of the current directory again. The program would be stuck in an infinite loop.

```
Option Explicit

' Initialize the file name.
Private Sub Form_Load()
Dim file_path As String

    file_path = App.Path
    If Right$(file_path, 1) <> "\" Then _
        file_path = file_path & "\"
    txtStartDir.Text = file_path
End Sub

' Search for subdirectories.
Private Sub cmdSearch_Click()
Dim start_dir As String

    Screen.MousePointer = vbHourglass
    txtResult.Text = ""
    DoEvents

    start_dir = txtStartDir.Text
    If Right$(start_dir, 1) <> "\" Then _
        start_dir = start_dir & "\"

    txtResult.Text = FindSubdirs(start_dir)

    Screen.MousePointer = vbDefault
End Sub

' Return a list of the subdirectories beneath
' this directory.
Private Function FindSubdirs(ByVal start_dir As String) As String
Dim dirs() As String
Dim num_dirs As Long
Dim sub_dir As String
Dim i As Integer
Dim txt As String

    ' Get the first subdirectory.
    sub_dir = Dir$(start_dir & "*", vbDirectory)
    Do While Len(sub_dir) > 0
        ' Add the subdirectory name to the list if
        ' it is a directory and it is not ., ..,
        ' or PAGEFILE.SYS.
```

```
        If UCase$(sub_dir) <> "PAGEFILE.SYS" And _
            sub_dir <> "." And sub_dir <> ".." _
        Then
            sub_dir = start_dir & sub_dir
            If GetAttr(sub_dir) And vbDirectory Then
                num_dirs = num_dirs + 1
                ReDim Preserve dirs(1 To num_dirs)
                dirs(num_dirs) = sub_dir & "\"
            End If
        End If

        ' Get the next subdirectory.
        sub_dir = Dir$(, vbDirectory)
    Loop

    ' Recursively search the subdirectories.
    For i = 1 To num_dirs
        ' Add this subdirectory and its subdirectory
        ' information to the result string.
        txt = txt & dirs(i) & vbCrLf & _
            FindSubdirs(dirs(i))
    Next i

    ' Return the string we have built.
    FindSubdirs = txt
End Function
```

160. Search for Files

☆ ☆
④ ⑤ ⑥

Directory: Search

The previous example uses the Dir$ function to search for directories beneath a starting directory. Using a similar technique, a program can search for other files beneath a start directory. Example program Search uses a similar technique to search for files matching a pattern. Enter a start directory and a file pattern. Then click the Search button to make the program locate files that match the pattern.

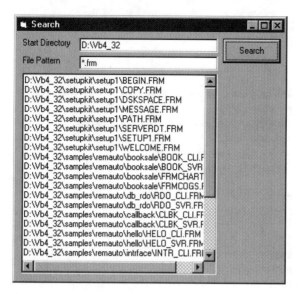

Program Search.

How It Works

Program Search is very similar to program SubDirs, described in the previous section. The difference is that this program uses a FindFiles function instead of a FindSubdirs function. Because this is the only difference between the two programs, only function FindFiles is shown here. For information on the other parts of the program, see the previous section.

Function FindFiles takes as parameters a directory name and a file-matching pattern. It begins by searching the directory for files that match the pattern. It adds the names of the files to its output text.

After it has listed all the matching files in the directory, the function searches for subdirectories exactly as function FindSubdirs does in the previous section. It uses the Dir$ function to fill an array with subdirectory names. It then calls itself recursively to find the files in those subdirectories that match the file pattern.

```
' Return a list of the files beneath this
' directory that match the pattern.
Private Function FindFiles(ByVal start_dir As String, _
    ByVal file_pattern As String) As String
Dim dirs() As String
Dim num_dirs As Long
```

```vb
Dim sub_dir As String
Dim file_name As String
Dim i As Integer
Dim txt As String

    ' Search for matching files in this directory.
    ' Get the first matching file.
    file_name = Dir$(start_dir & file_pattern, vbNormal)
    Do While Len(file_name) > 0
        ' Add the file to the return value.
        txt = txt & start_dir & file_name & vbCrLf

        ' Get the next matching file.
        file_name = Dir$(, vbNormal)
    Loop

    ' Get this directory's subdirectories.
    ' Get the first subdirectory.
    sub_dir = Dir$(start_dir & "*", vbDirectory)
    Do While Len(sub_dir) > 0
        ' Add the subdirectory name to the list if
        ' it is a directory and it is not ., ..,
        ' or PAGEFILE.SYS.
        If UCase$(sub_dir) <> "PAGEFILE.SYS" And _
            sub_dir <> "." And sub_dir <> ".." _
        Then
            sub_dir = start_dir & sub_dir
            If GetAttr(sub_dir) And vbDirectory Then
                num_dirs = num_dirs + 1
                ReDim Preserve dirs(1 To num_dirs)
                dirs(num_dirs) = sub_dir & "\"
            End If
        End If

        ' Get the next subdirectory.
        sub_dir = Dir$(, vbDirectory)
    Loop

    ' Recursively search the subdirectories.
    For i = 1 To num_dirs
        ' Add this subdirectory's matching files
        ' to the result string.
        txt = txt & FindFiles(dirs(i), file_pattern)
    Next i

    ' Return the string we have built.
    FindFiles = txt
End Function
```

161. Search for Files Using the API

Directory: Search2

The previous example uses the Dir$ function to locate files beneath a directory. This program is effective, but it is rather slow. A program can perform a similar search much more quickly using API functions. Example program Search2 uses this approach. Enter a start directory and a file pattern. Then click the Search button to make the program locate files that match the pattern.

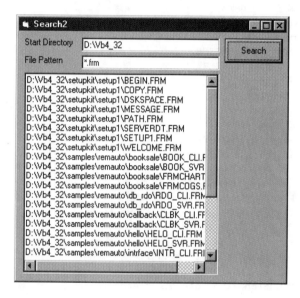

Program Search2.

How It Works

The only significant difference between program Search2 and program Search, described in the previous section, is in the FindFiles function. Because these programs are so similar, only the FindFiles code and the necessary API function declarations are shown here. To learn more about the rest of the code, read the previous two sections.

The version of FindFiles included in program Search2 uses the FindFirstFile API function to open a file search handle that identifies files that match the file pattern in the directory. FindFirstFile returns the file search handle and the first matching file name. The FindFiles function adds the file name to its return text. It then uses the FindNextFile API function to find the next matching file name. It continues using FindNextFile until it has read all the matching files. It then closes the file search handle with the FindClose API function.

Next, the function repeats this process to find the directory's subdirectories. It uses FindFirstFile to open the file search handle, saves the subdirectory name in the dirs array, and repeatedly uses FindNextFile to get the names of the other subdirectories.

Having read all of the subdirectories' names, the FindFiles function calls itself recursively to search for files inside those subdirectories.

```
Option Explicit

#If Win32 Then
    Private Const MAX_PATH = 260
    Private Type FILETIME
        dwLowDateTime As Long
        dwHighDateTime As Long
    End Type
    Private Type WIN32_FIND_DATA
        dwFileAttributes As Long
        ftCreationTime As FILETIME
        ftLastAccessTime As FILETIME
        ftLastWriteTime As FILETIME
        nFileSizeHigh As Long
        nFileSizeLow As Long
        dwReserved0 As Long
        dwReserved1 As Long
        cFileName As String * MAX_PATH
        cAlternate As String * 14
    End Type

    Private Declare Function FindFirstFile Lib "kernel32" _
        Alias "FindFirstFileA" (ByVal lpFileName As String, _
        lpFindFileData As WIN32_FIND_DATA) As Long
    Private Declare Function FindNextFile Lib "kernel32" _
        Alias "FindNextFileA" (ByVal hFindFile As Long, _
        lpFindFileData As WIN32_FIND_DATA) As Long
    Private Declare Function FindClose Lib "kernel32" ( _
        ByVal hFindFile As Long) As Long
    Private Declare Function GetLastError Lib "kernel32" () As Long

    Private Const ERROR_NO_MORE_FILES = 18&
    Private Const INVALID_HANDLE_VALUE = -1
    Private Const DDL_DIRECTORY = &H10
#End If

' Return a list of the files beneath this
' directory that match the pattern.
Private Function FindFiles(ByVal start_dir As String, _
    ByVal file_pattern As String) As String
Dim null_character As String
Dim dirs() As String
Dim num_dirs As Long
Dim sub_dir As String
Dim file_name As String
Dim i As Integer
Dim txt As String
Dim search_handle As Long
```

```
Dim file_data As WIN32_FIND_DATA

    ' ASCII character 0 terminates strings.
    null_character = Chr$(0)

    ' Search for matching files in this directory.
    ' Get the first matching file.
    search_handle = FindFirstFile( _
        start_dir & file_pattern, file_data)
    If search_handle <> INVALID_HANDLE_VALUE Then
        ' Save this file's name.
        Do While GetLastError <> ERROR_NO_MORE_FILES
            file_name = file_data.cFileName
            file_name = Left$(file_name, _
                InStr(file_name, null_character) - 1)
            If file_name <> "." And file_name <> ".." Then
                ' Add the file to the return value.
                txt = txt & start_dir & file_name & vbCrLf
            End If

            ' Get the next file.
            FindNextFile search_handle, file_data
        Loop

        ' Close the file search handle.
        FindClose search_handle
    End If

    ' Get this directory's subdirectories.
    ' Get the first subdirectory.
    search_handle = FindFirstFile( _
        start_dir & "*.*", file_data)
    If search_handle <> INVALID_HANDLE_VALUE Then
        ' Save this file's name.
        Do While GetLastError <> ERROR_NO_MORE_FILES
            ' Save the subdirectory name.
            If file_data.dwFileAttributes And DDL_DIRECTORY Then
                file_name = file_data.cFileName
                file_name = Left$(file_name, _
                    InStr(file_name, null_character) - 1)
                If file_name <> "." And file_name <> ".." Then
                    num_dirs = num_dirs + 1
                    ReDim Preserve dirs(1 To num_dirs)
                    dirs(num_dirs) = start_dir & file_name & "\"
                End If
            End If

            ' Get the next file.
            FindNextFile search_handle, file_data
        Loop
```

```
    ' Close the file search handle.
    FindClose search_handle
End If

    ' Recursively search the subdirectories.
For i = 1 To num_dirs
        ' Add this subdirectory's matching files
        ' to the result string.
        txt = txt & FindFiles(dirs(i), file_pattern)
    Next i

        ' Return the string we have built.
    FindFiles = txt
End Function
```

162. Find a Directory's Size

Directory: DirSize

The previous example shows how to search a directory hierarchy for files matching a pattern. It is easy to modify that program to find the files' sizes as well. Example program DirSize does that. Enter a start directory and a file pattern. Then click the Search button to make the program locate files that match the pattern and display their sizes.

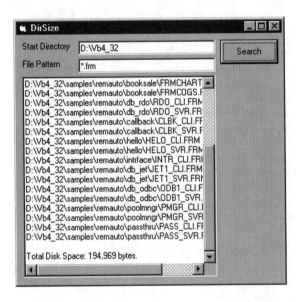

Program DirSize.

How It Works

Program DirSize is very similar to program Search2, described in the previous section. The only interesting difference is in the FindFiles function, so only it is presented here.

The new version of FindFiles uses Visual Basic's FileLen function to find the sizes of the files it locates. For more information about the FindFiles function and other parts of this program's code, see previous sections.

```
' Return a list of the files beneath this
' directory that match the pattern.
Private Function FindFiles(ByVal start_dir As String, _
    ByVal file_pattern As String, total_size As Long) As String
Dim null_character As String
Dim dirs() As String
Dim num_dirs As Long
Dim sub_dir As String
Dim file_name As String
Dim i As Integer
Dim txt As String
Dim search_handle As Long
Dim file_data As WIN32_FIND_DATA
Dim file_size As Long

    ' ASCII character 0 terminates strings.
    null_character = Chr$(0)

    ' Search for matching files in this directory.
    ' Get the first matching file.
    search_handle = FindFirstFile( _
        start_dir & file_pattern, file_data)
    If search_handle <> INVALID_HANDLE_VALUE Then
        ' Save this file's name.
        Do While GetLastError <> ERROR_NO_MORE_FILES
            file_name = file_data.cFileName
            file_name = Left$(file_name, _
                InStr(file_name, null_character) - 1)
            If file_name <> "." And file_name <> ".." Then
                ' Get the file's size.
                file_size = FileLen(start_dir & file_name)
                total_size = total_size + file_size

                ' Add the file to the return value.
                txt = txt & start_dir & file_name & _
                    " (" & Format$(file_size) & ")" & vbCrLf
            End If

            ' Get the next file.
            FindNextFile search_handle, file_data
        Loop
```

```
        ' Close the file search handle.
        FindClose search_handle
    End If


    ' Get this directory's subdirectories.
    ' Get the first subdirectory.
    search_handle = FindFirstFile( _
        start_dir & "*.*", file_data)
    If search_handle <> INVALID_HANDLE_VALUE Then
        ' Save this file's name.
        Do While GetLastError <> ERROR_NO_MORE_FILES
            ' Save the subdirectory name.
            If file_data.dwFileAttributes And DDL_DIRECTORY Then
                file_name = file_data.cFileName
                file_name = Left$(file_name, _
                    InStr(file_name, null_character) - 1)
                If file_name <> "." And file_name <> ".." Then
                    num_dirs = num_dirs + 1
                    ReDim Preserve dirs(1 To num_dirs)
                    dirs(num_dirs) = start_dir & file_name & "\"
                End If
            End If

            ' Get the next file.
            FindNextFile search_handle, file_data
        Loop

        ' Close the file search handle.
        FindClose search_handle
    End If

    ' Recursively search the subdirectories.
    For i = 1 To num_dirs
        ' Add this subdirectory's matching files
        ' to the result string.
        txt = txt & FindFiles(dirs(i), file_pattern, total_size)
    Next i

    ' Return the string we have built.
    FindFiles = txt
End Function
```

163. Copy a Directory Hierarchy ④ ⑤ ⑥

Directory: DirCopy

Visual Basic's FileCopy command allows a program to copy a single file. Unfortunately, Visual Basic does not have a command for copying a complete directory hierarchy. By modifying the techniques demonstrated in the previous examples, however, a program can copy a directory hierarchy.

Example program DirCopy allows you to copy files in a directory hierarchy. Enter the source and destination directories and a file pattern. The program will create the destination directory, so it must not yet exist. When you click the Copy button, the program copies the files in the source directory's hierarchy that match the pattern into the destination directory's hierarchy, creating subdirectories as needed.

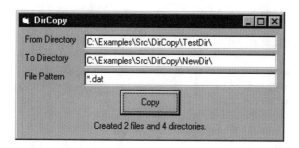

Program DirCopy.

How It Works

Program DirCopy is very similar to program Search2, described earlier. The main difference is in the CopyFiles subroutine. CopyFiles is a modified version of the function FindFiles used in program Search2. Because CopyFiles is the only interesting difference between the programs, only it is shown here.

When it starts, function CopyFiles uses Visual Basic's MkDir statement to create the destination directory. It then searches for files, much as function FindFiles does in program Search2. When it finds a file, however, CopyFiles does not save the file's name. Instead, it uses Visual Basic's FileCopy statement to copy the file to the destination directory.

Aside from these changes, CopyFiles is quite similar to function FindFiles. After it has copied all the files that match its file pattern, the function searches its directory for subdirectories. It then calls itself recursively to search its subdirectories and copy files that match the pattern. For a more complete description of these steps, see the section describing program Search2 earlier in this chapter.

```
' Copy the files beneath this directory that match
' the pattern.
```

```
Private Sub CopyFiles(ByVal from_dir As String, _
    ByVal to_dir As String, ByVal file_pattern As String, _
    files_copied As Long, dirs_created As Long)
Dim null_character As String
Dim dirs() As String
Dim to_dirs() As String
Dim num_dirs As Integer
Dim sub_dir As String
Dim file_name As String
Dim i As Integer
Dim txt As String
Dim search_handle As Long
Dim file_data As WIN32_FIND_DATA

    ' ASCII character 0 terminates strings.
    null_character = Chr$(0)

    ' Make the destination directory.
    MkDir to_dir
    dirs_created = dirs_created + 1

    ' Search for matching files in this directory.
    ' Get the first matching file.
    search_handle = FindFirstFile( _
        from_dir & file_pattern, file_data)
    If search_handle <> INVALID_HANDLE_VALUE Then
        ' Save this file's name.
        Do While GetLastError <> ERROR_NO_MORE_FILES
            file_name = file_data.cFileName
            file_name = Left$(file_name, _
                InStr(file_name, null_character) - 1)
            If file_name <> "." And file_name <> ".." Then
                ' Make sure this is not a directory.
                If (GetAttr(from_dir & file_name) And _
                        vbDirectory) = 0 Then
                    ' Copy the file.
                    FileCopy from_dir & file_name, to_dir & file_name
                    files_copied = files_copied + 1
                End If
            End If

            ' Get the next file.
            FindNextFile search_handle, file_data
        Loop

        ' Close the file search handle.
        FindClose search_handle
    End If

    ' Get this directory's subdirectories.
    ' Get the first subdirectory.
```

```
        search_handle = FindFirstFile( _
            from_dir & "*.*", file_data)
    If search_handle <> INVALID_HANDLE_VALUE Then
            ' Save this file's name.
        Do While GetLastError <> ERROR_NO_MORE_FILES
                ' Save the subdirectory name.
            If file_data.dwFileAttributes And DDL_DIRECTORY Then
                file_name = file_data.cFileName
                file_name = Left$(file_name, _
                    InStr(file_name, null_character) - 1)
                If file_name <> "." And file_name <> ".." Then
                    num_dirs = num_dirs + 1
                    ReDim Preserve dirs(1 To num_dirs)
                    dirs(num_dirs) = from_dir & file_name & "\"
                    ReDim Preserve to_dirs(1 To num_dirs)
                    to_dirs(num_dirs) = to_dir & file_name & "\"
                End If
            End If

                ' Get the next file.
            FindNextFile search_handle, file_data
        Loop

            ' Close the file search handle.
        FindClose search_handle
    End If

    ' Recursively search the subdirectories.
    For i = 1 To num_dirs
        CopyFiles dirs(i), to_dirs(i), file_pattern, _
            files_copied, dirs_created
    Next i
End Sub
```

164. Move a File into the Wastebasket ☆☆ ④⑤⑥

Directory: Waste

The Windows operating system has a wastebasket. Normally when you delete a file using Windows Explorer, the file is moved into the wastebasket. If you later decide you need the file, you can easily restore it.

Visual Basic's Kill statement deletes a file, but unfortunately it cannot place deleted files in the wastebasket. Once Kill deletes a file, it is gone.

Example program Waste moves files into the wastebasket. Enter the name of a file and click the Delete button to move the file into the wastebasket.

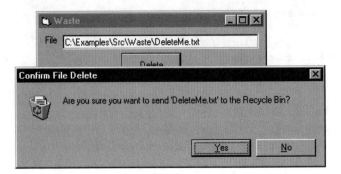

Program Waste.

How It Works

Program Waste is very simple. It uses the SHFileOperation API function to move the target file into the wastebasket. This function presents the user with a message confirming the deletion. If the user confirms the deletion, the function moves the file automatically.

```
Option Explicit

Private Type SHFILEOPSTRUCT
    hwnd As Long
    wFunc As Long
    pFrom As String
    pTo As String
    fFlags As Integer
    fAnyOperationsAborted As Long
    hNameMappings As Long
    lpszProgressTitle As Long
End Type
Private Declare Function SHFileOperation Lib "shell32.dll" _
    Alias "SHFileOperationA" (lpFileOp As SHFILEOPSTRUCT) As Long
Private Const FO_DELETE = &H3
Private Const FOF_ALLOWUNDO = &H40

' Initialize the file name.
Private Sub Form_Load()
Dim file_path As String

    #If Win32 = False Then
        MsgBox "This program only works in 32-bit Visual Basic."
        Unload Me
        Exit Sub
    #End If

    file_path = App.Path
    If Right$(file_path, 1) <> "\" Then _
        file_path = file_path & "\"
    txtTargetFile.Text = file_path & "DeleteMe.txt"
```

```
    End Sub

    ' Move the indicated file into the wastebasket.
    Private Sub CmdDelete_Click()
    Dim op As SHFILEOPSTRUCT

        With op
            .wFunc = FO_DELETE
            .pFrom = txtTargetFile.Text
            .fFlags = FOF_ALLOWUNDO
        End With
        SHFileOperation op
    End Sub
```

165. Display Disk Volume Information

☆ ☆
④ ⑤ ⑥

Directory: DiskInfo

Visual Basic provides a few statements such as FileLen and GetAttr for working with files, but it provides little support for working with a disk drive as a whole. The GetVolumeInformation API function allows a program to gather information about a disk volume. Example program DiskInfo uses GetVolumeInformation to describe a disk. Enter the name of the disk drive and click the Get Information button to make the program display information about the disk.

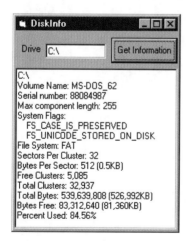

Program DiskInfo.

How It Works

Program DiskInfo is quite simple. It calls the GetVolumeInformation and GetDiskFree-Space API functions. The bulk of the code formats the results for display.

```
Option Explicit

Private Declare Function GetVolumeInformation Lib "kernel32" _
    Alias "GetVolumeInformationA" (ByVal lpRootPathName As String, _
    ByVal lpVolumeNameBuffer As String, ByVal nVolumeNameSize As Long, _
    lpVolumeSerialNumber As Long, lpMaximumComponentLength As Long, _
    lpFileSystemFlags As Long, ByVal lpFileSystemNameBuffer As String, _
    ByVal nFileSystemNameSize As Long) As Long

Private Const FS_CASE_IS_PRESERVED = &H2
Private Const FS_CASE_SENSITIVE = &H1
Private Const FS_UNICODE_STORED_ON_DISK = &H4
Private Const FS_PERSISTENT_ACLS = &H8
Private Const FS_FILE_COMPRESSION = &H10
Private Const FS_VOL_IS_COMPRESSED = &H8000&

Private Declare Function GetDiskFreeSpace Lib "kernel32" _
    Alias "GetDiskFreeSpaceA" (ByVal lpRootPathName As String, _
    lpSectorsPerCluster As Long, lpBytesPerSector As Long, _
    lpNumberOfFreeClusters As Long, lpTotalNumberOfClusters As Long) _
    As Long

' Display the disk information.
Private Sub cmdGetInfo_Click()
Dim txt As String
Dim volume_name As String
Dim file_system_name As String
Dim serial_number As Long
Dim component_length As Long
Dim system_flags As Long
Dim sectors_per_cluster As Long
Dim bytes_per_sector As Long
Dim free_clusters As Long
Dim total_clusters As Long
Dim total_bytes As Long
Dim free_bytes As Long

    volume_name = Space$(256)
    file_system_name = Space$(256)
    If GetVolumeInformation(txtDrive.Text, _
        volume_name, Len(volume_name), _
        serial_number, component_length, _
        system_flags, file_system_name, _
        Len(file_system_name)) = 0 _
    Then
        txt = "Error in GetVolumeInformation."
    Else
        txt = txtDrive.Text
        volume_name = Left$(volume_name, _
            InStr(volume_name, Chr$(0)) - 1)
        txt = txt & vbCrLf & "Volume Name: " & volume_name
        txt = txt & vbCrLf & "Serial number: " & Format$(serial_number)
```

```
            txt = txt & vbCrLf & "Max component length: " & _
                Format$(component_length)
            txt = txt & vbCrLf & "System Flags: "
        If system_flags And FS_CASE_IS_PRESERVED Then _
                txt = txt & vbCrLf & "    FS_CASE_IS_PRESERVED"
        If system_flags And FS_CASE_SENSITIVE Then _
                txt = txt & vbCrLf & "    FS_CASE_SENSITIVE"
        If system_flags And FS_UNICODE_STORED_ON_DISK Then _
                txt = txt & vbCrLf & "    FS_UNICODE_STORED_ON_DISK"
        If system_flags And FS_PERSISTENT_ACLS Then _
                txt = txt & vbCrLf & "    FS_PERSISTENT_ACLS"
        If system_flags And FS_FILE_COMPRESSION Then _
                txt = txt & vbCrLf & "    FS_FILE_COMPRESSION"
        If system_flags And FS_VOL_IS_COMPRESSED Then _
                txt = txt & vbCrLf & "    FS_VOL_IS_COMPRESSED"
            file_system_name = Left$(file_system_name, _
                InStr(file_system_name, Chr$(0)) - 1)
            txt = txt & vbCrLf & "File System: " & file_system_name
        End If


        If GetDiskFreeSpace(txtDrive.Text, _
            sectors_per_cluster, bytes_per_sector, _
            free_clusters, total_clusters) = 0 _
        Then
            txt = txt & vbCrLf & "Error in GetDiskFreeSpace."
        Else
            txt = txt & vbCrLf & "Sectors Per Cluster: " & _
                Format$(sectors_per_cluster)
            txt = txt & vbCrLf & "Bytes Per Sector: " & _
                Format$(bytes_per_sector) & _
                " (" & Format$(bytes_per_sector / 1024) & "KB)"
            txt = txt & vbCrLf & "Free Clusters: " & _
                Format$(free_clusters, "#,###")
            txt = txt & vbCrLf & "Total Clusters: " & _
                Format$(total_clusters, "#,###")
            total_bytes = total_clusters * sectors_per_cluster * _
                bytes_per_sector
            txt = txt & vbCrLf & "Total Bytes: " & _
                Format$(total_bytes, "#,###") & " (" & _
                Format$(total_bytes / 1024, "#,###") & "KB)"
            free_bytes = free_clusters * sectors_per_cluster * _
                bytes_per_sector
            txt = txt & vbCrLf & "Bytes Free: " & _
                Format$(free_bytes, "#,###") & " (" & _
                Format$(free_bytes / 1024, "#,###") & "KB)"
            txt = txt & vbCrLf & "Percent Used: " & _
                Format$(1 - (free_bytes / total_bytes), "0.00%")
        End If


    txtResults.Text = txt
End Sub
```

CHAPTER 19

Using the Registry

In early versions of Windows, a program stored configuration information in initialization files. With the introduction of Windows 95, Microsoft declared that programs should store configuration information in the system registry. Visual Basic provides commands that make using the registry in simple ways easy. This chapter explains some ways to use those commands and some API functions a program can employ to make more sophisticated use of the registry.

166. Track a Program's Usage

Directory: Usage

The intent of the registry is to store information for a program when it is not running. One way a program can use the registry is to track usage information. Example program Usage uses the registry to record the number of times it has run, the last time it ran, and the total time it has spent executing in the past.

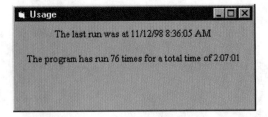

Program Usage.

How It Works

When program Usage loads, its Form_Load event handler saves the current time in the StartTime variable. It then uses Visual Basic's GetSetting function to read the last time it ran from the registry. If that value does not exist, it displays a string indicating this is the first time it has run. If the last time is present, the program also reads the number of times it has run and the total time it has spent executing. It displays its usage information in labels. Form_Load finishes by using Visual Basic's SaveSetting statement to save the current time as the program's last run time and to increment the number of times it has run.

When the program exits, its Form_Unload event handler uses DateDiff to determine the number of seconds that have elapsed since the program started. It adds that value to the number of seconds the program has run in the past, and it uses SaveSetting to store this value in the registry.

```
Option Explicit

' The application name and section used in
' SaveSetting and GetSetting.
Private Const APP_NAME = "Usage"
Private Const SECTION = "UsageInfo"

' The time this run started.
Private StartTime As Date

' The total time the program has been run.
Private NumSeconds As Long

' Load values from the registry.
Private Sub Form_Load()
Dim last_time As String
Dim num_times As Long
Dim num_seconds As Long
Dim txt As String

    ' Record the start time for this session.
    StartTime = Now

    ' Get the last run time.
    last_time = GetSetting(APP_NAME, SECTION, "LastTime", "")
```

```
        If last_time = "" Then
            ' No value was saved. This must be the first
            ' time the program has run.
            lblLastTime.Caption = _
                "This is the first time the program has run."
            num_times = 1
        Else
            ' Display the information.
            lblLastTime.Caption = "The last run was at " & last_time

            num_times = CLng(GetSetting(APP_NAME, SECTION, _
                "NumTimes", "0")) + 1
            txt = "The program has run " & Format$(num_times)

            NumSeconds = CLng(GetSetting(APP_NAME, SECTION, _
                "NumSeconds", "0"))
            num_seconds = NumSeconds
            txt = txt & " times for a total time of "

            ' Add the hours.
            txt = txt & Format$(num_seconds \ 3600) & ":"
            num_seconds = num_seconds Mod 3600

            ' Add the minutes.
            txt = txt & Format$(num_seconds \ 60, "00") & ":"
            num_seconds = num_seconds Mod 60

            ' Add the seconds.
            txt = txt & Format$(num_seconds, "00")
            lblNumTimes.Caption = txt
        End If

        ' Update the last run time and number of runs.
        SaveSetting APP_NAME, SECTION, "LastTime", Format$(Now)
        SaveSetting APP_NAME, SECTION, "NumTimes", Format$(num_times)
    End Sub

    ' Update the total run time.
    Private Sub Form_Unload(Cancel As Integer)
        NumSeconds = NumSeconds + DateDiff("s", StartTime, Now)
        SaveSetting APP_NAME, SECTION, "NumSeconds", NumSeconds
    End Sub
```

This may seem like a rather silly example, but it actually demonstrates a useful security technique. Each time the program runs, it displays the last time it ran. The user can glance at the time and verify that it makes sense. For instance, suppose you run the program on Monday and it says it last ran on Saturday. If you were not at work over the weekend, you know someone else ran the program. It is surprising how often this simple test can detect unauthorized computer use, particularly when the computer is attached to a network.

167. Use a One-Time Password

Directory: Password

Many programs prompt the user for a password the first time they run. Once the password has been entered correctly, the program does not prompt for the password again. Example program Password does this. When you first run the program, enter an invalid password to see how the program reacts. Run the program again, and enter the password "thepassword." Once you have entered the correct password, the program will not prompt you for a password again when you run it later.

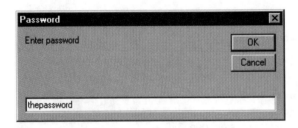

Program Password.

How It Works

An important fact about program Password is that it does not contain the password. That means even the cleverest hacker cannot take the program apart and read the password from its code. Actually, this example contains the password in a comment to make it easier for you to understand. In a real application, the password should not appear anywhere in the program.

Instead of storing the password, the program holds an encoded version of the password. When it starts, the program uses Visual Basic's GetSetting function to search for the encoded password in the system registry. If it finds the value and it matches the encoded value the program wants, the program runs normally.

If the program does not find the correctly encoded value in the registry, it prompts the user for the password. It encodes the result and compares it to the encoded password it wants. If the values match, the program runs normally. It also uses Visual Basic's SaveSetting statement to store the encoded password in the registry so that it does not need to ask for the password again later.

The encoding scheme used by program Password is ridiculously simple. It merely adds 1 to each letter in the password. For instance, the letter A becomes B in the encoding. A determined hacker would have little trouble figuring out how the program encodes passwords and then computing the correct password. A real application should use a more complicated encoding function.

Note that the program never decodes the password. It only encodes a value supplied by the user to see if the result matches the value it expects. That means you can use an encoding that is very hard or impossible to reverse because the program never needs to do that. Picking an encoding that is hard to reverse makes it harder for a hacker to determine what password to enter.

```vb
Option Explicit

' The application name and section used by
' SaveSetting and GetSetting.
Private Const APP_NAME = "Password"
Private Const SECTION = "Parameters"

' Make sure the user is authorized to run the
' program.
Private Sub Form_Load()
' This is the coded form of "thepassword"
Const WANTED_PASSWORD = "uifqbttxpse"

Dim coded_password As String
Dim plain_password As String

    ' See if the password is in the registry
    ' already.
    coded_password = GetSetting(APP_NAME, _
        SECTION, "Validation", "")

    If coded_password <> WANTED_PASSWORD Then
        ' The password is not saved or is incorrect.
        ' Ask the user for it.
        plain_password = InputBox("Enter password", APP_NAME, "")
        coded_password = Encode(plain_password)

        ' If the password is correct, save it in
        ' the registry.
        If coded_password = WANTED_PASSWORD Then
            SaveSetting APP_NAME, SECTION, _
                "Validation", coded_password
        End If
    End If

    ' If we did not get the right password, exit.
    If coded_password <> WANTED_PASSWORD Then
        MsgBox "Invalid password.", vbOK, "Invalid Password"
        Unload Me
        Exit Sub
    End If
End Sub

' Encode a text string by adding 1 to each letter.
' (This ridiculously weak scheme is for example
' purposes only.)
Private Function Encode(plain_text As String) As String
```

```
Dim i As Integer
Dim ch As String
Dim coded_text As String

    For i = 1 To Len(plain_text)
        ch = Mid$(plain_text, i, 1)
        ch = Chr$(Asc(ch) + 1)
        If ch > "~" Then ch = " "
        coded_text = coded_text & ch
    Next i
    Encode = coded_text
End Function
```

168. Perform One-Time Initialization

Directory: OneTime

The previous example shows how to prompt the user for a one-time password. Using a modified version of this technique, a program can perform one-time initialization. The first time it runs, the program can create directories, build files, set registry entries, and perform other initialization tasks.

Example program OneTime does this. The first time it runs, this program creates a registry entry indicating that it has been initialized.

Program OneTime.

How It Works

When program OneTime starts, it checks the registry for the value Initialized. If it finds this value, the program has already been initialized. If the value Initialized is missing, the program is uninitialized. It performs its one-time initialization and then continues as usual. This program presents a message indicating if it was already initialized or if it just initialized itself. A real application would probably not display this message.

```
Option Explicit

' The application name and section used by
' SaveSetting and GetSetting.
```

```
Private Const APP_NAME = "OneTime"
Private Const SECTION = "Initialization"

' Initialize the program if necessary.
Private Sub Form_Load()
    ' See if the program has already been initialized.
    If Len(GetSetting(APP_NAME, SECTION, _
        "Initialized", "")) = 0 _
    Then
            ' Not yet initialized.
            ' Do whatever is needed to initialize
            ' the application here.

            ' Record the fact that we are initialized.
            SaveSetting APP_NAME, SECTION, _
                "Initialized", "True"
            lblInitialized.Caption = "Initialized"
    Else
            ' The program is already initialized.
            lblInitialized.Caption = "Already initialized"
    End If
End Sub
```

169. Provide a Tip-of-the-Day

☆ ☆ ☆
④ ⑤ ⑥

Directory: Totd

A program can read tips from a file and display them to the user. It can use the registry to keep track of its position in the file so that the user does not see the same tip every day. Example program Totd displays tips in this manner.

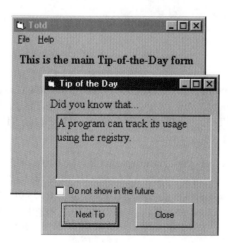

Program Totd.

How It Works

The Totd program includes two forms. TotdForm is the program's main form. TipForm is the form that displays the tips.

When it loads, TotdForm uses the GetSetting function to see if the value of HideTotd in the registry is True. If this value is not True, the program displays TipForm to show tips.

```
Option Explicit

' The application name and section used by
' GetSetting and SaveSetting.
Private Const APP_NAME = "Totd"
Private Const SECTION = "Parameters"

' Display the tip-of-the-day form.
Private Sub Form_Load()
    ' Make this form visible.
    Me.Show

    ' See if the tip-of-the-day is suppressed.
    If GetSetting(APP_NAME, SECTION, _
        "HideTotd", "") <> "True" _
    Then
        ' Display the tip-of-the-day.
        TipForm.Show
    End If
End Sub

' Unload the form.
Private Sub mnuFileExit_Click()
    Unload Me
End Sub

' Display the tip-of-the-day form.
Private Sub mnuHelpTotd_Click()
    TipForm.Show
End Sub
```

When TipForm loads, it checks the value of HideTotd in the registry. If that value is True, the program checks its check box so that the user can see that the form is marked as disabled in the registry. If HideTotd is not True, the form unchecks the check box. The form then calls its NextTip function to get the next tip's text.

When the form unloads, the Form_Unload event handler checks the state of the form's check box. If the box is checked, the user does not want to see the tips in the future so the program sets the value of HideTotd in the registry to True. If the box is unchecked, the program sets the value of HideTotd to False. The next time the program runs, the main form uses this value to decide whether it should display a tip-of-the-day.

The NextTip function fetches the NextOffset value from the registry. That gives the byte position of the next tip within the tip file. The function then calls function GetTipAtOffset to get the tip at that byte position. If the tip is blank, the program has read to the end of the tip file. NextTip starts over and returns the first tip in the file.

Function TipAtOffset returns the tip text starting at a specified byte position in the tip file. It begins by opening the tip file for binary input. It then uses Get to read MAX_TIP_LENGTH bytes from the file starting at the indicated offset. As you might guess from its name, MAX_TIP_LENGTH gives the length of the longest tip in the file.

The function then uses InStr to search for the carriage return and line feed that end the tip. If it does not find these characters, it returns an empty string to indicate that it is at the end of the file. If the function finds the end of the tip, it returns the tip and updates the file offset in the registry so that it skips this tip the next time it is called.

```
Option Explicit

' The application name and section used by
' GetSetting and SaveSetting.
Private Const APP_NAME = "Totd"
Private Const SECTION = "Parameters"

' Display the next tip.
Private Sub Form_Load()
    ' See whether the "Do not display in the future"
    ' box should be checked.
    If GetSetting(APP_NAME, SECTION, _
        "HideTotd", "") = "True" _
    Then
        chkHide.Value = vbChecked
    Else
        chkHide.Value = vbUnchecked
    End If

    ' Display the next tip.
    lblTip.Caption = NextTip
End Sub

' If the "Do not show in the future" box is
' checked, update the registry.
Private Sub Form_Unload(Cancel As Integer)
    If chkHide.Value = vbChecked Then
        SaveSetting APP_NAME, SECTION, _
            "HideTotd", "True"
    Else
        SaveSetting APP_NAME, SECTION, _
            "HideTotd", "False"
    End If
End Sub
```

```
' Load the next tip from the tip file.
Private Function NextTip() As String
Dim offset As Integer
Dim tip_text As String

    ' Read the registry to get the byte offset for
    ' the next tip in the tips file.
    offset = CInt(GetSetting(APP_NAME, _
        SECTION, "NextOffset", "1"))

    ' Get the tip.
    tip_text = TipAtOffset(offset)

    ' If the tip is blank, get the first tip.
    If tip_text = "" Then tip_text = TipAtOffset(1)

    NextTip = tip_text
End Function

' Load the indicated tip from the tip file.
Private Function TipAtOffset(ByVal offset As Integer) As String
Const MAX_TIP_LENGTH = 256

Dim fnum As Integer
Dim tip_buffer As String * MAX_TIP_LENGTH
Dim tip_text As String
Dim pos As Integer

    ' Open the tip file and read the next
    ' MAX_TIP_LENGTH bytes.
    fnum = FreeFile
    Open App.Path & "\tips.txt" For Binary As fnum
    Get #fnum, offset, tip_buffer
    Close fnum

    ' Find the end of the tip.
    tip_text = Trim$(tip_buffer)
    pos = InStr(tip_text, vbCrLf)
    If pos = 0 Then
        ' There is no vbCrLf. We are at the end of
        ' the file. Return a blank tip.
        offset = 1
        tip_text = ""
    Else
        tip_text = Left$(tip_text, pos - 1)
        offset = offset + pos + 1
    End If
    TipAtOffset = tip_text

    ' Save the offset for the next tip.
    SaveSetting APP_NAME, SECTION, _
```

```
                "NextOffset", Format$(offset)
End Function

' Unload the form.
Private Sub cmdClose_Click()
    Unload Me
End Sub

' Display the next tip.
Private Sub cmdNextTip_Click()
    lblTip.Caption = NextTip
End Sub
```

170. Save and Restore Settings   ④ ⑤ ⑥

Directory: SaveSet

The registry is a useful tool for applications that must save user configuration and other settings between runs. Example program SaveSet saves its caption and foreground and background colors. Enter a new caption in the TextBox and use the OptionButtons to select a color scheme. When you close the program, it saves those values in the registry. When you restart the program, it restores the caption and colors you previously selected.

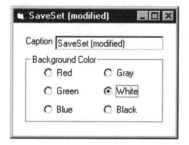

Program SaveSet.

How It Works

When program SaveSet loads, it uses GetSetting to read its configuration values from the registry. It sets the values of its TextBox and OptionButtons accordingly. The event handlers attached to those controls automatically apply the settings just as they do when the user modifies them interactively.

When program SaveSet unloads, its Form_Unload event handler saves the configuration settings in the registry. Note that this happens only when the form unloads normally. If the program stops unexpectedly because of a bug, operating system crash, power failure, or some other reason, the Form_Unload event handler does not execute, so the values are not saved. This can be annoying and frustrating to users.

If a program has important configuration parameters, it should save them as soon as they are changed rather than waiting for the form to unload. Then, even if the program crashes, the settings are safe.

```
Option Explicit

' The application name and section used by
' GetSetting and SaveSetting.
Private Const APP_NAME = "SaveSet"
Private Const SECTION = "Parameters"

' The selected color index.
Private ColorIndex As Integer

' Load saved configuration values.
Private Sub Form_Load()
Dim color_index As Integer

    ' Get the colors.
    color_index = CInt( _
        GetSetting(APP_NAME, SECTION, "ColorIndex", "3"))
    optColor(color_index).Value = True

    ' Get the caption.
    txtCaption.Text = _
        GetSetting(APP_NAME, SECTION, "Caption", "SaveSet")
End Sub

' Save configuration values.
Private Sub Form_Unload(Cancel As Integer)
    ' Save the selected color index.
    SaveSetting APP_NAME, SECTION, "ColorIndex", ColorIndex

    ' Save the caption.
    SaveSetting APP_NAME, SECTION, "Caption", Caption
End Sub

' Change the form's background color.
Private Sub optColor_Click(Index As Integer)
    ColorIndex = Index

    Select Case Index
        Case 0
            SetColors vbBlack, vbRed
        Case 1
            SetColors vbBlack, vbGreen
        Case 2
            SetColors vbWhite, vbBlue
```

```
        Case 3
            SetColors vbBlack, RGB(192, 192, 192)
        Case 4
            SetColors vbBlack, vbWhite
        Case 5
            SetColors vbWhite, vbBlack
    End Select
End Sub


' Change the form's caption.
Private Sub txtCaption_Change()
    Caption = txtCaption.Text
End Sub


' Set the colors for the form and controls.
Private Sub SetColors(ByVal fore_color As Long, _
    ByVal back_color As Long)
Dim ctl As Control

    ' Set the form's colors.
    BackColor = back_color
    ForeColor = fore_color

    ' Set the controls' colors, except for txtCaption.
    On Error Resume Next
    For Each ctl In Controls
        If ctl.Name <> "txtCaption" Then
            ctl.BackColor = back_color
            ctl.ForeColor = fore_color
        End If
    Next ctl
End Sub
```

☆ ☆

171. Read Unusual Registry Keys   ④ ⑤ ⑥

Directory: ReadKey

Visual Basic's SaveSetting and GetSetting statements allow a program to read and write registry values with little fuss. These routines take as parameters an application name, section name, key name, and key value. The key value is actually placed in the registry within the key:

```
HKEY_CURRENT_USERS\Software\VB and VBA Program Settings\
```

Using SaveSetting and GetSetting, a program can access only those values stored in this part of the registry. A program, though, may sometimes need to read values in other parts of the registry. It can do that using API functions.

Example program ReadKey lets you see key values in other parts of the registry. Use the OptionButtons to select a root key value. Enter a key and subkey value, and click the Find button to make the program display the subkey value.

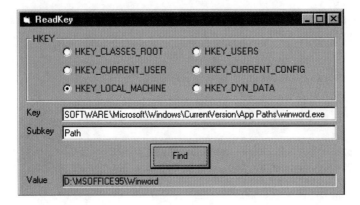

Program ReadKey.

How It Works

The most interesting part of program ReadKey is the GetKeyValue function. It starts by opening a registry to the key using the RegOpenKeyEx API function. It then uses the RegQueryValueEx API function to read the desired subkey value. GetKeyValue then uses RegCloseKey to close the key.

```
Option Explicit

Private Declare Function RegOpenKeyEx Lib "advapi32.dll" _
    Alias "RegOpenKeyExA" (ByVal hKey As Long, _
    ByVal lpSubKey As String, ByVal ulOptions As Long, _
    ByVal samDesired As Long, phkResult As Long) As Long
Private Declare Function RegQueryValueEx Lib "advapi32.dll" _
    Alias "RegQueryValueExA" (ByVal hKey As Long, _
    ByVal lpValueName As String, ByVal lpReserved As Long, _
    lpType As Long, lpData As Any, lpcbData As Long) As Long
Private Declare Function RegCloseKey Lib "advapi32.dll" ( _
    ByVal hKey As Long) As Long


Private Const ERROR_SUCCESS = 0&

Private Const HKEY_CLASSES_ROOT = &H80000000
Private Const HKEY_CURRENT_USER = &H80000001
Private Const HKEY_LOCAL_MACHINE = &H80000002
Private Const HKEY_USERS = &H80000003
Private Const HKEY_CURRENT_CONFIG = &H80000005
Private Const HKEY_DYN_DATA = &H80000006
```

```vb
Private Const STANDARD_RIGHTS_ALL = &H1F0000
Private Const KEY_QUERY_VALUE = &H1
Private Const KEY_SET_VALUE = &H2
Private Const KEY_CREATE_SUB_KEY = &H4
Private Const KEY_ENUMERATE_SUB_KEYS = &H8
Private Const KEY_NOTIFY = &H10
Private Const KEY_CREATE_LINK = &H20
Private Const SYNCHRONIZE = &H100000
Private Const KEY_ALL_ACCESS = _
    ((STANDARD_RIGHTS_ALL Or _
    KEY_QUERY_VALUE Or _
    KEY_SET_VALUE Or _
    KEY_CREATE_SUB_KEY Or _
    KEY_ENUMERATE_SUB_KEYS Or _
    KEY_NOTIFY Or KEY_CREATE_LINK) And _
    (Not SYNCHRONIZE))

' The selected HKEY option value.
Private SelectedHkey As Long

' Select HKEY_LOCAL_MACHINE.
Private Sub Form_Load()
    optHKEY(2).value = True
End Sub

' Set the HKEY value.
Private Sub optHKEY_Click(Index As Integer)
    Select Case Index
        Case 0
            SelectedHkey = HKEY_CLASSES_ROOT
        Case 1
            SelectedHkey = HKEY_CURRENT_USER
        Case 2
            SelectedHkey = HKEY_LOCAL_MACHINE
        Case 3
            SelectedHkey = HKEY_USERS
        Case 4
            SelectedHkey = HKEY_CURRENT_CONFIG
        Case 5
            SelectedHkey = HKEY_DYN_DATA
    End Select
End Sub

' Display the key/subkey value.
Private Sub cmdFind_Click()
    lblResult.Caption = _
        GetKeyValue(SelectedHkey, txtKey.Text, txtSubkey.Text)
End Sub

' Get the key/subkey value.
Private Function GetKeyValue(ByVal selected_hkey As Long, _
    ByVal key As String, ByVal subkey As String) As String
```

```
Dim hKey As Long
Dim value As String
Dim length As Long
Dim value_type As Long

    ' Open the key.
    If RegOpenKeyEx(selected_hkey, key, 0&, _
        KEY_ALL_ACCESS, hKey) <> ERROR_SUCCESS _
    Then
        GetKeyValue = "Error opening key."
        Exit Function
    End If

    ' Get the subkey's value.
    length = 256
    value = Space$(length)
    If RegQueryValueEx(hKey, subkey, _
        0&, value_type, ByVal value, length) _
            <> ERROR_SUCCESS _
    Then
        GetKeyValue = "Error getting subkey value."
    Else
        ' Remove the trailing null character.
        GetKeyValue = Left$(value, length - 1)
    End If

    ' Close the key.
    RegCloseKey hKey
End Function
```

172. Read Internationalization Keys ☆☆ ④⑤⑥

Directory: IntlInfo

Program ReadKey, described in the previous section, uses API functions to open a registry key, read a single subkey value, and close the key. The three-step process is rather complicated for a program that just needs to read a single registry value, but if a program must read multiple subkeys from within the same key, opening and closing the key in separate steps makes sense. The program can open the key, read several values, and then close the key.

Example program IntlInfo uses this method to read internationalization values from the registry. It opens the key HKEY_CURRENT_USER\Control Panel\International, reads a series of values, and closes the key.

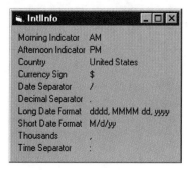

Program IntlInfo.

How It Works

Program IntlInfo's API declarations are the same as those used by program ReadKey. Because they are long and not particularly interesting, they are not repeated here. You can see them in the previous section's code if you like.

When program IntlInfo starts, its Form_Load event handler opens the key. It uses the GetSubkeyValue function to read a series of subkey values from the key. It then uses RegCloseKey to close the key.

The GetSubkeyValue function is relatively straightforward. It uses the RegQueryValueEx API function to read a single subkey value.

```
' Display internationalization information.
Private Sub Form_Load()
Dim hKey As Long

    ' Open the key.
    If RegOpenKeyEx(HKEY_CURRENT_USER, _
        "Control Panel\International", _
        0&, KEY_ALL_ACCESS, hKey) <> ERROR_SUCCESS _
    Then
        MsgBox "Error opening key."
        Exit Sub
    End If

    ' Get the subkeys' values.
    lblMorning.Caption = GetSubkeyValue(hKey, "s1159")
    lblAfternoon.Caption = GetSubkeyValue(hKey, "s2359")
    lblCountry.Caption = GetSubkeyValue(hKey, "sCountry")
    lblCurrencySign.Caption = GetSubkeyValue(hKey, "sCurrency")
    lblDateSep.Caption = GetSubkeyValue(hKey, "sDate")
    lblDecimalSep.Caption = GetSubkeyValue(hKey, "sDecimal")
    lblLongDate.Caption = GetSubkeyValue(hKey, "sLongDate")
    lblShortDate.Caption = GetSubkeyValue(hKey, "sShortDate")
```

```
        lblThousandsSep.Caption = GetSubkeyValue(hKey, "sThousand")
        lblTimeSep.Caption = GetSubkeyValue(hKey, "sTime")

    ' Close the key.
    RegCloseKey hKey
End Sub

' Return the registry value.
Private Function GetSubkeyValue(ByVal hKey As Long, _
    ByVal subkey_name As String) As String
Dim value As String
Dim length As Long
Dim value_type As Long

    length = 256
    value = Space$(length)
    If RegQueryValueEx(hKey, subkey_name, _
        0&, value_type, ByVal value, length) _
            <> ERROR_SUCCESS _
    Then
        value = "<error>"
    Else
        ' Remove the trailing null character.
        value = Left$(value, length - 1)
    End If

    GetSubkeyValue = value
End Function
```

Note that the internationalization information stored in your system registry may differ from the information shown here. The test shown here was performed on a computer running Windows NT. The same program cannot find any of these values on a typical Windows 95 system.

173. List Subkeys within a Key

⭐ ☆ ☆
④ ⑤ ⑥

Directory: RegTree

The previous sections described programs that read specific keys from the registry. Using the RegEnumKey API function, a program can recursively read all of the key values beneath a specific key. Example program RegTree lists the keys below a specified key.

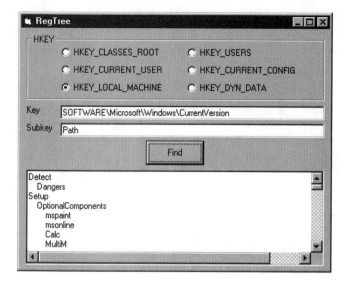

Program RegTree.

How It Works

This program's API declarations are similar to those used by program ReadKey. Because they are long and uninteresting, most of them are not repeated here. The RegEnumKey function is new, so its declaration is shown in the code that follows. You can see the rest of the declarations in the section describing program ReadKey earlier in this chapter.

The most interesting part of program RegTree is its EnumSubkeys function. EnumSubkeys opens the key where it will start searching. It then uses the RegEnumKey API function to examine the subkeys within that key. A program selects subkeys within a key by passing RegEnumKey the subkeys' indexes within the key. Program RegTree examines subkeys numbered 0, 1, 2, and so forth until it receives an error indicating there are no more subkeys.

Each time it finds a subkey, the program saves its name in the subkeys collection. It uses the RegQueryValue API function to get the subkey's value and saves the value in the subkey_values collection. When it has examined all of the subkeys, the program uses RegCloseKey to close the key.

The program then looks through its subkeys collection. For each subkey listed in the collection, the program adds the subkey's name and value to the function's return string.

The function then calls itself recursively to find information about the keys beneath that subkey. It increases the value of indent in its call to itself so that the subkeys farther down in the registry hierarchy are indented more.

```
Option Explicit
        :
    <code omitted>
        :
Private Declare Function RegEnumKey Lib "advapi32.dll" _
    Alias "RegEnumKeyA" (ByVal hKey As Long, ByVal dwIndex As Long, _
    ByVal lpName As String, ByVal cbName As Long) As Long
        :
    <code omitted>
        :

' Get the key information for this key and its
' subkeys. Separate keys from their values with
' vbTab. Separate keys with vbCrLf.
Private Function EnumSubkeys(ByVal selected_hkey As Long, _
    ByVal key_name As String, ByVal indent As Integer) As String
Dim subkeys As Collection
Dim subkey_values As Collection
Dim subkey_num As Integer
Dim subkey_name As String
Dim subkey_value As String
Dim length As Long
Dim hKey As Long
Dim txt As String

    Set subkeys = New Collection
    Set subkey_values = New Collection

    ' Open the key.
    If RegOpenKeyEx(selected_hkey, key_name, _
        0&, KEY_ALL_ACCESS, hKey) <> ERROR_SUCCESS _
    Then
        EnumSubkeys = "Error opening key."
    End If

    ' Enumerate the subkeys.
    subkey_num = 0
    Do
        ' Enumerate subkeys until we get an error.
        length = 256
        subkey_name = Space$(length)
        If RegEnumKey(hKey, subkey_num, _
            subkey_name, length) _
                <> ERROR_SUCCESS Then Exit Do
        subkey_num = subkey_num + 1
```

```
        subkey_name = Left$(subkey_name, _
            InStr(subkey_name, Chr$(0)) - 1)
        subkeys.Add subkey_name

        ' Get the subkey's value.
        length = 256
        subkey_value = Space$(length)
        If RegQueryValue(hKey, subkey_name, _
            subkey_value, length) _
            <> ERROR_SUCCESS _
        Then
            subkey_values.Add "Error"
        Else
            ' Remove the trailing null character.
            subkey_value = Left$(subkey_value, length - 1)
            subkey_values.Add subkey_value
        End If
    Loop

    ' Close the key.
    RegCloseKey hKey

    ' Recursively get information on the subkeys.
    For subkey_num = 1 To subkeys.Count
        txt = txt & Space$(indent) & _
            subkeys(subkey_num) & vbTab & _
            subkey_values(subkey_num) & vbCrLf
        txt = txt & EnumSubkeys(selected_hkey, _
            key_name & "\" & subkeys(subkey_num), _
            indent + 4)
    Next subkey_num

    EnumSubkeys = txt
End Function
```

To use this CD-ROM, your system must meet the following requirements:

A machine reasonably capable of running Visual Basic. Algorithms will run faster on machines with faster processors and more memory.

Hard drive space: To copy all the source code down to your hard drive, 15 MB.

Peripherals: CD-ROM drive.